M

ANN ARBOR DISTRICT LIBRARY

31621015720978

WITHDRAWN

A NEW CENTURY BOOK OF QUOTATIONS

\*\*\*

# PRACTICAL WISDOM

## &

# TIMELY ADVICE

Over 2,000 years of useful commentary
on human nature and life's big ideas

---

Compiled and Arranged
by
Richard Reed

Copyright © 1998 by Richard Reed

*All Rights Reserved*

ISBN 0-9666197-0-6


Library of Congress Catalog Card Number: 98-93856


Printed in the United States of America

10 9 8 7 6 5 4 3 2 1


Published by

Catawba Press
26450 Crocker, Suite 1213
Harrison Township, Michigan 48045

# TABLE OF CONTENTS

# INTRODUCTION

Some thirty years ago, back during my undergraduate days in the liberal arts, I happened to buy a copy of George Seldes' *The Great Quotations*. I've been an enthusiast and collector of quotations ever since. However much credit I owe Seldes' unique and celebrated anthology for pointing me down this particular path, the fortunate result has been a lasting appreciation for mankind's most independent, eloquent, irreverent, and timeless thinking.

Over the past years, I've gradually acquired several more books of quotations, as well as gleaned a multitude of quotes from newspapers and magazines. Such a collection is hardly unusual for we so-called prospectors of literary gems. Though we are a diverse group, our collective guide is a keen taste for the lucid thought or the well-turned phrase; and, in turn, we hold the fair belief that inspired words of style or substance are rare enough that their occasional appearance should not go unrecognized. This is not to say that as collectors we like quotations to the exclusion of everyone else. Daily life, after all, is filled with conversations in which someone relates a memorable line from a movie or TV show, or a book or magazine article. I think it's safe to say we all love a good quote, whether it be wicked or risqué, witty or wise. The difference is that some of us have our antennae especially attuned to these profound or provocative treasures, and through little more than sheer force of habit, clip them out or jot them down, preserving them as personal and precious artifacts to be filed and consulted.

Among the many books of quotations to choose from, there are, to be sure, books of better and lesser quality. My own eclectic collection contains many respected volumes, each having their own distinct style and purpose. And though they all deserve recommendation according to one's preference, I believe there are a handful that stand above all the rest. In addition to Mr. Seldes' *The Great Quotations*, there are especially *The New York Public Library Book of 20th Century American Quotations*, and Mortimer Adler and Charles Van Doren's monumental achievement, the *Great Treasury of Western Thought*. Having any one of these anthologies on hand provides a clear advantage in terms of understanding oneself, understanding others, or, more generally, helping us in Thomas Huxley's phrase to "learn what is true in order to do what is right."

Which brings up the obvious question, why another book of

quotations? Typically, books of quotations fall into one of two categories: those devoted to a single subject ( e.g. sports, movies or rock 'n' roll), and those which are, by and large, encyclopedic in nature. The latter try to cover everything under the sun, their subject headings frequently numbering in the hundreds. What makes *Practical Wisdom & Timely Advice* different is that it takes aim at a few subjects only, providing a full and thorough examination of each. Most important, these are subjects of the most practical and immediate sort, having to do with life delivered, as it were, "point blank." Here are quotations about life lived day-to-day, quotations solely about those ideas that we all must inescapably wrestle with and come to grips with. In short, what this book is about are those things that matter the most. Religion, Love, Marriage, Family, Government, Education, Work, Happiness. These are the ideas that everyday demand our attention and, consequently, everyday influence our actions. Here you will find these fundamental ideas fleshed out to their fullest, their eternal recurrence and relevance given their proper historical and philosophical due.

In *Meditations,* his learned collection of rules of practical morality, the Roman emperor Marcus Aurelius wrote, "Our life is what our thoughts make it." This is a famous example of the magic of a few words expressing a great truth. And it is a good example of the practical wisdom and timely advice that great quotations carry for their time and all generations that follow. In the following pages, you will find many more thoughtful insights and shrewd observations, some old some new, some short and some long. Read among them for pleasure or for profit. Browse and digest. In any case, my hope is whether you agree or disagree with any particular quote or passage, you will find there is always something to be gained from the encounter.

Richard Reed

Everthing has been said before, but since nobody listens we have to keep going back and beginning all over again.

*André Gide, French novelist [1869-1951]*

# CHAPTER - 1

# *GOD & RELIGION*

\*\*\*

You could not discover the frontiers of the soul even if you traveled every road to do so; such is the depth of its meaning.

-HERACLITUS, *Greek philosopher (c.540 - 480 B.C.)*

Concerning the gods, I am not able to know to a certainty whether they exist or not. For there are many things which prevent one from knowing, especially the obscurity of the subject, and the shortness of the life of man.

-PROTAGORAS, *Greek philosopher (485 - 410 B.C.)*

To escape from evil we must be made, as far as possible, like God; and this resemblance consists in becoming just, and holy, and wise.

-PLATO, *Greek philosopher (c.428 - c.347 B.C.)*

Reason is a light God has kindled in the soul.

-ARISTOTLE, *Greek philosopher (384 - 322 B.C.)*

God is completely inactive and unfettered by the need for occupation. He neither toils nor labors, but delights in his own wisdom and virtue. He knows for certain that He will always enjoy perfect and eternal pleasures. This is the God whom we can properly call happy. ...

But if the world itself is considered God, what could be less restful than to revolve at incredible speed around an axis, without a single moment of respite? Repose is a necessary condition for happiness. But on the other hand, if some god dwells in the world as its ruler and pilot, maintaining the course of the stars, the changes of season, and all the processes of creation, watching over all the interests of man on land and sea, what a bondage to tiresome and laborious business that would be.

*- CICERO, Roman orator, philosopher (106 - 43 B.C.)*

Religion is regarded by the common people as true, by the wise as false, and by the rulers as useful.

*- SENECA, Roman statesman, philosopher (c.4 B.C. - 65 A.D.)*

God said unto Moses, "I am that I am": and He said, Thus shalt thou say unto the children of Israel, 'I am' hath sent me unto you.

And God said moreover unto Moses, Thus shalt thou say unto the children of Israel, The Lord God of your fathers, the God of Abraham, the God of Isaac, and the God of Jacob, hath sent me unto you; this is my name for ever, and this is my memorial unto all generations.

*- EXODUS 3: 14 - 15*

Thou art a God ready to pardon, gracious and merciful, slow to anger, and of great kindness.

*- NEHEMIAH 9: 17*

The Lord is my light and my salvation; whom shall I fear? the Lord is the strength of my life; of whom

shall I be afraid?
*-PSALMS 27: 1*

O Lord, thou hast searched me, and known me.
Thou knowest my downsitting and mine upris-
ing, thou understandt my thought afar off.
Thou compasseth my path and my lying down,
and art acquainted with all my ways.
For there is not a word on my tongue, but, lo, O
Lord, thou knowest it altogether.
Thou hast beset behind and before, and laid
thine hand upon me.
Such knowledge is too wonderful for me; it is
high, I cannot attain unto it.
Whither shall I go from thy spirit? or whither
shall I flee thy presence?
If I ascend up into heaven, thou art there; if I
make my bed in hell, behold, thou art there.
If I take the wings of the morning, and dwell in
the uttermost parts of the sea;
Even there shall thy hand lead me, and thy
right hand shall hold me.
If I say, Surely the darkness shall cover me;
even the night shall be light about me.
Yea, the darkness hideth not from thee, but the
night shineth as the day: the darkness and the
light are both alike to thee.
*-PSALMS 139: 1 - 12*

Of making many books there is no end;
and much study is a weariness of the flesh.
Let us hear the conclusion of the whole
matter: Fear God, and keep his commandments; for this is the whole duty of man.

---

For God shall bring every work into judgement, with every secret thing, whether it be good, or whether it be evil.
-*ECCLESIASTES 12: 12 - 14*

Trust ye in the Lord for ever: for in the Lord Jehovah is everlasting strength.
-*ISAIAH 26: 4*

With God all things are possible.
-*MATTHEW 19: 26*

Beloved, let us love one another: for love is of God; and every one that loveth is born of God, and knoweth God.
He that loveth not knoweth not God; for God is love.
-*1 JOHN 4: 7 - 8*

God hath chosen the foolish things of the world to confound the wise; and God hath chosen the weak things of the world to confound the things that are mighty.
-*CORINTHIANS 1: 27*

All scripture is given by inspiration of God, and is profitable for doctrine, for reproof, for correction, for instruction in righteousness: That the man of God may be perfect, thoroughly furnished unto all good works.
-*TIMOTHY 3: 16 - 17*

God created only one single man, not, certainly, that he might be a solitary, bereft of all society, but that by this means the unity of society and the bond of concord might be more effectually commended to him, men being bound together not only by similarity of nature, but by family affection. And indeed He did not even create the woman that was to be given him as his wife as he created her out of the man, that the whole human race might derive from one man.

-*ST. AUGUSTINE, Church father, philosopher (354 - 430)*

God always is, nor has He been and is not, nor is but has not been, but as He never will not be; so He never was not.    -*ST. AUGUSTINE*

What is God? I asked the earth and it answered: "I am not He"; and all things that are in the earth made the same confession. ... And I turned to myself and said: "And you, who are you?" And I answered: "A man." Now clearly there is a body and a soul in me, one exterior, one interior. From which of these two should I have enquired of my God? I had already sought Him by my body, from earth to heaven, as far as my eye could send its beams on the quest. But the interior part is the better, seeing that all my body's messengers delivered to it, as ruler and judge, the answers that heaven and earth and all things in them made when they said: "We are not God," and, "He made us." The inner man knows these things through the ministry of the outer man. I the inner man knew them, I, I the soul, through the senses of the body. I asked the whole frame of the universe about my God and it answered me: "I am not He, but He made me."

-*ST. AUGUSTINE*

Understanding is the reward of faith. Therfore seek not to understand that thou mayest believe, but believe that thou mayest understand. -ST. AUGUSTINE

It is, if I may say so , by spiritually embracing Him that the intellectual soul is filled and impregnated with true virtues. We are enjoined to love this good with all our heart, with all our soul, with all our strength. To this good we ought to be led by those who love us, and to lead those we love. Thus are fulfilled those two commandments on which hang all law and the prophets: "Thou shalt love the Lord thy God with all thy heart, and with all thy mind, and with all thy soul"; and "Thou shalt love thy neighbor as thyself." For, that man might be intelligent in his self-love, there was appointed for him an end to which he might refer all his actions, that he might be blessed. For he who loves himself wishes nothing else than this. And the end set before him is "to draw near to God." And so, when one who has this intelligent self-love is commanded to love his neighbor as himself, what else is enjoined than that he shall do all in his power to commend to him the love of God? This is the worship of God, this is true religion, this right piety, this is the service due to God only.   -ST. AUGUSTINE

He who created us without our help will not save us without our consent.   -ST. AUGUSTINE

God changes not what is in people, until they change what is in themselves.
- THE KORAN

Although we do not know *what* God is, we infer from the existence of the world *that* He is, not that

He is any intelligible essence, but merely that He exists as the cause of all things. His inference is threefold. We observe that things are, and infer that their cause is. We observe that order of the universe, and infer that their cause is wise. We observe that things are in constant motion, being alive, and infer that their cause is life. Thus God, considered not in Himself but as the cause of all things, has three aspects: He is, He is wise, and He lives. His being is called the Father, His wisdom is called the Son, His life is called the Holy Ghost, words which denote not the three aspects themselves, but their relation to each other.

*-JOHN SCOTUS ERIGENA, Irish philosopher (810 - 877)*

God is that, the greater than which cannot be conceived.

*-ST. ANSELM, Benedictine monk (1033 - 1109)*

He who enters religion does not make professions to be perfect, but he professes to endeavour to attain perfection; even as he who enters the schools does not profess to have knowledge, but to study in order to acquire knowledge.

*-SAINT THOMAS AQUINAS, Italian theologian, philosopher (1225 - 1274)*

Man considers the actions, but God weighs the intentions.

*-THOMAS À KEMPIS, Dutch ecclesiastic, writer (1380 - 1471)*

I can't understand what must be in a man's mind if he doesn't feel seriously that there is a God when he sees the sun rise. It must at times occur to him that there are eternal things, or else he must push his face into the dirt like a sow. For its incredible that they [the planets] be observed to move without inquiring whether there isn't somebody who moves them.

-*MARTIN LUTHER, German religious reformer (1483 - 1546)*

Inasmuch as He is the one true God, wholly incomprehensible and inaccessible to man's understanding, it is reasonable, indeed inevitable, that His justice also should be incomprehensible.

-*MARTIN LUTHER*

The state of celibacy is great hypocrisy and wickedness. Christ with one sentence confutes all their arguments: God created them male and female.

-*MARTIN LUTHER*

God foreordained, for His own glory and the display of His attributes of mercy and justice, a part of the human race, without any merit of their own, to eternal salvation, and another part, in just punishment of their sin, to eternal damnation.

-*JOHN CALVIN, French theologian, reformer (1509 - 1564)*

Everyone is as God made him, and oftentimes a great deal worse.

-*MIGUEL DE CERVANTES, Spanish novelist (1547 - 1616)*

It is true, that a little philosophy inclineth man's mind to atheism; but depth in philosophy bringeth man's mind about to religion.

-*FRANCIS BACON, English essayist, philosopher (1561 - 1626)*

They that deny a God destroy men's nobility; for certainly man is of kin to the beasts by his body; and, if he be not of kin to God by his spirit, he is a base and ignoble creature.   -*FRANCIS BACON*

I count religion but a childish toy, and hold there is no sin but ignorance.
-*CHRISTOPHER MARLOWE, English playwright (1564 - 1593)*

Guide not the hand of God, nor order the finger of the almighty unto thy will and pleasure.
-*SIR THOMAS BROWNE, English physician, writer (1605 - 1682)*

If there is a God, He is infinitely incomprehensible, having neither parts nor limits. He has no relation to us. We are therefore incapable of knowing what He is, or whether He is. This being so, who will dare to solve the problem? Not we, who have no relation to Him.
You must wager. ... Which will you choose? ... Let us weigh the gain and loss in calling "heads" that God is. Let us weigh the two cases: if you win, you win all; if you lose you lose nothing. Wager then unhesitatingly that He is.
-*BLAISE PASCAL, French scientist, philosopher (1623 - 1662)*

True religion consists in annihilating self before that Universal Being, whom we have so often provoked, and who can justly destroy us at any time; in recognizing that we can do nothing without Him, and have deserved nothing from Him but His displeasure. It consists in knowing that there is an unconquerable opposition between us and God, and that without a mediator there can be no communion with Him.
-*BLAISE PASCAL*

How many natures lie in human nature?
-*BLAISE PASCAL*

If a true estimate were made of the morality and religions of the world, we would find that the far greater part of mankind received even those opinions and ceremonies they would die for, rather from the fashions of their countries and the constant practice of those about them, than from any conviction of their reason.

*-JOHN LOCKE, English philosopher (1632 - 1704)*

Men pretend to serve Almighty God who doth not need it, but make use of Him because they need Him.

*-SIR GEORGE SAVILE, English poltician, essayist (1633 - 1695)*

Religion is nothing else than love of God and man.

*- WILLIAM PENN, English Quaker, colonialist (1644 - 1718)*

That the universe was formed by a fortuitous concourse of the atoms, I will no more believe than that the accidental jumbling of the alphabet should fall into a most ingenious treatise on Philosophy.

*-JONATHON SWIFT, English satirist (1667 - 1745)*

We have just enough Religion to make us hate, but not enough to make us love one another.

*-JONATHON SWIFT*

Those who make religion to consist in the contempt of this world and its enjoyments, are under a very fatal and dangerous mission. As life is the gift of heaven, it is religion to enjoy it. He, therfore, who can be happy in himself, and who contributes all in his power toward the happiness of others, answers most effectually the ends of his creation, is an honor to his nature, and a pattern to mankind.

*-JOSEPH ADDISON, English essayist (1672 - 1719)*

It is absurd to call him a God of justice and goodness, who inflicts evil indiscriminately on the good and the wicked, upon the innocent and the guilty. It is idle to demand that the unfortunate should console themselves for their misfortunes in the very arms of the one who alone is the author of them.
-*JEAN MESLIER, French writer (1678 - 1733)*

Conscience is God's presence in man.
-*EMANUEL SWEDENBORG, Swedish theologian (1688 - 1772)*

Men are extremely inclined to the passions of hope and fear; a religion, therfore, that had neither a heaven nor a hell could hardly please them.
-*BARON DE MONTESQUIEU, French lawyer, philosopher (1689 - 1755)*

If God did not exist it would be necessary to invent Him. But all nature cries aloud that He does exist; that there is a supreme intelligence, an immense power, an admirable order, and everything teaches us our own dependence on it.
-*VOLTAIRE, French author, philosopher (1694 - 1778)*

All philosophers of the world who had a religion have said in all ages: "There is a God; and one must be just." That, then, is the universal religion established in all ages and throughout mankind. The point in which they all agree is therfore true; and the systems through which they differ therfore false.
-*VOLTAIRE*

After our holy religion (which is doubtless the only good one) which would be the least bad?
Wouldn't it be the simplest one? Wouldn't it be the one that taught a good deal of morality and very

little dogma? The one that tended to make men just, without making them absurd? The one that wouldn't command belief in impossible, contradictory things insulting to the Divinity and pernicious to mankind, and wouldn't dare to threaten with eternal punishment anyone who has common sense? Wouldn't it be the religion that didn't uphold its beliefs with executioners, and didn't inudate the world with blood for the sake of unintelligible sophisms? The one in which an ambiguity, a play on words, or two or three forged charters wouldn't make a sovereign and a god of a priest who is often a man who has committed incest, a murderer, and a poisoner? The one that wouldn't make kings subject to this priest? The one that taught nothing but the worship of a God, justice, tolerance and humanity?

*-VOLTAIRE*

If God created us in his own image we have more than reciprocated. *-VOLTAIRE*

I believe in one God, creator of the universe. That He governs it by His providence. That He ought to be worshipped. That the most acceptable service we render to Him is doing good to His other children. That the soul of man is immortal and will be treated with justice in another life respecting its conduct in this. These I take to be the fundamental principles of all sound religion.

*-BEN FRANKLIN, American statesman, writer, inventor (1706 - 1790)*

If men are so wicked with religion, what would they be without it. *-BEN FRANKLIN*

Many have quarreled about religion that have never practiced it. *-BEN FRANKLIN*

To be of no church is dangerous. Religion, of which the rewards are distant, and which is animated only by faith and hope, will glide by degrees out of the mind unless it be invigorated and reimpressed by external ordinances, by stated calls to worship, and the salutary influence of example.
*-SAMUEL JOHNSON, English lexicographer, writer (1709 - 1784)*

If *reason* be a gift of Heaven, and we can say as much of *faith*, Heaven has certainly made us two gifts not only incompatible but in direct contradiction to each other. In order to solve the difficulty, we are compelled to say either that faith is a chimera or that reason is useless.
*-DENIS DIDEROT, French philosopher (1713 - 1784)*

When God, from whom I have my reason, demands of me to sacrifice it, he becomes a mere juggler that snatches from me what he pretended to give.
*-DENIS DIDEROT*

I have only a small flickering light to guide me in the darkness of a thick forest. Up comes a theologian and blows it out. *-DENIS DIDEROT*

Nature is but a name for an effect, whose cause is God.
*-WILLIAM COWPER, English poet (1731 - 1800)*

Let us with caution indulge the supposition that morality can be maintained without religion. Whatever may be conceded to the influence of rational education on minds of peculiar structure, reason and experience both forbid us to expect that national morality can prevail in exclusion of religious principle.

*-GEORGE WASHINGTION, 1st President of the U.S. (1732 - 1799)*

Religion is as necessary to reason as reason is to religion. The one cannot exist without the other. A reasoning being would lose his reason, in attempting to account for the great phenomena of nature, had he not a Supreme Being to refer to; and well has it been said, that if there had been no God, mankind would have been obliged to imagine one.

*-GEORGE WASHINGTON*

The loss of paradise by eating a forbidden apple, has been many thousand years a lesson to mankind; but not much regarded. Moral reflections, wise maxims, religious terrors have little effect upon nations when they contradict a present passion, prejudice, imagination, enthusiasm or caprice.

*-JOHN ADAMS, 2nd President of the U.S. (1735 - 1826)*

Religion, or the duty which we owe to our Creator, and the manner of discharging it, can be directed only by reason and conviction, not by force or violence; and therfore all men are equally entitled to the free exercise of religion, according to the dictates of conscience; and that it is the mutual duty of all to practice Christian forbearance, love, and charity towards each other.

*-PATRICK HENRY, American statesman, orator (1736 - 1799)*

Question with boldness even the existence of God;

because, if there be one, he must more approve of the homage of reason than that of blindfolded fear.
- *THOMAS JEFFERSON, 3rd President of the U.S. (1743 - 1826)*

Say nothing of my religion. It is known to God and myself alone. Its evidence before the world is to be sought in my life: if it has been honest and dutiful to society the religion which has regulated it cannot be a bad one.   *-THOMAS JEFFERSON*

Man was not born to solve the problems of the universe, but to put his finger on the problem and then to keep within the limits of the comprehensible.
-*JOHANN WOLFGANG VON GOETHE, German poet, playwright (1749 - 1832)*

Mysteries are not necessarily miracles.   *- GOETHE*

It is proper to take alarm at the first experiment on our liberties. ... Who does not see that the same authority which can establish Christianity, in exclusion of all other Religions, may establish with the same ease any particular sect of Christians, in exclusion of all other Sects?
-*JAMES MADISON, 4th President of the U.S. (1751 - 1836)*

It is easy to understand God as long as you don't try to explain him.
-*JOSEPH JOUBERT, French moralist (1754 - 1824)*

All religions united with government are more or less inimical to liberty. All separated from government are compatible with liberty.
-*HENRY CLAY, American politician (1777 - 1852)*

How can you have order in a state without religion?

For, when one man is dying of hunger near another who is ill of surfeit, he cannot resign himself to this difference unless there is an authority which declares, "God wills it thus." Religion is excellent stuff for keeping common people quiet.
*-NAPOLEON BONAPARTE, Emperor of France (1769 - 1821)*

Religion is the masterpiece of the art of animal training, for it trains people as to how they shall think.
*-ARTHUR SCHOPENHAUER, German philosopher (1788 - 1860)*

God - but a word invoked to explain the world.
*-ALPHONSE DE LAMARTINE, French poet (1790 - 1869)*

If Jesus Christ were to come today, people would not even crucify him. They would ask him to dinner, and hear what he had to say, and make fun of it.
*- THOMAS CARLYLE, Scottish essayist, historian (1795 - 1881)*

A man lives by believing something, not by debating and arguing about many things.   *-THOMAS CARLYLE*

God will forgive me; that's his business.
*-HEINRICH HEINE, German poet, critic (1797 - 1856)*

Religion finds the love of happiness and the principles of duty separated in us; and its mission - its masterpiece is, to reunite them.
*-ALEXANDRE VINET, Swiss theologian (1797 - 1847)*

Religion is an illusion of childhood, outgrown under proper education.
*-AUGUSTE COMTE, French philosopher (1798 - 1857)*

Religion has its own enlargement, and an

enlargement, not of tumult, but of peace. It is often remarked of uneducated persons, who have hitherto thought little of the unseen world, that, on their turning to God, looking into themselves, regulating their hearts, reforming their conduct, and meditating on death and judgement, heaven and hell, they seem to become, in point of intellect, different beings from what they were. Before, they took things as they came, and thought no more of one thing than another. But now every event has a meaning; they have their own estimate of whatever happens to them; they are mindful of times and seasons, and compare the present with the past; and the world, no longer dull, monotonous, unprofitable, and hopeless, is a various and complicated drama, with parts and an object, and an awful moral.

*-JOHN HENRY NEWMAN, English prelate, writer (1801 - 1890)*

I do not see the difference between avowing that there is no God, and implying that nothing definite can for certain he known about Him.

*-JOHN HENRY NEWMAN*

God enters by a private door into every individual.

*-RALPH WALDO EMERSON, American poet, essayist (1803 - 1882)*

I like the silent church before the service begins, better than any preaching.    *-RALPH WALDO EMERSON*

God offers to every mind a choice between truth and repose. Take which you please - you can never have both.    *-RALPH WALDO EMERSON*

The great writers to whom the world owes what religious liberty it possesses, have mostly asserted freedom of conscience as an indefeasible right, and denied absolutely that a human being is accountable to others for his religious belief. Yet so natural to mankind is intolerance in whatever they really care about, that religious freedom has hardly anywhere been practically realized.

*-JOHN STUART MILL, English philosopher (1806 - 1873)*

It is conceivable that religion may be morally useful without being intellectually sustainable.

*-JOHN STUART MILL*

In practice all men are atheists; they deny their faith by their actions.

*-LUDWIG FEUERBACH, German philosopher (1804 - 1872)*

Man, himself, is the crowning wonder of creation; the study of his nature the noblest study the world affords.

*-WILLIAM GLADSTONE, English politician (1809 - 1898)*

The mystery of the beginning of all things is insoluble by us; and I for one must be content to remain agnostic.

*-CHARLES DARWIN, English naturalist, writer (1809 - 1882)*

We, on our side, are praying Him to give us victory, because we believe we are right; but those on the other side pray Him, too, for victory, believing they are right. What must He think of us?

*-ABRAHAM LINCOLN, 16th President of the U.S. (1809 - 1865)*

To exclude the Church, founded by God Himself, from life, from laws, from the education of youth, from domestic society, is a grave and fatal error. A

state from which religion is banished can never be well regulated.
-*LEO X111, Pope from 1878 (1810 - 1903)*

Temptations without imply desires within; men ought not to say, "How powerfully the devil tempts," but "How strongly I am tempted."
-*HENRY WARD BEECHER, American cleric, writer (1813 - 1887)*

Prayer does not change God, but it changes him who prays.
-*SÖREN KIERKEGAARD, Danish philosopher, theologian (1813 - 1855)*

Both [Church and State] have the same principle as their point of departure: that of the natural wickedness of man, which can be vanquished, according to the Church, only by divine grace and the death of the natural man in God; and according to the State, only by law and the immolation of the individual upon the altar of the State. Both strive to transform man, the one into a saint, the other into a citizen. But the natural man must die, for the religions of the Church and of the State unanimously pronounce his sentence.
-*MIKHAIL BAKUNIN, Russian writer, anarchist (1814 - 1876)*

All temporal and human power proceeds directly from spiritual or divine authority.
But authority is the negation of liberty. God, or rather the fiction of God, is thus the sanction and the intellectual and moral cause of all slavery on earth, and the liberty of men will not be complete unless it will have completely annihilated the inauspicious fiction of a heavenly master.   -*MIKHAIL BAKUNIN*

The best religion is humanity, the best divine service, love thy neighbor as thyself. The motto which we inscribe on our banner is the fatherhood of God and the brotherhood of man.

- MAX LILIENTHAL, American rabbi (1815 - 1882)

The church is a sort of hospital for men's souls, and as full of quackery as the hospital for their bodies.

- HENRY DAVID THOREAU, American essayist, naturalist (1817 - 1862)

I distrust those people who know so well what God wants them to do, because I notice it always coincides with their own desires.

- SUSAN B. ANTHONY, American suffragist (1820 - 1906)

No one will say, that it is admittedly certain and verifiable, that there is a personal first cause, the moral and intelligent governor of the universe, whom we may call 'God' if we will. But that all things seem to us to have what we call a law of their being and to tend to fulfill it, is certain and admitted; though whether we will call this 'God' or not, is a matter of choice. Suppose, however, we call it 'God', we then give the name of 'God' to a certain and admitted reality; this, at least, is an advantage.

- MATTHEW ARNOLD, English poet, critic (1822 - 1888)

Religion, if we follow the intention of human thought and human language in the use of the word, is ethics heightened, enkindled, lit up by feeling; the passage from morality to religion is made when to morality is applied emotion.    -MATTHEW ARNOLD

Leave the matter of religion to the family alter, the church and the private school, supported entirely by private contributions. Keep the Church and the State forever separate.

*-ULYSSES S. GRANT, 18th President of the U.S. (1822 - 1885)*

Agnosticism, in fact, is not a creed, but a method, the essence of which lies in the rigorous application of a single principle. That principle is of great antiquity; it is as old as Socrates, as old as the writer who said, "Try all things, hold fast by that which is good"; it is the foundation of the Reformation, which simply illustrated the axiom that every man should be able to give a reason for the faith that is in him; it is the great principle of Descartes; it is the fundamental axiom of modern science.

Positively the principle may be expressed: In matters of the intellect, follow your reason as far as it will take you, without regard to any other consideration. And negatively: In matters of the intellect, do not pretend that conclusions are certain which are not demonstrated or demonstrable. That I take to be the agnostic faith, which if a man keep whole and undefiled, he shall not be ashamed to look the universe in the face, whatever the future may have in store for him.

*- THOMAS HUXLEY, English biologist, writer (1825 - 1895)*

The essence of religion consists solely in the answer to the question, "Why do I live, and what is my relation to the infinite universe around me?"

All the metaphysics of religion, all the doctrines about deites and about the origin of the world, and all external worship - which all usually supposed to be religion - are but indications (differing according to geographical, ethnographical and historical circumstances) of the existence of religion. There is no religion from the most elevated to the coarsest that has not at its root this establishing of man's relation to the surrounding universe or to its first cause. There is no religious rite however coarse, nor any cult however refined, that has not this at its root. Every religious teaching is the expression which the founder of that religion has given of the relation he considered himself (and consequently all other people also) to occupy as a man towards the universe and its origin and first cause.

*-LEO TOLSTOY, Russian novelist (1828 - 1910)*

The worst moment for the atheist is when he is really thankful, and has nobody to thank.

*-DANTE GABRIEL ROSSETTI, English poet, painter (1828 - 1882)*

Our hope of immortality does not come from any religion, but clearly all religions come from that hope.

*-ROBERT INGERSOLL, American lawyer, orator (1833 - 1899)*

A competent religious guide must be clear and intelligible to all, so that every one may fully understand the true meaning of the instructions it contains. Is the Bible a book intelligible to all? Far from it; it is full of obscurities and dfficulties not only for the illiterate, but even for the learned.

*-JAMES CARDINAL GIBBONS, American Roman Catholic prelate (1834 - 1921)*

In the best sense of the word, Jesus was a radical. ... His religion has so long been identified with conservatism ... that it is almost startling sometimes to remember that all the conservatives of his own times were against him; that it was the young, free, restless, sanguine, progressive part of the people who flocked to him.

-*PHILLIPS BROOKS, American religious leader (1835 - 1893)*

Man is a Religious Animal. He is the only Religious Animal. He is the Only animal that has the True Religion - several of them. He is the only animal that loves his neighbor as himself and cuts his throat if his theology isn't straight.

-*MARK TWAIN, American writer, humorist (1835 - 1910)*

The motto ("In God We Trust") stated a lie. If this nation ever trusted in God, that time has gone by; for nearly half a century its entire trust has been in the Republican Party and the dollar - mainly the dollar.

-*MARK TWAIN*

It is the fool who saith in his heart there is no God. But what shall we call the man who tells us that with this sort of world God bids us be content?

-*HENRY GEORGE, American economist, writer (1839 - 1897)*

Christian, n. One who believes that the New Testament is a divinely inspired book admirably suited to the spiritual needs of his neighbor. One who follows the teachings of Christ in so far as they are not inconsistent with a life of sin.

-*AMBROSE BIERCE, American journalist, writer (1842 - c.1914)*

Scriptures, n. The sacred books of our holy religion, as distinguished from the false and profane writings on which all other faiths are based.

-*AMBROSE BIERCE*

Infidel, n. In New York, one who does not believe in the Christian religion; in Constantinople, one who does. -*AMBROSE BIERCE*

Religion, n. A daughter of Hope and Fear, explaining to Ignorance the nature of the Unknowable.
-*AMBROSE BIERCE*

The pivot round which the religious life, as we have traced it, revolves, is the interest of the individual in his private personal destiny. Religion, in short, is a monumental chapter in the history of human egotism.
- *WILLIAM JAMES, American philosopher, psychologist (1842 - 1910)*

We can act *as if* there were a God; feel *as if* we were free; consider Nature *as if* she were full of special designs; lay plans *as if* we were to be immortal; and we find then that these words do make a genuine difference in our moral life. -*WILLIAM JAMES*

The highest flights of charity, devotion, trust, patience, bravery to which wings of human nature have spread themselves have been flown for religious ideals. -*WILLIAM JAMES*

What is it: is man only a blunder of God, or God only a blunder of man.
-*FRIEDRICH WILHELM NIETZSCHE , German philosopher, poet (1844 - 1900)*

I have never seen the slightest scientific proof of the religious theories of heaven and hell, of future life for individuals, or of a personal God.
- *THOMAS EDISON, American inventor (1847 - 1931)*

We hear much nowadays of the danger of

"suppressed complexes". It is indeed in the discovery of the danger of these complexes and the methods of their cure that the main originality of the Freudian school consists. Man finds himself in inevitable conflict with some and often many elements in his environment; he shirks the conflict. Just because it is harassing and depressing, he forcibly drives it out of his conscious life. But his unconscious life is beyond his control. Into that unconscious stratum the conflict sinks and lives there an uninterrupted life.

Now the function of religion is to prevent, to render needless, just this suppression of conflict. Man has made for himself representations of beings stronger and more splendid than himself; he has lost all sense that they are really projections of his own desire, and to these beings he hands over his conflict; he no longer needs to banish the conflict into the unconscious, but gods will see to it and fight on his side: "God is our refuge and strength," "Cast all your care upon Him, for He careth for you." The function of theology is to keep the conflict that would be submerged in the sphere of the conscious and prevent its development into a mischievous subliminal complex.

*-JANE ELLEN HARRISON, English scholar, author (1850 - 1928)*

I do not love my neighbor as myself, and apologize to no one. I treat my neighbor as fairly and politely as I hope to be treated, but there is no law in nature or common sense ordering me to go beyond that.

*-EDGAR WATSON HOWE, American journalist, editor (1853 - 1937)*

It always strikes me, and it is very peculiar, that,

3  1621  00860  7554

whenever we see the image of indescribable and unutterable desolation - of loneliness, poverty, and misery, the end and extreme of things - the thought of God comes into one's mind.

-*VINCENT VAN GOGH, Dutch painter (1853 - 1890)*

Every saint has a past and every sinner has a future.

-*OSCAR WILDE, Irish poet, playwright, wit (1854 - 1900)*

I sometimes think that God, in creating man, somewhat overestimated his ability. *-OSCAR WILDE*

Men are not punished for their sins, but by them.

-*ELBERT HUBBARD, American writer, publisher (1856 - 1915)*

God will not look you over for medals, degrees, or diplomas, but for scars. *-ELBERT HUBBARD*

Religion is an attempt to get control over the sensory world, in which we are placed, by means of the wish-world, which we have developed inside us as a result of biological and psychological necessities.

-*SIGMUND FREUD, Austrian neurologist, psychoanalyst (1856 - 1939)*

If one wishes to form a true estimate of the full grandeur of religion, one must keep in mind what it undertakes to do for men. It gives them information about the source and origin of the universe, it assures them of protection and final happiness amid the changing vicissitudes of life, and it guides their thoughts and motions by means of precepts which are backed by the whole force of its authority.

-*SIGMUND FREUD*

In my 'Future of an Illusion' I was concerned much

less with the deepest sources of religious feeling than with what the ordinary man understands by his religion, that system of doctrines and pledges that on the one hand explains the riddle of this world to him with enviable completeness, and on the other assures him that a solicitous Providence is watching over him and will make up to him in a future existence for any shortcomings in this life. The ordinary man cannot imagine this Providence in any other form but that of a greatly exalted father, for only such a one could understand the needs of the sons of men, or be softened by their prayers and placated by the signs of their remorse. The whole thing is so patently infantile, so incongruous with reality, that to one whose attitude to humanity is friendly it is painful to think that the great majority of mortals will never be able to rise above this view of life.

*- SIGMUND FREUD*

Even those who do not regret the disappearance of religious illusions from the civilized world of today will admit that so long as they were in force they offered those who were bound by them the most powerful protection against the danger of neurosis.

*- SIGMUND FREUD*

Religion is a great force - the only real motive force in the world. But you must get at a man through his own religion, not yours.

*- GEORGE BERNARD SHAW, British playwright, critic (1856 - 1950)*

The fact that a believer is happier than a skeptic is no more to the point than the fact that a drunken man is happier than a sober one.     *-GEORGE BERNARD SHAW*

The truth is, no one really believes in immortality. Belief must mean something more than desire or hope.
*-CLARENCE DARROW, American lawyer (1857 - 1938)*

In spite of all the yearnings of men, no one can produce a single fact or reason to support the belief in God and in personal immortality.
*-CLARENCE DARROW*

I say that religion is the belief in future life and in God. I don't believe in either. *-CLARENCE DARROW*

I do not consider it an insult, but rather a compliment to be called an agnostic. I do not pretend to know where many ignorant men are sure - that is all agnosticism means. *-CLARENCE DARROW*

An atheist is a man who believes himself an accident.
*-FRANCIS THOMPSON, English poet (1859 - 1907)*

Then God, if he is good, is not the author of all things, as the many assert, but he is the cause of a few things only, and not of most things that occur to men. For few are the goods of human life, and many are the evils, and the good is to be attributed to God alone; of the evils the causes are to be sought elsewhere, and not in him.
*-MAX PLANCK, German scientist (1858 - 1947)*

What would have been the effect upon religion if it had come to us through the minds of women?
*-CHARLOTTE PERKINS GILMAN, American feminist, writer (1860 - 1935)*

Many people believe that they are attracted by God,

or by Nature, when they are only repelled by man.
 -*WILLIAM RALPH INGE, English prelate, writer (1860 - 1954)*

If we have to give up either religion or education, we should give up education.
 -*WILLIAM JENNINGS BRYAN, American politician, fundamentalist (1860 - 1925)*

The brute necessity of believing something so long as life lasts does not justify any belief in particular.
 -*GEORGE SANTAYANA, American philosopher, poet (1863 - 1952)*

That fear first created the gods is perhaps as true as anything so brief could be on so great a subject.
 -*GEORGE SANTAYANA*

Each religion, by the help of more or less myth which it takes more or less seriously, proposes some method of fortifying the human soul and enabling it to make its peace with its destiny.   -*GEORGE SANTAYANA*

What religion a man shall have is a historical accident, quite as much as what language he shall speak.   -*GEORGE SANTAYANA*

Faith is in its essence simply a matter of will, not reason, and to believe is to wish to believe, and to believe in God is, before all and above all, to wish that there may be a God.
 -*MIGUEL DE UNAMUNO, Spanish writer (1864 - 1936)*

All outward forms of religion are almost useless, and are the causes of endless strife. ... Believe there is a great power silently working all things for good, behave yourself and never mind the rest.
 -*BEATRIX POTTER, English writer, illustrator (1866 - 1943)*

Religion teaches those who toil in poverty all their lives to be resigned and patient in this world, and consoles them with the hope of reward in heaven. As for those who live upon the labor of others, religion teaches them to be charitable in earthly life, thus providing a cheap justification for their whole exploiting existence and selling them at a reasonable price tickets to a heavenly bliss. "Religion is the opium of the people." (Marx). Religion is a kind of spiritual intoxicant, in which the slaves of capital drown their humanity and blunt their desires for some sort of decent human existence.

*-V. I. LENIN, Russian communist leader (1870 - 1924)*

It is easier to fight for one's principles than to live up to them.

*-ALFRED ADLER, Austrian psychiatrist (1870 - 1937)*

If I were personally to define religion I would say that it is a bandage that man has invented to protect a soul made bloody by circumstance.

*-THEODORE DREISER, American editor, author (1871 - 1945)*

I do not pretend to be able to prove that there is no God. I equally cannot prove that Satan is a fiction. The Christian God may exist; so may the Gods of Olympus, or of ancient Egypt, or of Babylon. But no one of these hypotheses is more probable than any other: they lie outside the region of even probable knowledge, and therfore there is no reason to consider any of them.

*-BERTRAND RUSSELL, English philosopher (1872 - 1970)*

God and Satan alike are essentially human figures,

the one a projection of ourselves, the other of our enemies. -*BERTRAND RUSSELL*

The most savage controversies are those about matters as to which there is no good evidence either way. Persecution is used in theology, not in arithmetic. -*BERTRAND RUSSELL*

I admit that the love of God, if there were a God, would make it possible for human beings to be better than is possible in a Godless world.
-*BERTRAND RUSSELL*

The extraordinary sway which the Christian story exercised over the minds of men is easily understood. No interpretation of the life of mankind ever more exactly reflected the experience, or more effectively responded to the hopes of average men. To be aware of present trials and misfortunes, to look back with fond memories to the happier times (imagined so at least) of youth, to look forward with hope to a more serene and secure old age - what could more adequately sum up the experience of the great majority? And what was the Christian story if not an application of this familiar individual experience to the life of mankind? Mankind had its youth, its happier time in the Garden of Eden, to look back upon, its present middle period of misfortunes to endure, its future security to hope for. The average man needed no theology to understand universal experience when presented in terms so familiar; and it consoled him - it no doubt added something to his sense of personal significance - to realize that his own life, however barren and limited it might be, was but a concrete exemplification of the experience which God had decreed for all the generations of men.

But better than all that - best of all - he could understand that there should sometimes be an end made, a judgement pronounced upon the world of men and things, a day of reckoning in which evil men would be punished and good men rewarded; he could believe that with all his heart, with a conviction fortified by the stored-up memories of the injustices he had witnessed, the unmerited injuries he had suffered. The average man could believe all that; and in the measure that he could believe it he could hope, he could so easily convince himself, that on that last day he would be found among those judged good, among those to be admitted into that other world in which things would be forever right.

*-CARL BECKER, American historian (1873 - 1945)*

I don't know why it is that the religious never ascribe common sense to God.

*-SOMERSET MAUGHAM, English novelist, playwright (1874 - 1965)*

There is no higher religion than human service. To work for the common good is the greatest creed.

*-ALBERT SCHWEITZER, French clergyman, physician, philosopher (1875 - 1965)*

Those psychiatrists who are not superficial have come to the conclusion that the vast neurotic misery of the world could be termed a neurosis of emptiness. Men cut themselves off from the rest of their being, from God, and then life turns empty, inane, meaningless, without purpose. So when God goes, goal goes. When goal goes, meaning goes. When

meaning goes, value goes, and life turns dead on our hands.
-*CARL JUNG, Swiss psychiatrist (1875 - 1961)*

Fortunately, in her kindness and patience, Nature has never put the fatal question as to the meaning of their lives into the mouths of most people. And where no one asks, no one needs to answer.   *-CARL JUNG*

Once there was God, now there is no God, some day there will be a God again.
-*RAINER MARIA RILKE, German poet (1875 - 1926)*

The fact that astronomies change while the stars abide is a true analogy of every realm of human life and thought, religion not least of all. No existent theology can be a final formulation of spiritual truth.
-*HARRY EMERSON FOSDICK, American clergyman (1878 - 1969)*

There need not be in religion, or music, or art, or love, or goodness, anything that is against reason; but never while the sun shines will we get great religion, or music, or art, or love, or goodness, without going beyond reason.   *-HARRY EMERSON FOSDICK*

No man can be wrong with man and right with God.
-*HARRY EMERSON FOSDICK*

Evil is here in the world, not because God wants it or uses it here, but because He knows not how at the moment to remove it; or knowing, has not the skill or power to achieve His end. Evil, therefore, is a fact not to be explained away, but to be accepted; and accepted not to be endured, but to be conquered. It is a challenge neither to our reason nor to our patience, but to our courage.

*-JOHN HAYNES HOLMES, American clergyman (1879 - 1964)*

The whole Christian system, like every other similar system, goes to pieces upon the problem of evil. Its most adept theologians, attempting to reconcile the Heavenly Father of their theory with the dreadful agonies of man in His world, can only retreat behind Chrysostom's despairing maxim, that "a comprehended God is no God".

*-H.L. MENCKEN, American editor, satirist (1880 - 1956)*

We must respect the other fellow's religion, but only in the sense and to the extent that we respect his theory that his wife is beautiful and his children smart. *-H.L. MENCKEN*

I believe that religion, generally speaking, has been a curse to mankind - that its modest and greatly overestimated services on the ethical side have been more than overcome by the damage it has done to clear and honest thinking.

I believe that no discovery of fact, however trivial, can be wholly useless to the race, and that no trumpeting of falsehood, however virtuous in intent, can be anything but vicious. ...

I believe that the evidence for immortality is no better than the evidence of witches, and deserves no more respect.

I believe in the complete freedom of thought and speech.

I believe in the capacity of man to conquer his world, and to find out what it is made of, and how it is run.

I believe in the reality of progress.
I -
But the whole thing, after all, may be put very simply. I believe that it is better to tell the truth than to lie. I believe that it is better to be free than to be a slave. And I believe that it is better to know than to be ignorant.   *-H.L. MENCKEN*

All great religions, in order to escape absurdity, have to admit a dilution of agnosticism. It is only the savage, whether of the African bush or the American gospel tent, who pretends to know the will and the intent of God exactly and completely.   *-H.L. MENCKEN*

Cruel persecutions and intolerance are not accidents, but grow out of the very essence of religion, namely, its absolute claims.
*-MORRIS COHEN, American professor of philosophy, (1880 - 1947)*

The day will come when after harnessing the ether, the winds, the tides, gravitation, we shall harness for God the energies of love. And on that day for the second time in the history of the world, man will have discovered fire.
*- TEILHARD DE CHARDIN, French paleontologist, philosopher (1881 - 1955)*

To be thoroughly religious, one must, I believe, be sorely disappointed. One's faith in God increases as one's faith in the world decreases. The happier the man, the farther he is from God.
*- GEORGE NATHAN, American editor, author (1882 - 1958)*

I find in the universe so many forms of order, organization, system, law, and adjustment of means to ends, that I believe in a cosmic intelligence and I conceive God as the life, mind, order, and law of the world.

- *WILL DURANT, American historian (1885 - 1981)*

Is Christianity dying? Is the religion that gave morals, courage, and art to Western civilization suffering slow decay through the spread of knowledge, the widening of astronomic, geographical, and historical horizons, the realization of evil in history and the soul, the decline of faith in an afterlife and of trust in a benevolent guidance of the world? If this is so, it is the basic event of modern times, for the soul of a civilization is its religion, and it dies with its faith.    -*WILL DURANT*

Doubt isn't the opposite of faith; it is an element of faith.

- *PAUL TILLICH, American theologian (1886 - 1965)*

The important thing is not that people go more to church, listen to evangelists and join churches. The important thing is that the younger generation asks the right questions ... the meaning of our life, the conflicts of our existence, the way to deal with anxiety in our life, the feeling of guilt, the feeling of emptiness.    -*PAUL TILLICH*

The "establishment of religion" clause of the First Amendment means at least this: Neither a state or the Federal Government can set up a church. Neither can pass laws which aid one religion, aid all religions, or prefer one religion over another.

- *HUGO BLACK, U.S. Supreme Court Justice (1886 - 1971)*

Often in history we see that religion, which was

meant to raise us and make us better and nobler, has made people behave like beasts. Instead of bringing enlightenment to them, it has often tried to keep them in the dark; instead of broadening their minds, it has frequently made them narrow-minded and intolerant of others.

-*JAWAHARLAL NEHRU, Prime Minister of India (1889 - 1964)*

God is really another artist. He invented the giraffe, the elephant and the cat. He has no real style. He just goes on trying other things.

-*PABLO PICASSO, Spanish painter, sculptor (1881 - 1973)*

I believe that the scientist is trying to express absolute truth and the artist absolute beauty, so that I find in science and art, and in an attempt to lead a good life, all the religion that I want.

-*J.B.S. HALDANE, British scientist (1892 - 1964)*

There appear to be three alternatives. God may not be wholly benevolent. If He is not, He is not worthy of our worship. ... Or God may not be omniscient. But if He is not, how can we be sure He is wiser than some of our wise men?

The third alternative is Plato's final conviction, that God was not coercive, but only persuasive. And is this not Christianity?

-*CHARLES P. CURTIS, American lawyer, writer, educator (1891 - 1959)*

There can be no conflict between science and religion. Science is a reliable method of finding truth. Religion is the search for a satisfying way of life. Science is growing; yet a world that has science needs, as never before, the inspiration that religion

offers.
*-ARTHUR HOLLY COMPTON, American physicist (1892 - 1962)*

We have grasped the mystery of the atom, and rejected the Sermon on the Mount.
*-OMAR BRADLEY, American general (1893 - 1981)*

How could science be any enemy of religion when God commanded man to be a scientist the day He told him to rule the earth and subject it?
*-FULTON J. SHEEN, American prelate (1895 - 1979)*

Many souls fail to find God because they want a religion which will remake society without remaking themselves. *-FULTON J. SHEEN*

A vital religion proves itself both by moral responsibility in creating tolerable forms of community and justice, and by a humble awareness of human imperfectibility. Above all, it preserves a sense of ultimate majesty and meaning, transcending all our little majesties and meanings.
*-REINHOLD NIEBUHR, American theologian, (1892 - 1971)*

Religious faith is not a storm cellar to which men and women can flee for refuge from the storms of life. It is, instead, an inner spiritual strength which enables them to face those storms with hope and serenity. Religious faith has the miraculous power to lift ordinary human beings to greatness in seasons of stress.
*-SAM ERVIN, U.S. Senator (1896 - 1985)*

No one is without Christianity, if we agree on what we mean by the word. It is every individual's individual code of behavior by means of which he makes himself a better human being than his nature wants to be, if he followed his nature only.

*- WILLIAM FAULKNER, American novelist (1897 - 1962)*

I remember that when Christian teachers told me long ago that I must hate a bad man's actions but not the man, I used to think this a silly, straw-splitting distinction: how could you hate what a man did and not hate the man? But years later it occurred to me that there was one man to whom I had been doing this all my life - namely, myself.

*-C.S. LEWIS, English writer (1898 - 1963)*

Men may believe what they cannot prove. They may not be put to the proof of their religious doctrines or beliefs. Religious experiences which are as real as life to some may be incomprehensible to others.

*- WILLIAM O. DOUGLASS, U.S. Supreme Court Justice (1898 - 1980)*

What do I believe? As an American I believe in generosity, in liberty, in the rights of man. These are social and political faiths that are part of me, as they are, I suppose part of all of us. Such beliefs are easy to express. But part of me too is my relation to all life, my religion. And this is not so easy to talk about. Religious experience is highly intimate and, for me, ready words are not at hand.

*-ADLAI STEVENSON, American politician, statesman (1900 - 1965)*

The Lord works from the inside out. The world works from the outside in. The world would take people out of the slums. Christ takes the slums out of the people, and then they take themselves out of the slums. The world would mold men by changing their environment. Christ changes men, who then change their environment. The world would shape human behavior, but Christ can change human nature.

-EZRA TAFT BENSON, American government official, religious leader (1899 - 1994)

It is an open question whether any behavior based on fear of eternal punishment can be regarded as ethical or should be regarded as merely cowardly.

-MARGARET MEAD, American anthropologist (1901 - 1978)

If a man without a sense of smell declared that this yellow rose I hold had no scent we should know that he was wrong. The defect is in him, not in the flower. It is the same with a man who says there is no God. It merely means that he is without the capacity to discern his presence.

-SIR RALPH RICHARDSON, English actor (1902 - 1983)

We have to believe in free-will. We've got no choice.

-ISAAC BASHEVIS SINGER, American Yiddish writer (1904 - 1991)

There is no God and no prevenient design which can adapt the world and all its possibilities to my will. When Descartes said, "Conquer yourself rather than the world" what he meant was, at bottom, the same thing.

-JEAN -PAUL SARTRE, French philosopher, writer (1905 - 1980)

In this life you sometimes have to choose between pleasing God and pleasing man. In the long run it's better to please God - he's more apt to remember.

-HARRY KEMELMAN, American author (1908 - 1996)

We cannot know whether we love God, although there may be strong reasons for thinking so, but there can be no doubt about whether we love our neighbor or no.

-*MOTHER TERESA, Yugosalvian-born nun, missionary (1910 - 1997)*

To me, God and compassion are one and the same. Compassion is the joy of sharing. It's doing small things for the love of each other - just a smile, or carrying a bucket of water, or showing some simple kindness. These are the small things that make up compassion.

It is only pride and selfishness and coldness that keep us from having compassion. When we ultimately go home to God, we are going to be judged on what we were to each other, what we did for each other, and, especially, how much love we put in that. It's not how much we give, but how much love we put in the *doing* - that's compassion in action.

One's religion has nothing to do with compassion. It's our love for God that is the main thing. Many Christians and non-Christians alike come to help in our houses in Calcutta and throughout the world. We have volunteers of all religions working with our aides day and night. Religion is meant to help us come closer to God, not meant to separate us. All God really wants is for us to love Him. The way we can show our love for Him is to serve others.

-*MOTHER TERESA*

Often God has to shut a door in our face, so that He can subsequently open the door through which He wants us to go.

-*CATHERINE MARSHALL, American writer (1914 - 1983)*

Sometimes I think we're alone in the universe, and sometimes I think we're not. In either case, the idea is quite staggering.

-*ARTHUR C. CLARKE, English science-fiction writer*

Religions should grow as our knowledge and understanding grow. Our idea of God cannot remain a static one if we believe we have been given the gift of reason, and are created in the image of His thought. Our capacity to learn more about ourselves and the cosmos is the imprint of divinity that marks us off from the rest of the animal world. To reject our new knowledge out of hand is surely to worship a false idol.

-*SYDNEY J. HARRIS, American newspaper columnist (1917 - 1986)*

Religious zealots who attempt to play God to history are not enacting religion. They are betraying religion, or at least they are betraying Christianity. For the profoundest Christian tradition is to recognize the frailty and weakness of erring mortals and to emphasize the unfathomable distance between man and God. The pretense that human sinners can penetrate to the divine purpose is surely presumptuous when not egomaniacal. Religion calls rather for humility before the impenetrable mystery.

-*ARTHUR SCHLESINGER JR., American historian*

I believe in an America where the separation of church and state is absolute - where no Catholic prelate would tell the President (should he be a Catholic) how to act and no Protestant minister would tell his parishioners for whom to vote - where no church or church school is granted any public funds or political preference - and where no man is denied public office merely because his religion differs from the President who might appoint him or the people who might elect him.

-*JOHN F. KENNEDY, 35th President of the U.S. (1917 - 1963)*

I'm not going to heaven because I've preached to great crowds of people. I'm going to heaven because Christ died on that cross. None of us are going to heaven because we're good. And we're not going to heaven because we've worked. We're not going to heaven because we pray and accept Christ. We're going to heaven because of what He did on the Cross. All I have to do is receive Him. And it's so easy to receive Christ that millions stumble over its sheer simplicity.

-*BILLY GRAHAM, American evangelist*

Whatever you love most, be it sports, pleasure, business, or God, that is your God.   -*BILLY GRAHAM*

A real Christian is a person who can give his pet parrot to the town gossip.   -*BILLY GRAHAM*

If the concept of God has any validity or any use, it can only be to make us larger, freer, and more loving. If God cannot do this, then it is time we got rid of him.

-*JAMES BALDWIN, American novelist, essayist (1924 - 1987)*

The idea of a good society is something you do not need a religion and eternal punishment to buttress; you need a religion if you are terrified of death.

-*GORE VIDAL, American novelist, essayist*

It is obviously possible for individuals to keep high moral standards and be irreligious. I strongly doubt whether it is possible for civilizations. Absent religious tradition, what reason is there for a society to respect human rights and the dignity of man? What is human dignity, scientifically speaking? A superstition?

Empirically, men are demonstrably unequal. How can we justify equality? Human rights is an unscientific idea. As the poet Czeslaw Milosz says, these values are rooted in a transcendent dimension.

-*LESZEK KOLAKOWSKI, Polish professor of philosophy*

The United States of America was not a secular state. It might more accurately be described as a moral and ethical society without a state religion. Clearly, those who created it saw it as an entity, to use Lincoln's later phrase, "Under God." The Declaration of Independence in its first paragraph invokes "the Laws of Nature and of Nature's God" as the entitlement of the American people to choose separation from Britain. It insists that men have the right to "Life, Liberty, and the pursuit of Happiness" because they are so "endowed by their creator." The men who wrote it appeal, in their conclusion, to "the Supreme Judge of the world" and express their confidence in "the Protection of Divine Providence."

Equally, the men called to govern the new state saw a political society within a religious framework. George Washington began his first inaugural address with a prayer to "that Almighty Being, who rules over the universe, who presides in the councils of nation," asking Him to bless a government

consecrated "to the liberties and happiness of the people." He was certain that his prayer expressed the sentiments of Congress as well as his own, for "no people can be bound to acknowledge and adore the invisible hand which conducts the affairs of men more than the people of the United States. Every step by which they have advanced to the character of an independent nation seems to have been distinguished by some token of providential agency."
-*PAUL JOHNSON,* English historian

We Americans cannot save the world. Even Christ failed at that. We Americans have our hands full trying to save ourselves.
-*EDWARD ABBEY,* American author (1927 - 1989)

The church must be reminded that it is not the master or servant of the state, but rather the conscience of the state. It must be the guide and the critic of the state, and never its tool. If the church does not recapture its prophetic zeal, it will become an irrelevant social club without moral or spiritual authority.
-*MARTIN LUTHER KING, JR.,* American clergyman, reformer (1929 - 1968)

Deep down in every man, woman and child, is the fundamental idea of God. It may be obscured by calamity, by pomp, by worship of other things, but in some form or other it is there. For faith in a power greater than ourselves, and miraculous demonstrations of that power in human lives, are facts as old as man himself.
-*ALCOHOLICS ANONYMOUS*

God, grant me the serenity to accept the things I cannot change, courage to change the things I can and wisdom to know the difference.

-*prayer of ALCOHOLICS ANONYMOUS*

The essence of all religions is love, compassion and tolerance. Kindness is my true religion. No matter whether you are learned or not, whether you believe in the next life or not, whether you believe in God or Buddha or some other religion or not, in day-to-day life you must be a kind person. When you are motivated by kindness, it doesn't matter whether you are a practitioner a lawyer, a politician, an administrator, a worker, or an engineer: Whatever your profession or field, deep down you are a kind person.

Love, compassion, and tolerance are necessities, not luxuries. Without them, humanity cannot survive. If you have a particular faith or religion, that is good. But you can survive without it if you have love, compassion, and tolerance. The clear proof of a person's love of God is if that person genuinely shows love to fellow human beings.

-*HIS HOLINESS THE DALAI LAMA*

A synagogue or church that admitted only saints would be like a hospital that admitted only healthy people. It would be a lot easier to run, and a more pleasant place to be, but I'm not sure it would be doing the job it is here to do.

-*RABBI HAROLD KUSHNER, American writer*

I don't like the notion that when we pray and don't get answers, God has considered our request and said

no. I don't know anything about God. But I know prayer makes life better and richer for me.
*-RABBI HAROLD KUSHNER*

"By prayer, I don't mean shouting and mumbling and wallowing like a hog in religious sentiment. Prayer is only another name for good, clean, direct thinking. When you pray, think. Think well what you're saying, and make your thoughts into things that are solid. In that way, your prayer will have strength, and that strength will become a part of you in body, mind and spirit."
*-WALTER PIDGEON, Canadian-born actor (1897 - 1984). As a preacher in, "How Green Was My Valley." 1941*

"Hey, old man, you home tonight? ... I know I ain't got no call to ask for much. But even so, you got to admit you ain't dealt me no cards in a long time. You got things fixed so I can't never win. ... You made me like I am. Just where am I supposed to fit in? What you got in mind for me? What do I do now?"
*-PAUL NEWMAN, American actor. As a prisoner addressing God in, "Cool Hand Luke." 1967*

When we talk to God, we're praying. When God talks to us we're schizophrenic.
*-LILY TOMLIN, American actress, comedian*

I do occasionally envy the person who is religious naturally, without being brainwashed into it or suckered into it by all the organized hustles. Just like having an ear for music or something. It would just never occur to such a person for a second that the world isn't about something.
*-WOODY ALLEN, American actor, writer, film director*

If it turns out there is a God, I don't think He's evil. The worst thing you can say about Him is that He's basically an underachiever. *-WOODY ALLEN*

If only God would give me a clear sign! Like making a large deposit in my name at a Swiss bank.
*-WOODY ALLEN*

I'm an existentialist humanist. I think that morality and ethics come from us. There is no God who says you must behave this way. References to God, religion, historical and political imperatives are all meaningless unless you realize that we have invented all that to make sense of our lives, and that we control it. That's what existentialism is all about - that we're condemned to be free. To be an existentialist is to be a humanist because you're saying, "It's us, it's all us."
*-DAVID CRONENBERG, Canadian writer, film director*

Leibniz, too, counted Necessary Being among the Godhead's perfection. God exists as a matter of logical necessity; it is because He harbors the reason for His existence in His nature that He, and He alone, can furnish the last link in the great explanatory chain, the ultimate answer to the question "Why is there something rather than nothing?" There is a world because God created it out of nothing, through his own free choice. This not only explains why *a* world exists, Leibniz contended, but also accounts for the selection of this particular world: since God's creative act was motivated by His infinite goodness, the world He brought into being must be the best of all possible worlds - and, adds the cynic, everything in it is a necessary evil. (A physicist I know claims that things make much more sense if you assume the world was created not by an all-good and all-powerful being but by one that is 100 percent malevolent but only 90 percent effective.)

-*JIM HOLT,* American writer

Somewhere, and I can't find where, I read about an Eskimo hunter who asked the local missionary priest, "If I did not know about God and sin, would I go to hell?" "No," said the priest, "not if you did not know." "Then why," asked the Eskimo earnestly, "did you tell me?"

-*ANNIE DILLARD,* American writer

What's definitely new is the angel 'business'. That there's so much money in angels is an amazing thing. ... The reason people have always liked angels is that they want to believe God is in the details. But the fact is that God may *not* be in the details. God may be busy. And angels *are* in the details. Angels have time for your flat tire or your parking space.

-*NORA EPHRON,* American writer

What is the province of religion? You look at the Bible and you can see great literature and poetry, morals and ethics; you can see the churches and synagogues as centers of community and family, teachers of values about charity and cherishing our fellows. But these are not scientific institutions. The Bible is not a scientific book, or not lately. The science in the Bible is mainly what the Jews during the Babylonian captivity got from the Babylonians

2,600 years ago. And that was the best science on the planet in 600 B.C., but we've learned a lot since. If, as fundamentalists do, you take the Bible as the literal word of God, dictated to a perfect stenographer with no room for metaphor or allegory, then you run into deep trouble because the Bible is demonstrably wrong in areas of science. But if you take it as the work of inspired humans, if you believe that there's room for allegory and metaphor as most mainstream Jewish, Protestant and Roman Catholic sects do, then there's no problem, there's no conflict. Science and religion each are in their own sphere, and they're in fact mutually supportive.

-CARL SAGAN, American astronomer, astrophysicist (1934 - 1997)

Some scientists suspect they are religious because both science and religion share a search for certainty, for higher laws. Albert Einstein attributed a physicist-friend's persistence at difficult work to the "longing to behold ... preestablished harmony." Religious people have the same longing, he said, and a "legitimate conflict between science and religion cannot exist." I agree with Einstein.

"Science without religion is lame," he went on to say, "religion without science is blind." I'm not sure what he meant by that, but it sounds right. The world is complicated and people, who are also complicated, have a lot of questions. Some questions - the simple, concrete ones - science can answer. Other questions - the ones about how best to live and find meaning in life - only religion can answer. I can't imagine living without both scientific knowledge and religious faith.

-ANN FINKBEINER, American science writer

It is important that we understand how profoundly we all felt the needs that religion, down the ages, has satisfied. I would suggest that these needs are of three types: firstly, the need to be given an articulation of our half-glimpsed knowledge of exaltation, of awe, of wonder; life is an awesome experience, and religion helps us understand why life so often makes us feel small, by telling us what we are *smaller than*; and, contrariwise, because we also have a sense of being special, of being *chosen*, religion helps us by telling us what we have been chosen by, and what for. Secondly, we need answers to the unanswerable: how did we get here? How did "here" get here in the first place? Is this, this brief life all there is? How can it be? What would be the point of that? And, thirdly, we need codes to live by, "rules for every damn thing." The idea of god is at once a repository for our awestruck wonderment at life and an answer to the great questions of existence, and a rulebook, too. The soul needs all these explanations - not simply rational explanations, but explanations of the heart.

*-SALMAN RUSHDIE, Indian writer*

What New Age cultivars have in common with each other may be best summarized by the magazine, *Gnosis*, the ancient Greek word for knowledge. Ancient Gnosticism coexisted with and influenced Christianity in the first and second centuries A.D., but was smothered as heretical soon after. Its central tenet, outlined in second-century texts that were rediscovered in 1945, is that self-knowledge is knowledge of God: The self and God are one and the same. This precept links Gnosticism - and its many derivatives - more closely with Eastern metaphysical systems and paganism than with mainstream Christianity. For a generation of lapsed Catholics, Protestants, and Jews, the do-it-yourself aspect of self-knowledge is an attractive alternative to organized religion. The pursuit of enlightenment needs no intermediaries, no tedious Sunday sermons, no church socials or collection plates. There is no hierarchy, no central religious figure. In Gnostic terms, Christ was an illuminated teacher who brought the world gnosis, rather than the son of God who died to atone for human sins.

Yet fealty to a powerful, charismatic leader is the antithesis of Gnosticism and its New Age offshoots. And what creates a Jonestown or a Rancho Santo Fe is exactly that. Applewhite, and others like him, exploit universal needs: the craving to belong, the desire for orderliness and certainty, the wish to connect to something larger than oneself, the secret hope of finding an all-caring parent who offers protection and comfort.

-ERICA GOODE, American writer (writing about the mass suicide by followers of Marshall Appplewhite in Rancho Santo Fe, California. In U.S. News & World Report)

When you take a chance on anything you are gambling. God thought he had created only a good world and he lost.

-JOE LIGHT, American artist

The only real hope of people today is probably an renewal of our certainty that we are rooted in the earth and, at the same time, the cosmos. This awareness endows us with the capacity for self-transcendence. Politicians at international forums may reiterate a thousand times that the basis of the new world order must be universal respect for human rights, but it will mean nothing as long as this imperative does not derive from the respect of the miracle of Being, the miracle of the universe, the miracle of nature, the miracle of our own existence. Only someone who submits to the authority of the universal order and of creation, who values the right to be part of it and a participant in it, can genuinely value himself and his neighbors, and thus honor their rights as well.

It logically follows that, in today's multicultural world, the truly reliable path to coexistence, to peaceful coexistence and creative cooperation, must start from what is at the root of all cultures and what lies infinitely deeper in human hearts and minds than political opinion, convictions, antipathies or sympathies: It must be rooted in self-transcendence. Transcendence as a hand reached out to those close to us, to foreigners, to the human community, to all living creatures, to nature, to the universe; transcendence as a deeply and joyously experienced need to be in harmony even with what we ourselves are not, what we do not understand, what seems distant from us in time and space, but with which we are nevertheless mysteriously linked because, together with us, all this constitutes a single world. Transcendence as the only real alternative to extinction.

The Declaration of Independence adopted 218

years ago in this building, states that the Creator gave man the right to liberty. It seems man can realize that liberty only if he does not forget the One who endowed him with it.

*-VACLAV HAVEL, Czech writer, President of Czech Republic (from a speech delivered July 4, 1994 at Independence Hall in Philadelphia)*

All religions teach us to help people whenever we can. All religions teach us to play fair and not to hit or kill or steal or cheat. All religions teach us we should be forgiving and cut people some slack when they mess up, because someday we will mess up too. All religions teach us to love our families, to respect our parents and to make new families when we grow up. Religions all over the world teach the same right way to live.

*-RABBI MARC GELMAN and MSGR. THOMAS HARTMEN, American clergymen, authors*

# CHAPTER - 2

# *LOVE & MARRIAGE*

## ***

They are not wise , then, who stand forth to buffet against Love; for Love rules the gods as he will, and me.

*-SOPHOCLES, Greek playwright (496 - 406 B.C.)*

Drunkenness is always improper, except at the festivals of the God who gave wine; and peculiarly dangerous, when a man is engaged in the business of marriage; at such a crisis of their lives a bride and bridegroom ought to have all their wits about them.

*-PLATO, Greek philosopher (c.428 - c.347 B.C.)*

It is pleasant to be loved, for this makes a man see himself as the possessor of goodness, a thing that every being that has a feeling for it desires to possess: to be loved means to be valued for one's own personal qualities.

*-ARISTOTLE, Greek philosopher (384 - 322 B.C.)*

The pleasure of the eye is the beginning of love. For no one loves if he has not first been delighted by the form of the beloved; but he who delights in the form of another does not, for all that, love her, but only does so when he also longs for her when absent and craves for her presence.  *-ARISTOTLE*

It is not good that the man should be alone.
- GENESIS 2: 18

To keep thee from the evil woman, from the flattery
of the tongue of a strange woman.
Lust not after her beauty in thine heart; neither
let her take thee with her eyelids.
For by means of a whorish woman a man is
brought to a piece of bread: and the adultress will
hunt for the precious life.
Can a man take fire in his bosom, and his
clothes not be burned?
Can one go upon hot coals, and his feet
not be burned?
So he that goeth to his neighbor's wife;
whosoever toucheth her shall not be innocent.
- PROVERBS 6: 24 - 29

Lust is an enemy to the purse, a foe to the person, a
canker to the mind, a corrosive to the conscience, a
weakness of the wit, a besotter of the senses, and,
finally, a mortal bane to all the body.
- PLINY THE ELDER, Roman scholar (23 - 79 A.D.)

His first wife was Papiria, the daughter of Maso, who
had formerly been consul. With her he lived a
considerable time in wedlock, and then divorced her,
though she had made him the father of noble
children, being mother of the renowned Scipio and
Fabius Maximus. The reason of this separation has
not come to our knowledge; but there seems to be a
truth conveyed in the account of another Roman's
being divorced from his wife, which may be
applicable here. This person being highly blamed by

his friends, who demanded, "Was she not chaste? was she not fair? was she not fruitful?" holding out his shoe, asked them, whether it was not new and well made. "Yet," added he, "none of you can tell where it pinches me."

*-PLUTARCH, Greek biographer (c.46 - c.120)*

When Philip was trying to force a woman against her will she said to him, "Let me go. All women are alike when the light is out." This is an excellent answer to adulterers and licentious men, but a married woman ought not be like any chance female when the light is out. It is when her body is invisible that her virtue and her sole devotion and affection for her husband should be evident.   *-PLUTARCH*

I in my great worthlessness - for it was greater thus early - had begged You for chastity, saying "Grant me chastity and continence, but not yet." For I was afraid that You would hear my prayer too soon, and too soon would heal me from the disease of lust which I wanted satisfied rather than extinguished.

*-ST. AUGUSTINE, Church father, philosopher (354 - 430)*

The virtue of chastity most of all makes men apt for contemplation, since sexual pleasures most of all weigh down the mind to sensible objects.

*-ST. THOMAS AQUINAS, Italian theologian, philosopher (1225 - 1274)*

"Choose, now," said she, "one of these two things, aye,
To have me foul and old until I die,
And be to you a true and humble wife,
And never anger you in all my life;

Or else to have me young and very fair
And take your chance with those who will repair
Unto your house, and all because of me,
Or in some other place, as well may be.
Now choose which you like better and reply."
*- GEOFFREY CHAUCER, English poet (1340 - 1400)*

The wedlock of minds will be greater than that of bodies.
*- ERASMUS, Dutch scholar (1466 - 1536)*

God uses lust to impel men to marriage, ambition to office, avarice to earning, and fear to faith.
*- MARTIN LUTHER, German religious reformer (1483 - 1546)*

He who is not impatient is not in love.
*- PIETRO ARETINO, Italian writer (1492 - 1556)*

The concern that some women show at the absence of their husbands does not arise from their not seeing them and being with them, but from the apprehension that their husbands are enjoying pleasures in which they do not participate, and which, from their being at a distance, they have not the power of interrupting.
*- MICHEL DE MONTAIGNE, French moralist, essayist (1533 - 1592)*

If there is no end to avarice and ambition, neither is there any to lechery. It still lives after satiety; no constant satisfaction or end can be prescribed to it, for it always goes beyond its possession.
*- MICHEL DE MONTAIGNE*

The woman who goes to bed with a man should put off her modesty with her skirt and put it on again with her modesty. *-MICHEL DE MONTAIGNE*

A good marriage would be between a blind wife and a deaf husband. *-MICHEL DE MONTAIGNE*

A good marriage, if such there be, rejects the company and conditions of love. It tries to reproduce those of friendship. It is a sweet association in life, full of constancy, trust, and an infinite number of useful and solid services and mutual obligations. No woman who savors the taste of it ... would want to have the place of a mistress or paramour to her husband. If she is lodged in his affection as a wife, she is lodged there much more honorably and securely. When he dances ardent and eager attention elsewhere, still let anyone ask him then on whom he would rather have some shame fall, on his wife or his mistress; whose misfortune would afflict him more; for whom he wishes more honor. These questions admit of no doubt in a sound marriage.
*-MICHEL DE MONTAIGNE*

Love and marriage are two intentions that go by separate and distinct roads. A woman may give herself to a man whom she would not at all want to have married; I do not mean because of the state of his fortune, but because of his personal qualities. Few men have married their mistresses who have not repented it. *-MICHEL DE MONTAIGNE*

Love is a power too strong to be overcome by anything but flight.
*-MIGUEL DE CERVANTES, Spanish novelist, poet (1547 - 1616)*

"Do not forget, Sancho," replied Don Quixote, "that there are two kinds of beauty, one being of the soul and the other of the body. That of the soul is revealed through intelligence, modesty, right conduct, generosity, and good breeding, all of which qualities may exist in an ugly man; and when one's gaze is fixed upon beauty of this sort and not upon that of the body, love is usually born suddenly and violently." *-MIGUEL DE CERVANTES*

Love and War are the same thing, and stratagems and policy are as allowable in the one as in the other.
*-MIGUEL DE CERVANTES*

Remember, that if thou marry for beauty, thou bindest thyself all thy life for that which perchance will neither last nor please thee one year; and when thou hast it, it will be to thee of no price at all; for the desire dieth when it is attained, and the affection perisheth when it is satisfied.
*-SIR WALTER RALEIGH, English courtier, historian (1552 - 1618)*

Love is a sour delight, a sugar'd grief,
A living death, an ever-dying life;
A breach of Reason's law, a secret thief,
A sea of tears, an everlasting strife;
A bait for fools, a scourge of noble wits,
A deadly wound, a shot which ever hits.
*-THOMAS WATSON, English poet (1557 - 1592)*

Wives are young men's mistresses; companions for middle age; and old men's nurses.
*-FRANCIS BACON, English essayist, philosopher (1561 - 1626)*

*Rosalind.* Love is merely a madness, and I tell you, deserves as well a dark house and a whip as madmen do; and the reason why they are not so punished and cured is that the lunacy is so ordinary that the whippers are in love too.

*- WILLIAM SHAKESPEARE, English playwright (1564 - 1616). From "As You Like It.'*

Love and a cough cannot be hid.

*- GEORGE HERBERT, English clergyman, poet (1593 - 1633)*

We may, it seems to me, find differences in love according to the esteem which we bear to the object loved as compared with oneself; for when we esteem the object of love less than ourselves, we have only a simple affection for it; when we esteem it equally with ourselves, that is called friendship; and when we esteem it more, the passion which we have may be called devotion.

*- RENÉ DESCARTES, French philosopher (1596 - 1650)*

Vows made in storms are forgotten in calm.

*- THOMAS FULLER, English clergyman (1608 - 1661)*

A man knows his companion in a long journey and a little inn.  *-THOMAS FULLER*

In the human heart new passions are for ever being born; the overthrow of one almost always means the rise of another.

*-FRANÇOIS DE LA ROCHEFOUCAULD, French moralist (1613 - 1680)*

There are few people who are not ashamed of their love affairs when the infatuation is over.

*- LA ROCHEFOUCAULD*

If one judges love by most of its results it is closer to hatred than friendship.  *-LA ROCHEFOUCAULD*

We are nearer loving those who hate us than those who love us more than we wish.   -*LA ROCHEFOUCAULD*

There is no disguise which can for long conceal love where it exists or simulate it where it does not.
-*LA ROCHEFOUCAULD*

If you think you love your mistress for her own sake, you are quite mistaken.   -*LA ROCHEFOUCAULD*

There are two kinds of faithfulness in love: one is based on forever finding new things to love in the loved one; the other is based on our pride in being faithful.   -*LA ROCHEFOUCAULD*

Passion often turns the cleverest men into idiots and makes the greatest blockheads clever.
-*LA ROCHEFOUCAULD*

A mighty pain to love it is,
And 'tis a pain that pain to miss;
But of all pains, the greatest pain
It is to love, but love in vain.
-*ABRAHAM COWLEY*, English poet (1618 - 1667)

With regard to marriage, it is plain that it is in accordance with reason, if the desire of connection is engendered not merely by external form, but by a love of begetting children and wisely educating them; and if, in adddition, the love both of the husband and wife has for its cause not external form merely, but chiefly liberty of the mind.
-*BENEDICT SPINOZA*, Dutch philosopher (1632 - 1677)

A woman with eyes only for one person, or with eyes

always averted from him, creates exactly the same impression.

-*JEAN DE LA BRUYÈRE,* French essayist, moralist (1645 - 1696)

Love begins with love; friendship, however warm, cannot change to love, however mild.

-*JEAN DE LA BRUYÈRE*

Their [the Lilliputians] maxim is, that among people of quality, a wife should be always be a reasonable and agreeable companion, because she cannot always be young.

-*JONATHAN SWIFT,* English satirist, poet (1667 - 1745)

Thus grief still treads upon the heels of
    pleasure;
Married in haste, we may repent at leisure.

-*WILLIAM CONGREVE,* English playwright (1670 - 1729)

Two persons who have chosen each other out of all the species, with the design to be each other's mutual comfort and entertainment, have, in that action, bound themselves to be good-humored, affable, discreet, forgiving, patient, and joyful, with respect to each other's frailties and perfections, to the end of their lives.

-*JOSEPH ADDISON,* English essayist, (1672 - 1719)

All the reasons of man cannot outweigh a single feeling of a woman.

-*VOLTAIRE,* French author, philosopher (1694 - 1778)

Marriage is the only adventure open to the cowardly.

-*VOLTAIRE*

One good husband in worth two good wives; for the scarcer things are the more they are valued.
-*BEN FRANKLIN, American statesman, writer, scientist (1706 - 1790)*

It is the man and woman united that make the complete human being. Separate, she wants his force of body and strength of reason; he, her softness, sensibility and acute discernment. Together, they are most likely to succeed in the world.   *-BEN FRANKLIN*

Where there's marriage without love, there will be love without marriage.   *-BEN FRANKLIN*

I desire of philosophers to grant that there is in some (I believe in many) human breasts a kind and benevolent disposition, which is gratified by contributing to the happiness of others. That in this gratification alone, as in friendship, in parental and filial affection, as indeed in general philanthropy, there is a great and exquisite delight. That if we will not call such disposition love, we have no name for it. That though the pleasures arising from such pure love may be heightened and sweetened by the assistance of amorous desires, yet the former can subsist alone, nor are they destroyed by the intervention of the latter.

Lastly, that esteem and gratitude are the proper motives to love, as youth and beauty are to desire, and, therfore, though such desire may naturally cease, when age or sickness overtakes its object; yet these can have no effect on love, nor ever shake or remove, from a good mind, that sensation or passion which hath gratitude and esteem for its basis.
-*HENRY FIELDING, English novelist (1707 - 1754)*

Marriage has many pains, but celibacy has no
pleasures.
*-SAMUEL JOHNSON, English lexicographer, writer (1709 - 1784)*

There are few things that we so unwillingly give up,
even in advanced age, as the supposition that we have
still the power of ingratiating ourselves with the fair
sex.   *-SAMUEL JOHNSON*

Marriage is the strictest tie of perpetual friendship,
and there can be no friendship without confidence,
and no confidence without integrity, and he must
expect to be wretched, who pays to beauty, riches, or
politeness that regard which only virtue and piety can
claim.   *-SAMUEL JOHNSON*

*Boswell.* "Pray, sir, do you not suppose that there are
fifty women in the world, with any one of whom a
man may be as happy, as with any one woman in
particular?" *Johnson.* "Ay, sir, fifty thousand."
*Boswell.* "Then, sir, you are not of opinion with
some who imagine that certain men and certain
women are made for each other; and that they cannot
be happy if they miss their counterparts?" *Johnson.*
"To be sure not, sir. I believe marriages would in
general be as happy, and often more so, if they were
all made by the Lord Chancellor, upon a due
consideration of characters and circumstances,
without the parties having any choice in the matter."
*-JAMES BOSWELL, English biographer (1740 - 1795). From "Life of Johnson".*

To argue from her [Mrs. Johnson's] being much older
than Johnson, or any other circumstances, that he
could not really love her, is absurd; for love is not a

subject of reasoning, but of feeling, and therfore there are no common principles upon which one can persuade another concerning it. Every man feels for himself, and knows how he is affected by particular qualities in the person he admires, the impressions of which are too minute and delicate to be substantiated in language. -JAMES BOSWELL

A gentleman who had been very unhappy in marriage, married immediately after his wife died; Johnson said, it was the triumph of hope over experience. -JAMES BOSWELL

The domestic relations are founded on marriage, and marriage is founded upon the natural reciprocity or intercommunity of the sexes. This natural union of the sexes proceeds according to the mere animal nature, or according to the law. The later is marriage which is the union of two persons of different sex for life-long reciprocal possession of their sexual faculties. The end of producing and educating children may be regarded as always the end of nature in implanting mutual desire and inclination in the sexes; but it is not necessary for the rightfulness of marriage that those who marry should set this before themselves as the end of their union, otherwise the marriage would be dissolved of itself when the production of children ceased.

-IMMANUEL KANT, German philosopher (1724 - 1804)

The Christian religion, by confining marriage to pairs, and rendering the relation indissoluble, has by these two things done more toward the peace, happiness, settlement, and civilization of the world, than by any other part in this whole scheme of divine wisdom.

-*EDMUND BURKE, British diplomat orator, writer (1729 - 1779)*

We attract hearts by the qualities we display; we retain them by the qualities we possess.

-*JEAN BAPTISTE ANTOINE SUARD, French journalist (1734 - 1817)*

Love is blind, but marriage restores its sight.

-*GEORG CHRISTOPH LICHTENBERG, German physicist, writer (1742 - 1799)*

Only choose in marriage a woman whom you would choose as a friend if she were a man.

-*JOSEPH JOUBERT, French essayist (1754 - 1824)*

I went to the Garden of Love,
And saw what I never had seen:
A Chapel was built in the midst,
Where I used to play on the green.

And the gates of this chapel were shut,
And "Thou shalt not" writ over the door;
So I turned to the Garden of Love,
That so many sweet flowers bore;

And I saw it was filled with graves,
And tombstones where flowers should be;
And priests in black gowns were walking their rounds,
And binding with briars my joys and desires.

-*WILLIAM BLAKE, English artist, poet (1757 - 1827)*

Egotism erects its center in itself; love places it out of itself in the axis of the universal whole. Love aims at unity, egotism at solitude. Love is the citizen ruler of a flourishing republic, egotism is a despot in a devastated creation.

*-FRIEDRICH VON SCHILLER, German dramatist, poet (1759 - 1805)*

Love is an ideal thing, marriage a real thing; a confusion of the real with the ideal never goes unpunished.

*-JOHANN WOLFGANG VON GOETHE, German poet, playwright (1749 - 1832)*

Let a woman once give you a task and you are hers, heart and soul; all your care and trouble lend new charms to her for whose sake they are taken. To rescue, to revenge, to instruct, or to protect a woman, is all the same as to love her.

*-JEAN PAUL RICHTER, German novelist, humorist (1763 - 1825)*

Love is the whole history of a woman's life, it is but an episode in a man's.

*-MADAME DE STAËL, French author (1766 - 1817)*

The man's desire is for the woman; but the woman's desire is rarely other than for the desire of the man.

*-SAMUEL TAYLOR COLERIDGE, British poet, critic (1772 - 1834)*

Corporeal charms may indeed gain admirers. but there must be mental ones to retain them.

*-CHARLES COLEB COLTON, English clergyman (1780 - 1832)*

All love, however ethereally it may bear itself, is rooted in the sexual impulse alone, nay, it absolutely is only a more definitely determined, specialised, and indeed in the strictest sense individualized sexual impulse.

*-ARTHUR SCHOPENHAUER, German philosopher (1788 - 1860)*

The sexual impulse ... next to the love of life ... shows itself the strongest and most powerful of motives; constantly lays claim to half the powers and thoughts of the younger portion of mankind, to the ultimate goal of almost all human efforts, interrupts the most serious occupations every hour, sometimes embarrasses for a while even the greatest minds, does not hesitate to intrude with its trash, interfering with the negotiations of statesmen and the investigations of men of learning, knows how to slip its love letters and locks of hair even into ministerial portfolios and philosophical manuscripts, and no less devises daily the most entangled and the worst actions, destroys the most valuable relationships, breaks the firmest bond, demands the sacrifice sometimes of life or health, sometimes of wealth, rank, and happiness, nay, robs those who are otherwise honest of all conscience, makes those who have hitherto been faithful, traitors; accordingly on the whole, appears as a malevolent demon that strives to pervert, confuse and overthrow everything.
*-ARTHUR SCHOPENHAUER*

In her first passion woman loves her lover,
In all the others, all she loves is love.
*-LORD BYRON, English poet (1788 - 1824)*

'Tis melancholy and a fearful sign
Of human frailty, folly, also crime,
That love and marriage rarely can combine,
Although they both are born in the same clime.
*-LORD BYRON*

A husband and wife ought to continue so long united

as they love each other, and any law which would bind them to cohabitation for one moment after the decay of their affection would be a most intolerable tyranny, and the most unworthy of toleration
-*PERCY BYSSHE SHELLEY, English poet (1792 - 1822)*

Men are so made that they can resist sound argument, and yet yield to a glance.
-*HONORÉ DE BALZAC, French novelist (1799 - 1850)*

Marriage should war incessantly with that monster that is the ruin of everything. This is the monster of habit. *-HONORÉ DE BALZAC*

So heavy is the chain of wedlock that it needs two to carry it, and sometimes three.
-*ALEXANDRE DUMAS, French novelist, playwright (1802 - 1870)*

The first symptom of love in a young man, is timidity; in a girl, it is boldness. The two sexes have a tendency to approach, and each assumes the qualities of the other.
-*VICTOR HUGO, French author (1802 - 1885)*

The greatest happiness of life is the conviction that we are loved, loved for ourselves, or rather loved in spite of ourselves. *-VICTOR HUGO*

Wedlock's like wine, not properly judged of till the second glass.
-*DOUGLASS JERROLD, English playwright, editor (1803 - 1857)*

Is not marriage an open question, when it is alleged, from the beginning of the world, that such as are in the institution wish to get out, and such as are out

wish to get in?
-*RALPH WALDO EMERSON, American poet, essayist (1803 - 1882)*

Never self-possessed, or prudent, love is all abandonment   -*RALPH WALDO EMERSON*

The magic of first love is our ignorance that it can ever end.
-*BENJAMIN DISRAELI, British Prime Minister, author (1804 - 1881)*

Caresses, expressions of one sort or another, are as necessary to the life of the affections as leaves are to the life of a tree. If they are wholly restrained, love will die at the roots.
-*NATHANIEL HAWTHORNE, American novelist (1804 - 1864)*

Man has his will - but woman has her way!
-*OLIVER WENDELL HOLMES, SR., American writer (1809 - 1894)*

It is better to have loved and lost, than not to love at all.
-*ALFRED, LORD TENNYSON, English poet (1809 - 1892)*

I have urged on woman independence of man, not that I do not think the sexes are mutually needed by one another, but because in woman this fact has led to excessive devotion, which has cooled love, degraded marriage and prevented either sex from being what it should be to itself or the other. ... That her hand may be given with dignity, she must be able to stand alone.
-*MARGARET FULLER, American writer, social reformer (1810 - 1850)*

We never know how much one loves till we know how much he is willing to endure and suffer for us;

and it is the suffering element that measures love. The characters that are great, must, of necessity, be characters that shall be willing, patient, and strong to endure for others. To hold our nature in the willing service of another, is the divine idea of manhood, of the human character.

-*HENRY WARD BEECHER, American clergyman, writer (1813 - 1887)*

Young love is a flame; very pretty, often hot and fierce, but still only light and flickering. The love of the older and disciplined heart is as coals, deep-burning, unquenchable. *-HENRY WARD BEECHER*

Well married, a man is winged; ill-matched, he is shackled. *-HENRY WARD BEECHER*

There is no disparity in marriage like unsuitability of mind and purpose.

-*CHARLES DICKENS, English novelist (1812 - 1870)*

Romantic love can very well be represented in the moment, but conjugal love cannot, because an ideal husband is not one who is such once in his life, but one who everyday is such.

-*SÖREN KIERKEGAARD, Danish philosopher, theologian (1813 - 1855)*

A happy marriage is a new beginning in life, a new starting point for happiness and usefulness

-*ARTHUR PENRHYN STANLEY, English clergyman (1815 - 1881)*

The one who will be found in trial capable of great acts of love is ever the one who is always doing considerate small ones.

-*FREDERICK WILLIAM ROBERTSON, English clergyman (1816 - 1853)*

There is more of good nature than of good sense at the bottom of most marriages.
-*HENRY DAVID THOREAU, American essayist, naturalist (1817 - 1862)*

I believe that love produces a certain flowering of the whole personality which nothing else can achieve.
-*IVAN TURGENEV, Russian writer (1818 - 1883)*

It is a common enough case, that of a man being suddenly captivated by a woman nearly the opposite of his ideal.
-*GEORGE ELIOT, English novelist (1819 - 1880)*

Marriage, by making us more contented, causes us often to be less enterprising.
-*CHRISTIAN NESTELL BOVEE, American author (1820 - 1904)*

All men from their very earliest years know that besides the good of their animal personality there is another, or better, good in life, which is not only independent of the gratification of the appetites of the animal personality, but on the contrary the greater the renunciation of the welfare of the animal personality the greater this good becomes.

This feeling, solving all life's contradictions and giving the greatest good to man, is known to all. That feeling is *love.*

Life is activity of animal personality subjected to the law of reason. Reason is the law to which, for his own good, man's animal personality must be subjected. Love is the only reasonable activity of man.
-*LEO TOLSTOY, Russian novelist (1828 - 1910)*

Love is a sport in which the hunter must contrive to

to have the quarry in pursuit.
-*ALEXANDER KERR, American educator (1828 - 1919)*

The fate of love is that it always seems too little or too much.
-*AMELIA BARR, American writer (1831 - 1919)*

A woman springs a sudden reproach upon you which provokes a hot retort - and then she will presently ask you to apologize.
-*MARK TWAIN, American writer, humorist (1835 - 1910)*

Of the delights of *this* world man cares *most* for sexual intercourse. He will go any length for it - risk fortune, character, reputation, life itself. And what do you think he has done? In a thousand years you would never guess - *He has left it out of his heaven! Prayer takes its place.*   -*MARK TWAIN*

To live is like to love - all reason is against it, and all healthy instinct for it.
-*SAMUEL BUTLER, English writer, satirist (1835 - 1902)*

'Tis better to have loved and lost, than never to have lost at all.   -*SAMUEL BUTLER*

The longest absence is less perilous to love than the terrible trials of incessant proximity.
-*MARIE LOUISE DE LA RAMEÉ, English novelist (1839 - 1908)*

Of all sexual aberrations, chastity is the strangest.
-*ANATOLE FRANCE, French writer (1844 - 1924)*

Love is the state in which man sees things most widely different from what they are. The force of illusion reaches its zenith here, as likewise the sweetening and transfiguring power. When a man is in love he endures more than at other times; he submits to everything.

*- FRIEDRICH WILHELM NIETZSCHE, German philosopher, poet (1844 - 1900)*

Love matches, as they are called, have illusion for their father and need for their mother.

*- FRIEDRICH WILHELM NIETZSCHE*

God created woman. And boredom did indeed cease from that moment - but many other things ceased as well. Woman was God's second mistake.

*- FRIEDRICH WILHELM NIETZSCHE*

Love when felt at all deeply has an element of transcendentalism in it, which makes it the most natural thing in the world for the two lovers - even though drawn together by a passing sex-attraction - to swear eternal truth to each other; but there is something quite diabolic and mephistophelean in the practice of the Law, which creeping up behind, as it were, at the critical moment, and overhearing the two pledging themselves, claps his book together with a triumphant bang and exclaims, "There now, you are married and done for, for the rest of you natural lives."

*- EDWARD CARPENTER, English poet, essayist (1844 - 1929)*

Love is moral even without legal marriage, but marriage is immoral without love.

*- ELLEN KEY, Swedish educator, writer (1849 - 1926)*

The substance of our lives is women. All other things are irrelevancies, hypocrisies, subterfuges. We sit talking of sports and politics, and all the while

our hearts are filled with memories of women and the capture of women.
-*GEORGE MOORE, Irish novelist, essayist (1852 - 1933)*

Love is born with the pleasure of looking at each other, it's fed with the necessity of seeing each other, it is concluded with the impossibility of separation.
-*JOSÉ MARTI, Cuban poet, essayist (1853 - 1895)*

It is a great mistake for men to give up paying compliments, for when they give up saying what is charming, they give up thinking what is charming.
-*OSCAR WILDE, Irish poet, playwright, wit (1854 - 1900)*

One should always be in love. That is the reason one should never marry. -*OSCAR WILDE*

Those who love deeply never grow old; they may die of old age, but they die young.
-*SIR ARTHUR WING PINERO, English playwright, actor (1855 - 1934)*

A man is as good as he has to be, and a woman as bad as she dares.
-*ELBERT HUBBARD, American writer, publisher (1856 - 1915)*

I'll believe it when girls of twenty with money marry male paupers, turned sixty.
-*ELBERT HUBBARD*

The trouble with many married people is that they are trying to get more out of marriage than there is in it.
-*ELBERT HUBBARD*

A man who marries a woman to educate her falls into the same fallacy as the woman who marries a man to reform him.    *-ELBERT HUBBARD*

Those who talk most about the blessings of marriage and the constancy of its vows are the very people who declare that if the chain were broken and the prisoners were left free to choose, the whole social fabric would fly asunder. You can't have the argument both ways. If the prisoner is happy, why lock him in? If he is not, why pretend that he is?

*- GEORGE BERNARD SHAW, British playwright, critic (1856 - 1950)*

The whole world is strewn with snares, traps, gins and pitfalls for the capture of men by women.

*- GEORGE BERNARD SHAW*

Marriage is popular because it combines the maximum of temptation with the maximum of opportunity.    *GEORGE BERNARD SHAW*

There is no doubt about this: the promise of mutual exclusive and everlasting love is a promise that cannot be kept and should not be made. It cannot form a permanent basis of marriage. ... Yet, there has been a general conspiracy not merely to preserve that fiction but to put it at the front as the primary condition of marrriage.

*- HAVELOCK ELLIS, English physician (1859 - 1939)*

Love is either the shrinking remnant of something which was once enormous; or else it is part of something which will grow in the future into something enormous. But in the present it does not satisfy. It gives much less than one expects.

*- ANTON CHEKHOV, Russian author (1860 - 1904)*

Sex endows the individual with a dumb and powerful instinct, which carries his body and soul continually toward another; makes it one of the dearest employments of his life to select and pursue a companion, and joins to possession the keenest pleasure, to rivalry the fiercest rage, and to solitude an eternal melancholy.
*- GEORGE SANTAYANA, American philosopher, poet (1863 - 1952)*

Love is a brillant illustration of a principle everywhere discoverable: namely, that human reason lives by turning the friction of material forces into the light of ideal goods. There can be no philosophic interest in disguising the animal basis of love, or in denying its spiritual sublimations, since all life is animal in its origin and all spiritual in its possible fruits. *-GEORGE SANTAYANA*

It takes patience to appreciate domestic bliss; volatile spirits prefer unhappiness.
*- GEORGE SANTAYANA*

In how many lives does Love really play a dominant part? The average taxpayer is no more capable of a grand passion than of a grand opera.
*- ISRAEL ZANGWILL, English playwright, novelist (1864 - 1926)*

A man and woman should choose each other for life. A long life is barely enough for a man and woman to understand each other; and to understand is to love. The man who understands *one* woman is qualified to understand pretty well everything.
*- WILLIAM BUTLER YEATS, Irish poet, playwright (1865 - 1939)*

Love, the strongest and deepest element in all lives,

the harbinger of hope, of joy, of ecstasy; love, the defier of all laws, of all conventions; love, the freest, the most powerful moulder of human destiny; how can such an all-compelling force be synonymous with that poor little State and Church-begotten weed, marriage?

*-EMMA GOLDMAN, American feminist, writer, anarchist (1869 - 1940)*

It is this slavish acquiescence to a man's superiority that has kept the marriage institution seemingly intact for so long a period. Now that a woman is coming into her own, now that she is actually growing aware of herself as a being outside of the master's grace, the sacred institution of marriage is gradually being undermined, and no amount of sentimental lamentation can stay it.

*-EMMA GOLDMAN*

Marriage is a natural thing in life, and to consider it derogatory in any sense is wholly wrong. The ideal is to look upon marriage as a sacrament and therfore to lead a life of self-restraint in the married state.

*-MOHANDAS GANDHI, Indian nationlist leader (1869 - 1948)*

It is seldom indeed that one parts on good terms, because if one were on good terms one would not part.

*-MARCEL PROUST, French novelist (1871 - 1922)*

In its early stage love is shaped by desire; later on it is kept alive by anxiety. In painful anxiety as in joyful desire, love insists upon everything. It is born and it thrives only if something remains to be won.

*-MARCEL PROUST*

There is not a woman in the world the possession of whom is as precious as that of the truth which she reveals to us by causing us to suffer.   -MARCEL PROUST

There is nothing like sexual desire to keep our words from having anything to do with our thoughts.
-MARCEL PROUST

When love is concerned, it is easier to renounce a feeling than to give up a habit.   -MARCEL PROUST

You walk into a room, see a woman, and something happens. It's chemical. What are you going to do about it?
-THEODORE DREISER,  American editor, author (1871 - 1945)

The real value of love is the increased general vitality it produces.
-PAUL AMBROISE VALÉRY,  French poet, philsospher (1871 - 1945)

Civilized people cannot fully satisfy their sexual instinct without love.
-BERTRAND RUSSELL, English philosopher (1872 - 1970)

It is possible for a civilized man and woman to be happy in marriage, although if this is to be the case a number of conditions must be fulfilled. There must be a feeling of complete equality on both sides; there must be no interference with mutual freedom; there must be the most complete physical and mental intimacy; and there must be a certain similarity in regard to the standards of values. (It is fatal, for example, if one values only money while the other values only good work.) Given all these conditions, I believe marriage to be the best and most important relation that can exist between two human beings. If it has not often been realized hitherto, that is chiefly because husband and wife have regarded themselves as each other's policeman. If marriage is to achieve its possibilities, husbands and wives must learn to understand that whatever the law may say, in their private lives they must be free.   *-BERTRAND RUSSELL*

To fear love is to fear life, and those who fear life are already three parts dead.   *-BERTRAND RUSSELL*

The way to love anything is to realize it might be lost.
*-GILBERT KEITH CHESTERTON, English journalist, author (1874 - 1936)*

Love is an irresistible desire to be irresistibly desired.
*-ROBERT FROST, American poet (1874 - 1963)*

A good marriage is that in which each appoints the other guardian of his solitude. Once the realization is accepted that even between the closest human beings infinite distances continue to exist, a wonderful living side by side can grow up, if they succeed in loving the distance between them which makes it possible for each to see the other whole and against a wide sky.
*-RAINER MARIA RILKE, German poet (1875 - 1926)*

Marriage is that relation between man and woman in which the independence is equal, the dependence mutual, and the obligation reciprocal.
*-LOUIS ANSPACHER, American playwright, (1878 - 1947)*

Who are happy in marriage? Those with so little

imagination that they cannot picture a better state, and those so shrewd that they prefer quiet slavery to hopeless rebellion.

-*H.L. MENCKEN, American editor, satirist (1880 - 1956)*

Tis more blessed to give than receive, for example, wedding presents. -*H.L. MENCKEN*

I married beneath me. All women do.

-*NANCY ASTOR, American-born English politician, socialite (1879 - 1964)*

Never try to impress a woman. Because if you do she'll expect you to keep up to the standard for the rest of your life. And the pace, my friends, is devastating.

-*W.C. FIELDS, American comedian, actor (1880 - 1940)*

The only thing which is not purely mechanical about falling in love is its beginning. Although all those who fall in love do so in the same way, not all fall in love for the same reason. There is no single quality which is universally loved.

-*JOSE ORTEGA Y GASSET, Spanish philosopher, politician (1883 - 1955)*

Even as love crowns you so shall he crucify you. Even as he is for your growth so is he for your pruning.

-*KAHIL GIBRAN, Syrian poet, novelist (1883 - 1931)*

Love and attraction between men and women, in many cases, is the very finest relationship; it has nothing to do with bearing a child. That's secondary many, many times.

-*MARGARET SANGER, Founder Planned Parenthood Federation (1884 - 1966)*

The love we have in our youth is superficial compared to the love that an old man has for his old wife.
-*WILL DURANT, American historian (1885 - 1981)*

He gave her a look you could have poured on a waffle.
-*RING LARDNER, American writer (1885 - 1933)*

No love, no friendship, can cross the path of our destiny without leaving some mark on it forever.
-*FRANCOIS MAURIAC, French author (1885 - 1970)*

Many a man has fallen in love with a girl in a light so dim he would not have chosen a suit by it.
-*MAURICE CHEVALIER, French actor (1888 - 1972)*

The emotion of love, in spite of the romantics, is not self-sustaining; it endures only when the lovers love many things together, and not merely each other.
-*WALTER LIPPMANN, American journalist (1889 - 1974)*

There are two arts of love and it makes a considerable difference which one is meant. There is the art of love as Casanova, for example, practiced it. It is the art of seduction, courtship, and sexual gratification: it is an art which culminates in the sexual act. It can be repeated with the same lover and with other lovers, but it exhausts itself in the moment of ecstasy. When that moment is reached, the work of art is done, and the lover as artist "after an interval, perhaps of stupor and vital recuperation," must start all over again, until at last the rhythm is so stale it is a weariness to start at all; or the lover must find new lovers and new resistances to conquer. The aftermath of romantic love - that is, of love that is consumated in sexual ecstasy - is either tedium in middle age or the compulsive adventurousness of the libertine.

Now this is not what Mr. Ellis means when he talks about love as an art. "The act of intercourse," he says, "is only an incident, and not an essential in love." Incident to what? His answer is that it is an incident to an "exquisitely and variously and harmoniously blended activity of all the finer activities of the organism, physical and psychic." I take this to mean that when a man and woman are successfully in love, their whole activity is energized and victorious. They walk better, their digestion improves, they think more clearly, their secret worries drop away, the world is fresh and interesting, and they can do more than they dreamed that they could do. In love of this kind sexual intimacy is not the dead end of desire as it is in romantic or promiscuous love, but periodic affirmation of the inward delight of desire pervading an active life. Love of this sort can grow: it is not, like youth itself, a moment that comes and is gone and remains only a memory of something which cannot be recovered. It can grow because it has something to grow upon and to grow with; it is not contracted and stale because it has for its object, not the mere relief of physical tension, but all the objects with which the two lovers are concerned. They desire their worlds in each other, and therfore their love is as interesting as their worlds and their worlds are as interesting as their love. *-WALTER LIPPMAN*

What love does is to arm. It arms the worth of life in spite of life.
-*ARCHIBALD MACLEISH, American poet (1892 - 1982)*

Love is not all ...
Love cannot fill the thickened lung with
    breath,
Nor clean the blood, nor set the fractured
    bone;
Yet many a man is making friends with
    death
Even as I speak, for lack of love alone.
-*EDNA ST. VINCENT MILLAY, American poet (1892 - 1950)*

I play no favorites. There's something about every man. A man may be short, dumpy, and rapidly getting bald - but if he has fire, women will like him.
-*MAE WEST, American movie actress (c.1893 - 1980)*

When women go wrong, men go right after them.
-*MAE WEST*

It is better to be looked over than overlooked.
-*MAE WEST*

In real love you want the other person's good. In romantic love you want the other person.
-*MARGARET ANDERSON, American editor (1893 - 1973)*

Never feel remorse for what you have thought about your wife;  she has thought much worse things about you.
-*JEAN ROSTAND, French biologist, writer (1894 - 1977)*

A lady of 47 who has been married 27 years and has six children knows what love really is and once

described it for me like this: "Love is what you've been through with somebody."
-JAMES THURBER, American author (1894 - 1961)

Be of love (a little) more careful than of anything.
-e. e. cummings, American poet, painter (1894 - 1962)

They make a business out of [marriage]. When you work too hard at a business you get tired; and when you get tired you get grouchy; and when you get grouchy you start fighting; and when you start fighting you're out of business.
-GEORGE BURNS, American comedian (1896 - 1996)

The women who take husbands not out of love but out of greed, to get their bills paid, to get a fine house and clothes and jewels; the women who marry to get out of a tiresome job, or to get away from disagreeable relatives, or to avoid being called an old maid - these are whores in everything but name. The only difference between them and my girls is that my girls gave a man his money's worth.
-POLLY ADLER, American businesswoman, madam (1900 - 1962)

It is only with the heart that one can see rightly; what is essential is invisible to the eye.
-ANTOINE DE SAINT-EXUPÉRY, French author (1900 - 1944)

There is hardly any activity, any enterprise, which is started with such tremendous hopes and expectations and yet which fails so regularly as love.
-ERICH FROMM, American pyschoanalyst, philosopher (1900 - 1980)

To make love the requirement of lifelong marriage is exceedingly difficult, and only a very few people can

achieve it. I don't believe in setting up universal standards that a large proportion of people can't reach.
*-MARGARET MEAD, American anthropologist (1901 - 1978)*

In America sex is an obsession, in other parts of the world it is a fact.
*-MARLENE DIETRICH, German-born American actress (1901 - 1992)*

"A thing happened to me that usually happens to men. You see a man can meet two, three or four women and fall in love with all of them, and then, by a process of - er - interesting elimination, he is able to decide which he prefers; but a woman must decide purely on instinct, guesswork, if she wants to be considered nice."
*-MIRIAM HOPKINS, American actress (1902 - 1972). In "Design for Living". 1933*

There is only one situation I can think of in which men and women make an effort to read better than they usually do. When they are in love and reading a love letter, they read for all they are worth. They read every word three ways; they read between the lines and in the margins. They may even take the punctuation into account. Then, if never before or after, they read.
*-MORTIMER ADLER, American philosopher, author*

There is radicalism in all getting, and a conservatism in all keeping. Love-making is radical, while marriage is conservative.
*-ERIC HOFFER, American author (1902 - 1983)*

At the end of what is called the 'sexual life' the only love which has lasted is the love which has everything, every disappointment, every failure and every betrayal, which has accepted even the sad fact that in the end there is no desire so deep as the simple desire for companionship.

-*GRAHAM GREENE, English author*

An occasional lucky guess as to what makes a wife
    tick is the best a man can hope for.
Even then, no sooner has he learned how to cope
    with the tick than she tocks.

-*OGDEN NASH, American writer, poet (1902 - 1971)*

To keep your marriage brimming,
With love in the loving cup,
Whenever you're wrong, admit it,
Whenever you're right, shut up.

-*OGDEN NASH*

A man who won't lie to a woman has very little consideration for her feelings.

-*BERGEN EVANS, American educator, author, TV personality (1904 - 1978)*

Sometimes love is stronger than a man's convictions.

-*ISAAC BASHEVIS SINGER, American Yiddish writer (1904 - 1991)*

To love means to communicate to the other that you are all for him, that you will never fail him or let him down when he needs you, but that you will always be standing by with all the necessary encouragements. It is something one can communicate to another only if one has it.

-*ASHLEY MONTAGU, American anthropologist, biologist*

Love is an expression and assertion of self-esteem, a response to one's values in the person of another.

One gains a profoundly personal, selfish joy from the mere existence of the person one loves. It is one's own personal, selfish happiness that one seeks, and derives from love.

-*AYN RAND, American writer (1905 - 1982)*

What makes love a rare game is there are either two winners or none.

-*FRANKLIN P. JONES, American author*

Almost all of our relationships begin and most of them continue as forms of mutual exploitation, a mental or physical barter, to be terminated when one or both parties run out of goods.

-*W.H. AUDEN, American poet, playwright (1907 - 1973)*

Any marriage, happy or unhappy, is infinitely more interesting and significant than any romance, however passionate.   -*W.H. AUDEN*

Marriage is a very alienating institution, for men as well as for women. ... It's a very dangerous institution - dangerous for men who find themselves trapped, saddled with a wife and children to support; dangerous for women, who aren't financially independent and end up depending on men who can throw them out when they are 40, and dangerous for children because their parents vent all their frustrations on them.

-*SIMONE DE BEAUVOIR, French writer, activist, feminist (1908 - 1986)*

Opposites may attract, but similarities endure.

-*LEO ROSTEN, American author, humorist (1908 - 1997)*

The difficulty with marriage is  that we fall in love

with a personality, but we must live with a character.

-*PETER DE VRIES, American author*

You mustn't force sex to do the work of love or love to do the work of sex.

-*MARY McCARTHY, American novelist (1912 - 1989)*

When things don't work well in the bedroom, they don't work well in the living room either.

-*WILLIAM MASTERS, American biologist, sexual therapist*

So long as the emotional feelings between the couple are right, so long as there is mutual trust and love, their bodies will invariably make the appropriate responses.

-*DAVID R. MACE, American educator, therapist*

As a general thing, people marry most happily with their own kind. The trouble lies in the fact that people usually marry at an age when they do not really know what their own kind is.

-*ROBERTSON DAVIES, Canadian writer (1913 - 1995)*

No one has ever loved anyone the way everyone wants to be loved.

-*MIGNON McLAUGHLIN, American writer, editor, humorist*

Desire can be as fragile as it is sudden.

-*FRANÇOISE GIROUD, Franch writer, editor*

Most marriages recognize this paradox: Passion destroys passion; we want what puts an end to wanting what we want.

-*JOHN FOWLES, English writer*

We in the West laugh or sneer or reproach the old

custom in India of parents arranging a marriage between teenagers who may not have yet even met one another. But there is no hard evidence that such arranged marriages are less successful or happy or enduring than our own.

One reason for this, perhaps, is that happiness as such is not one of the main criteria for a good marriage in the East. Nor was it in the West until this century. If someone had asked my mother if she was happy in her marriage, she would have thought the questioner crazy. The thought would not have occurred to her. You didn't marry to be happy; that was a by-product; if it came, it was something extra; if not, you shrugged and made do.

In this land and era of rising expectations, our expectations for marriage have risen along with our social and economic ambitions. But greater freedom to choose has not necessarily been accompanied by better judgement in choosing, and all we can say is that we prefer making our own mistakes to having them made for us by others.

*-SYDNEY J. HARRIS, American newspaper columnist (1917 - 1986)*

Love is the word used to label the sexual excitement of the young, the habituation of the middle-aged, and the mutual dependence of the old.

*-JOHN CIARDI, American poet, educator, critic (1916 - 1986)*

I want a man who's kind and understanding. Is that too much to ask of a millionaire?

*-ZSA ZSA GABOR, Hungarian-born American actress*

Getting divorced just because you don't love a man is almost as silly as getting married just because you do.   -ZSA ZSA GABOR

I never hated a man enough to give his diamonds back.   -ZSA ZSA GABOR

My wife and I were happy for twenty years. Then we met.
-RODNEY DANGERFIELD, American comedian

Americans, who make more of marrying for love than any other people, also break up more of their marriages (close to 1.2 million annually), but the figure reflects not so much the failure of love as the determination of people not to live without it.
-MORTON HUNT, American writer

If divorce has increased by one thousand percent, don't blame the women's movement. Blame the obsolete sex roles on which our marriages were based.
-BETTY FRIEDAN, American writer, feminist

Love is simple to understand if you haven't got a mind soft and full of holes. It's a crutch, that's all, and there isn't any one of us that doesn't need a crutch.
-NORMAN MAILER, American writer

There are four stages in a marriage. First there's the affair, then the marriage, then children and finally the fourth stage, without which you cannot know a woman, the divorce.   -NORMAN MAILER

Being divorced is like being hit by a Mack truck - if you survive you start looking very carefully to the

right and left.
-*JEAN KERR, American essayist, playwright*

Love is many things. But more than anything it is a disturbance of the digestive system.
-*GABRIEL GARCÍA MÁRQUEZ, Columbian author*

Age does not protect you from love but love to some extent protects you from age.
-*JEANNE MOREAU, French actress*

Brevity may be the soul of wit, but not when someone's saying, "I love you." When someone's saying "I love you," he always ought to give a lot of details: Like, Why does he love you? And, How much does he love you? And, When and where did he first begin to love you? Favorable comparisons with all the other women he ever loved are also welcome. And even though he insists it would take forever to count the ways in which he loves you, let him start counting.
-*JUDITH VIORST, American author*

One advantage of marriage, it seems to me, is that when you fall out of love with him, or he falls out of love with you, it keeps you together until you maybe fall in again.    *-JUDITH VIORST*

I have no personal life at the moment and that's liberating.
-*CAROL BURNETT, American comedian, actress*

A liberated woman is one who has sex before marriage and a job after.
-*GLORIA STEINEM, American writer, feminist*

What is most beautiful in virile men is something feminine; what is most beautiful in feminine women is something masculine.
-*SUSAN SONTAG, American essayist, novelist*

I've watched myself and my friends in relationships and something isn't right. At first we can't wait to get under the same roof and into the same bed with our chosen mate. Then, after a few years, we can't wait to get away, listing a million reasons why it was a bad idea in the first place.

It can't be that people shouldn't live together, because so much indicates that we want to. But we make it hard on each other, and hardest of all seems to be the notion that people in love don't need time alone. It's no wonder that some people eventually drag themselves away, wearied by the effort of living their lives welded at the wrist to the person they thought they loved.

Relationships I've observed that seem to be working accept this need to be alone. Partners spend time apart from each other in separate rooms, even go on trips alone, without suffering cynicism or mistrust. If more men and women had rooms of their own - places to go where no questions are asked - perhaps more relationships would succeed. Perhaps some separations are really a final, desperate means of getting space.
-*PAT PAQUIN, American writer*

Love is the answer, but while you're waiting for the answer, sex raises some pretty good questions.
-*WOODY ALLEN, American actor, writer, film director*

Sex alleviates tension. Love causes it. *-WOODY ALLEN*

I thought of that old joke, you know, this guy goes to a psychiatrist and says, "Doc, my brother's crazy. He thinks he's a chicken." And the doctor says, "Why don't you turn him in?" And the guy says, "I would but I need the eggs." Well, I guess that's pretty much how I feel about relationships. You know, they're totally irrational and crazy and absurd ... but I guess we keep going through it because most of us need the eggs. *-WOODY ALLEN, from the film "Annie Hall". 1977*

I wish I could introduce The Rules Girl to a friend who tells each of her daughters, "Be yourself. The only man you will scare off is your future ex-husband."
*-ELLEN GOODMAN, American journalist, author*

Even when you lack self confidence, keep in mind that if you want a woman to think you're a prince, you should treat her like a queen.
*-MARILYN VOS SAVANT, American writer, columnist*

Americans, at least tacitly, have all but given up on the notion that the appropriate premarital state is one of chastity. The Bible may have warned that like the denizens of Sodom and Gomorah, those who give "themselves over to fornication" will suffer "the vengeance of eternal fire." Yet for most Americans, adult premarital sex has become the "sin" they not only wink at but endorse. On television, adult virgins are as rare as caribou in Manhattan. Several studies have found the prime-time network shows implicitly condone premarital sex, and air as many as

8 depictions of it for every 1 of sex between married couples. And a *U.S News* poll shows that while most Americans - 74 percent - have serious qualms about teens having sex before mariage, more than half believe it is not at all wrong, or wrong only sometimes, for *adults* to have premarital sex.
- *DAVID WHITMAN, American journalist. In "U.S. News & World Report"*

My fellow Americans, we must be candid. There is sex. Now, can we please change the subject.
- *MAUREEN DOWD, American newspaper columnist*

There isn't any clear line to be drawn between ourselves and the people we love. We are them in a certain sense; if we weren't we wouldn't mind what happened to them.
- *WENDELL BERRY, American poet, author*

You see an awful lot of smart guys with dumb women, but you hardly ever see a smart woman with a dumb guy.
- *ERICA JONG, American writer, feminist*

Many of the complaints about family life in the 1990's sound an awful lot like those voiced in the 1950's, an era we look upon with nostalgia. We often forget that the current gold standard of family life - the family built upon an intimate marital relationship - was regarded with great suspicion when it made its debut. The middle-class nuclear family that became the norm at mid-century was a stripped down version of the extended families of previous decades. Kingsley Davis observed that a host of social ills could be traced to this new form of family: "The family union has been reduced to its lowest common denominator - married couple with children. The family aspect of our culture has become couple-centered with only one or two children eventually entering the charmed circle," he wrote.

Ernest Burgess, one of the most respected sociologists of his generation, wrote in 1953 that urbanization, greater mobilization, individualization, increased secularization, and the emancipation of women had transformed the family from an institution based on law and custom to one based on companionship and love. Despite believing that the changes taking place in the family were largely beneficial to society, Burgess acknowledged the enormous pressure that would be placed on the marital relationship to meet new expectations for intimacy. Burgess and Davis correctly predicted that divorce would rise because of the tremendous strain placed on couples to manage the growing demands for congeniality and cooperation.

*-FRANK F. FURSTENBERG, American sociologist, author. In 'American Demographics "*

When you look at relationships that make it, the people are good friends and treat each other with respect; they have shared values and they trust one another. Trust is the foundation. Without it, you don't feel safe.

If you don't feel safe, you can't be vulnerable. If you're not vulnerable, you can't be intimate.

*-LONNIE BARBACH, American psychologist, writer*

Often the difference between a successful marriage and a mediocre one consists of leaving about three or

four things a day unsaid.
-*HARLAN MILLER, American writer*

The Japanese have a word for it. It's judo - the art of conquering by yielding. The Western equivalent of judo is, "Yes, dear."
-*J.P. McEVOY, American writer*

Myth: *Affairs prove that love has gone from the marriage.*
The reasons for affairs are rich and varied. Most of the reasons have to do with the ego state of the person having the affair rather than the person against whom the infidelity is being committed. Even if someone did not love the spouse, an infidelity would be a rather complicated and indirect way to say so, and an inefficient way to approach the problems in a marriage. The feelings one spouse has for another are complicated from the beginning. The degree of complexity of the emotions in long-standing marriages is staggering. To reduce this complexity to a question as adolescent as the presence or absence of "love" is idiocy of the highest order. That question is best left to the petals of daisies.
-*FRANK PITTMAN, American psychiatrist, family therapist*

Some years ago, I wrote about four couple-friends who were getting divorced and implied that somehow those couples hadn't tried hard enough to stay together. I believed then that marriage was a matter of intention, not attention, and that if a couple was committed enough, it would work out. Last forever. Till death do us part.

I no longer believe it's that simple. Marriage is wonderful when it lasts forever, and I envy the old couples in *When Harry Met Sally* who reminisce tearfully about the day they met 50 years before. I no longer believe, however, that a marriage is a failure if it doesn't last forever. It may be a tragedy, but it is not necessarily a failure. And when a marriage does last forever with love alive, it is a miracle.

Love is a fluid process, and marriage is inherently ambiguous. As such, they both require care and maintenance. When we prefer to believe that marriage will automatically take care of itself, we may neglect to tend to it. The marriages that last with love alive are made of individuals who are willing to attend to and appreciate the marriage bond, not rely on it. Indeed, rather than being aghast that so many marriages are ending, we might look in awe at how many are surviving or beginning anew.

-*PEGGY O'MARA, American writer*

# CHAPTER - 3

## *FAMILY & CHILDREN*

### ***

Amongst mortals I do assert that they who are wholly without experience and have never had children far surpass in happiness those who are parents. The childless, because they have never proved whether children grow up to be a blessing or curse to men are removed from all share in many troubles; whilst those who have a sweet race of children growing up in their houses do wear away, as I perceive, their whole life through; first with the thought how they may train them up in virtue, next how they shall leave their sons the means to live; and after all this 'tis far from clear whether on good or bad children they bestow their toil.

But one last crowning woe for every mortal man I now will name: suppose that they have found sufficient means to live, and seen their children grow up to man's estate, and walk in virtue's path, still if fortune so befall, comes Death and bears the children's bodies off to Hades. Can it be any profit to the gods to heap upon us mortal men, beside our other woes, this further grief for children lost, a grief surpassing all?

*- EURIPIDES, Greek playwright (480 - 406 B.C.)*

When my sons are grown up, I would ask you, O my friends, to punish them; and I would have you trouble them, as I have troubled you, if they seem to care about riches, or anything, more than about virtue; or if they pretend to be something when they are really nothing, - then reprove them as I have reproved you, for not caring about that for which they ought to care, and thinking they are something when they are really nothing. And if you do this, both I and my sons will have received justice at your hands.

-SOCRATES, Greek philosopher (c.469 - 399 B.C.)

Between man and wife friendship seems to exist by nature; for man is naturally inclined to form couples - even more than to form cities, inasmuch as the household is earlier and more necessary than the city, and reproduction is more common to man with the animals. With the other animals the union extends only to this point, but human beings live together not only for the sake of reproduction but also for the purposes of life; for from the start the functions are divided, and those of man and woman are different; so they help each other by throwing their peculiar gifts into the common stock.

It is for these reasons that both utility and pleasure seem to be found in this kind of friendship. But this friendship may be based on virtue, if the parties are good; for each has its own virtue and they will delight in the fact. And children seem to be a bond of union (which is the reason why childless people part more easily); for children are a good common to both and what is common holds them together. -ARISTOTLE, Greek philosopher (384 - 322 B.C.)

Small children disturb your sleep, big children your life.
- *YIDDISH PROVERB*

Train up a child in the way he should go; and when he is old, he will not depart from it.
- *PROVERBS 22:6*

They who care for the rest rule - the husband the wife, the parents the children, the masters the servants; and they who are cared for obey - the women their husbands, the children their parents, the servants their masters. But in the family of the just man who lives by faith ... even those who rule serve those whom they seem to command; for they rule not from a love of power, but from a sense of the duty they owe to others - not because they are proud of authority, but because they love mercy.
- *ST. AUGUSTINE, Church father, philosopher (354 - 430)*

You fathers and you mothers fond, also,
If you have children be it one or two,
Yours is the burden of their wise guidance
The while they are within your governance.
Beware that not from your own lax living,
Or by your negligence in chastening
They fall and perish; for I dare will say,
If that should chance you'll dearly have to pay.
Under a shepherd soft and negligent
Full many a sheep and lamb by wolf is rent.
- *GEOFFREY CHAUCER, English poet (1340 - 1400)*

No man is so virtuous as to marry a wife only to have children.    -*MARTIN LUTHER, German religious reformer (1483 - 1546)*

It is wrong and foolish to prohibit children who have come of age from being famliar with their fathers, and to prefer to maintain an austere and disdainful gravity toward them, hoping thereby to keep them in fear and obedience. For that is a very futile farce, which makes fathers annoying to their children and what is worse, ridiculous. They have in their hands youth and vigor, and consequently the wind and favor of the world behind them; and they receive with mockery these fierce and tyrannical looks from men who have no blood left in either heart or veins - real scarecrows in a hemp field. Even if I could make myself feared, I would much rather make myself loved.

*-MICHEL DE MONTAIGNE, French moralist, essayist, (1533 - 1592)*

But though there be a time when a child comes to be free from subjection to the will and command of his father as he himself is free from subjection to the will of anybody else, and they are both under no other restraint but that which is common to them both, whether it be the law of Nature or the munincipal law of their country, yet this freedom exempts not a son from that honor which he ought, by the law of God and Nature, to pay his parents, God having made the parents instruments in His great design of continuing the race of mankind and the occasions of life to their children. As He hath laid on them an obligation to nourish, preserve, and bring up their offspring, so He has laid on the children a perpetual obligation of honoring their parents, which, containing in it an inward esteem and reverence to be shown by all outward expressions, ties up the child

from anything that may ever injure or affront, disturb or endanger the happiness or life of those from whom he received his, and engages him in all actions of deference, relief, assistance, and comfort of those by whose means he entered into being and has been made capable of any enjoyments of life. From this obligation no state, no freedom, can absolve children.
*-JOHN LOCKE, English philosopher (1632 - 1704)*

The power, then, that parents have over their children arises from that duty which is incumbent on them, to take care of their offspring during the imperfect state of childhood. To inform the mind, and govern the actions of their yet ignorant nonage, till reason shall take its place and ease them of that trouble, is what the children want, and the parents are bound to. For God having given man an understanding to direct his actions, has allowed him a freedom of will and liberty of acting, as properly belonging therunto within the bounds of that law he is under. But whilst he is in an estate wherin he has no understanding of his own to direct his will, he is not to have any will of his own to follow. He that understands for him must will for him too; he must prescribe to his will and regulate his actions, but when he comes to the estate that made his father a free man, the son is a free man too.    *-JOHN LOCKE*

Children are overwhelming, supercilious, passionate, envious, inquisitive, egotistical, idle, fickle, timid, intemperate, liars and disemblers; they laugh and weep easily, are excessive in their joys and sorrow, and that about the most trifling subjects; they bear no pain, but like to inflict it on others; already they are

men.
*-JEAN DE LA BRUYÈRE, French essayist, moralist (1645 - 1696)*

Civilization varies with the family, and the family with civilization. Its highest and most complete realization is found where enlightened Christianity prevails; where woman is exalted to her true and lofty place as equal with the man; where husband and wife are one in honor, influence, and affection, and where children are a common bond of care and love. This is the idea of a perfect family.
*- WILLIAM AIKMAN, Scottish painter (1682 - 1731)*

What maintains one Vice would bring up two Children.
*-BEN FRANKLIN, American statesman, writer, scientist (1706 - 1790)*

Unlike grownups, children have little need to deceive themselves.
*-JOHANN WOLFGANG VON GOETHE, German poet, playwright (1749 - 1832)*

Correction does much, but encouragement does more. Encouragement after censure is as the sun after a shower.   *-GOETHE*

The words a father speaks to his children in the privacy of the home are not overheard at the time, but, as in whispering galleries, they will be clearly heard at the end and by posterity.
*-JEAN PAUL RICHTER, German novelist (1763 - 1825)*

Why does it follow that women are fitted for nothing but the cares of domestic life, for bearing children, and cooking the food of a family, devoting all their time to the domestic circle - to promoting the immediate personal comfort of their husbands, brothers, and sons? ... The mere departure of a woman from the duties of the domestic circle, far from being a reproach to her, is a virtue of the highest order, when it is done from purity of motive, by appropriate means, and the purpose good.

*-JOHN QUINCY ADAMS, 6th President of the U.S. (1767 - 1848)*

Nobody, who has not been in the interior of a family, can say what the difficulties of any individual of that family may be.

*-JANE AUSTEN, English novelist (1775 - 1817)*

Whether it be for good or evil, the education of the child is principally derived from its own observation of the actions, words, voice, and looks of those with whom it lives. The friends of the young, then, cannot be too circumspect in their presence to avoid every and the last appearance of evil.

*-JOHN JEBB, English cleric (1775 - 1883)*

If children were brought into the world by an act of pure reason alone, would the human race continue to exist? Would not a man rather have so much sympathy with the coming generation as to spare it the burden of existence, or at any rate not to take it upon himself to impose that burden upon it in cold blood.

*-ARTHUR SCHOPENHAUER, German philosopher (1788 - 1860)*

There is no absurdity so palpable but that it may be firmly planted in the human head if only you begin to inculcate it before the age of five, by constantly

repeating it with an air of great solemnity.
-ARTHUR SCHOPENHAUER

The tasks set to children should be moderate. Over-exertion is hurtful both physically and intellectually, and even morally. But it is of the utmost importance that they should be made to fulfill all their tasks correctly and punctually. This will train them for an exact and conscientious discharge of their duties in later life.
-AUGUSTUS and JULIUS HARE, English clerygymen (1792, 1795 - 1834, 1855)

There never was a child so lovely but his mother was glad to get him asleep.
-RALPH WALDO EMERSON, American poet, essayist (1803 - 1882)

I remember the very place in Hyde Park where, in my fourteenth year, on the eve of leaving my father's house for a long absence, he told me that I should find, as I got acquainted with new people, that I had been taught many things which youths of my age did not commonly know; and that many persons would be disposed to talk to me of this, and to compliment me upon it. What other things he said on this topic I remember very imperfectly; but he wound up by saying, that whatever I knew more than others, could not be ascribed to any merit in me, but to the very unusual advantage which had fallen to my lot, of having a father who was able to teach me, and willing to give the necessary trouble and time; that it was no matter of praise to me, if I knew more than those who had not had a similar advantage, but the deepest disgrace to me if I did not.
-JOHN STUART MILL, English philosopher (1806 - 1873)

The duties of parents to their children are those which are indissolubly attached to the fact of causing the existence of a human being. The parent owes to society to endeavour to make the child a good and valuable member of it, and owes to the children to provide, so far as depends on him, such education and such appliances and means, as will enable them to start with a fair chance of achieving by their own exertions a successful life. To this every child has a claim; and I cannot admit, that as a child he has a claim to more.  -*JOHN STUART MILL*

Oh for boyhood's painless play,
Sleep that wakes in laughing day,
Health that mocks the doctor's rules,
Knowledge never learned of schools.
-*JOHN GREENLEAF WHITTIER, American poet (1807 - 1892)*

As the vexations men receive from their children hasten the approach of age, and double the force of years, so the comforts they reap from them are balm to all their sorrows, and disappoint the injuries of time. Parents repeat their lives in their offspring; and their esteem for them is so great, that they feel their sufferings and taste their enjoyments as much as if they were their own.
-*RAY PALMER, American clergyman (1808 - 1887)*

It always grieves me to contemplate the initiation of children into the ways of life when they are scarcely more than infants. It checks their confidence and simplicity, two of the best qualities that heaven gives them, and demands that they share our sorrows before they are capable of enterng into our

---

enjoyments.
-*CHARLES DICKENS, English novelist (1812 - 1870)*

You cannot teach a child to take care of himself
unless you will let him try to take care of himself.
He will make mistakes; and out of these mistakes
will come his wisdom.
-*HENRY WARD BEECHER, American cleric, writer (1813 - 1887)*

I have no sympathy with the old idea that children
owe such immense gratitude to their parents that they
can never fulfill their obligations to them. I think the
obligation is all on the other side. Parents can never
do too much for their children to repay them for the
injustice of having brought them into the world,
unless they have insured them high moral and
intellectual gifts, fine physical health, and enough
money and education to render life something more
than one ceaseless struggle for necessaries.
-*ELIZABETH CADY STANTON, American suffragist (1815 - 1902)*

Children do not know how their parents love them,
and they never will till the grave closes over those
parents, or till they have children of their own.
-*PHILIP PENDLETON COOKE, American author (1816 - 1850)*

We are always too busy for our children; we never
give them the time or interest they deserve. We
lavish gifts upon them; but the most precious gift -
our personal association, which means so much to
them - we give grudgingly.
-*MARK TWAIN, American writer, humorist (1835 - 1910)*

When I was a boy of 14, my father was so ignorant I
could hardly stand to have the old man around. But

when I got to be 21, I was astonished at how much the old man had learned in seven years.    -MARK TWAIN

Familiarity breeds contempt - and children.
-MARK TWAIN

Our Gilded Youths should be packed off to coal and iron mines, to freight trains, to fishing fleets in December, to dishwashing and clothes-washing, to road building and tunnel making, according to their choice, to get the childishness knocked out of them, and to come back into society with healthier sympathies and soberer ideas.
- WILLIAM JAMES, American philosopher, psychologist (1842 - 1910)

The family is the miniature commonwealth upon whose integrity the safety of the larger commonwealth depends.
-FELIX ADLER, American educator, reformer (1851 - 1933)

Families with babies and families without babies are sorry for each other.
-EDGAR WATSON HOWE, American journalist, essayist (1853 - 1937)

From the time of puberty onward the human individual must devote himself to the great task of *freeing himself from the parents*; and only after this detachment is accomplished can he cease to be a child and so become a member of the social community. For a son, the task consists in releasing his libidinal desires from his mother, in order to employ them in the quest of an external love-object in reality; and in reconciling himself with his father if he has remained antagonistic to him, or in freeing himself from his donimation if, in the reaction to the infantile revolt, he has lapsed into subservience to him.

These tasks are laid down for every man; it is noteworthy how seldom they are carried through ideally, that is, how seldom they are solved in a manner psychologically as well as socially satisfactory. In neurotics, however, this detachment from the parents is not accomplished at all ; the son remains all his life in subjection to his father, and incapable of transfering his libido to a new sexual object. In the reversed relationship the daughter's fate may be the same. In this sense the Oedipus complex is justifiably regarded as the kernal of the neuroses.

*-SIGMUND FREUD, Austrian neurologist, psychoanalyst (1856 - 1939)*

The family only represents one aspect, however important an aspect, of a human being's functions and activities. ... A life is beautiful and ideal or the reverse, only when we have taken into our consideration the social as well as the family relationship.

*-HAVELOCK ELLIS, English scientist, author (1859 - 1939)*

Perhaps I may record here my protest against the efforts, so often made, to shield children and young people from all that has to do with death and sorrow, to give them a good time at all hazards on the assumption that the ills of life will come soon enough. Young people themselves often resent this attitude on the part of their elders; they feel set aside and belittled as if they were denied the common human experience.

*-JANE ADDAMS, American social worker, activist (1860 - 1935)*

Nature kindly warps our judgement about our children, especially when they are young, when it would be a fatal thing for them if we did not love them.
- *GEORGE SANTAYANA, American philosopher, poet (1863 - 1952)*

Nature makes boys and girls lovely to look upon so they can be tolerated until they acquire some sense.
- *WILLIAM LYON PHELPS, American educator (1865 - 1943)*

I have certainly known more men destroyed by the desire to have a wife and child and to keep them in comfort than I have seen destroyed by drink and harlots.
- *WILLIAM BUTLER YEATS, Irish poet, playwright (1865 - 1939)*

As for boys and girls, it is one of the sorriest mistakes to talk down to them: almost always your lad of fifteen thinks more simply, more fundamentally than you do; and what he accepts as good coin is not facts or precepts, but feelings and convictions.
- *DAVID GRAYSON, American journalist (1870 - 1946)*

Hope is the last gift given to man, and the only gift not given to youth. Youth is pre-eminently the period in which a man can be lyric, fanatical, poetic; but youth is the period in which a man can be hopeless. The end of every episode is the end of the world. But the power of hoping through everything, the knowledge that the soul survives its adventures, that great inspiration comes to the middle-aged.
- *GILBERT KEITH CHESTERTON, English journalist, author (1874 - 1936)*

Give me four years to teach the children and the seed

I have sown will never be uprooted.

- *V.I. LENIN, Russian Communist leader (1870 - 1924)*

After a certain age, the more one becomes oneself, the more obvious one's family traits become.

- *MARCEL PROUST, French novelist (1871 - 1922)*

The father is always a Republican toward his son, and his mother's always a Democrat.

- *ROBERT FROST, American poet (1874 - 1963)*

If there is anything we wish to change in the child, we should first examine it and see whether it is not something that could better be changed in ourselves.

- *CARL JUNG, Swiss psychiatrist (1875 - 1961)*

Nothing has a stronger influence psychologically on their environment, and especially on their children, than the unlived life of the parents.   - *CARL JUNG*

Infancy isn't what it is cracked up to be. Children, not knowing that they are having an easy time, have a good many hard times. Growing and learning and obeying the rules of their elders, or fighting against them, are not easy things to do.

- *DON MARQUIS, American writer, humorist (1878 - 1937)*

Childhood - a period of waiting for the moment when I could send everyone and everything connected with it to hell.

- *IGOR STRAVINSKY, Russian-born American composer (1882 - 1971)*

You may give them your love but not your thoughts.
For they have their own thoughts.

You may house their bodies but not their
souls,
    For their souls dwell in the house of tomorrow,
which you cannot visit, not even in your dreams.
    You may strive to be like them, but
seek not to make them like you,
    For life goes not backward nor tarries
with yesterday.
    You are the bows from which your children
as living arrows are sent forth.
*-KAHIL GIBRAN, Syrian poet, painter (1883 - 1931)*

I have found the best way to give advice to your
children is to find out what they want and then advise
them to do it.
*-HARRY TRUMAN, 33rd President of the U.S. (1884 - 1972)*

You can never really live anyone else's life, not even
your child's. The influence you exert is through your
own life, and what you've become yourself.
*-ELEANOR ROOSEVELT, American First Lady (1884 - 1962)*

The average child is an almost non-existent myth. To
be normal one must be peculiar in some way or
another.
*-HEYWOOD BROUN, American journalist (1888 - 1939)*

The vast army of children all over the world,
outwardly different in many ways, speaking different
languages, wearing different kinds of clothes and yet
so very like one another. If you bring them together,
they play or quarrel but even their quarrelling is
some kind of play. They do not think of differences
amongst themselves, differences of class or caste or

color or status. They are wiser than their fathers and mothers. As they grow up, unfortunately, their natural wisdom is often eclipsed by the teaching and behaviour of their elders. At school they learn many things which are no doubt useful but they gradually forget that the essential thing is to be human, and kind and playful and to make life richer for ourselves and others.

*-JAWAHARLAL NEHRU, Indian nationalist, Prime Minister (1889 - 1964)*

The commonest axiom of history is that every generation revolts against its fathers and makes friends with its grandfathers.

*-LEWIS MUMFORD, American cultural historian (1895 - 1990)*

A boy may be a brilliant mathematician at the age of thirteen. But I never knew a child of that age who had much that was useful to say about the ends of human life.

*-ROBERT MAYNARD HUTCHINS, American educator (1899 - 1977)*

I'm convinced that every boy, in his heart, would rather steal second base than an automobile.

*-TOM C. CLARKE, U.S. Supreme Court justice (1899 - 1977)*

What the world needs is not romantic lovers who are sufficient unto themselves, but husbands and wives who live in communities, relate to other people, carry on useful work and willingly give time and attention to their children.

*-MARGARET MEAD, American anthropologist (1901 - 1978)*

No matter how many communes anybody invents, the family always creeps back. *-MARGARET MEAD*

The more people have studied different methods of bringing up children the more they have come to the conclusion that what good mothers and fathers instinctively feel like doing for their babies is the best after all.

*-BENJAMIN SPOCK, American pediatrician, author (1903 - 1998)*

The best upbringing that children can receive is to observe their parents taking excellent care of themselves - mind, body, spirit. Children, being the world's greatest mimics, naturally and automatically model their parents behavior. *-BENJAMIN SPOCK*

I can't help but think that the more books you read, the more differences of opinion you read and the more confused you get. I find that authors of books for parents tend to offer tricks - rewards for children who eat their vegetables, or the "timeout" [as a tool for discilpline]. The timeout isn't necessarily wrong or harmful, but it suggests that the way to manage children is through tricks. I always strive to get back to the fundamental relationship between you and the kid - that you do the most to guide your child all the way along by a mutually respecting and loving relationship. *-BENJAMIN SPOCK*

There is always one moment in childhood when the door opens and lets the future in.

*-GRAHAM GREENE, English author*

A child as well as an adult needs plenty of what in German is called *Spieraum*. Now, *Spieraum* is not primarily a 'room to play in.' While the word also means that, its primary meaning is 'free scope, plenty of room' - to move not only one's elbows, but also one's mind, to experiment with things and ideas at one's leisure or, to put it colloquially, to toy with ideas. The biographies of creative people of the past are full of accounts of long hours they spent sitting by a river as teenagers, thinking their own thoughts, roaming through the woods with their faithful dogs or dreaming their own dreams. But who today has the leisure and the opportunities for this? If a youngster tries it, as likely as not his parents will fret that he is not using his time constructively, that he is daydreaming when he should be tackling the serious business of life. However, developing an inner life, including fantasies and daydreams, is one of the most constructive things a growing child can do. The days of most middle-class children are filled with scheduled activities - Boy or Girl Scouts meetings, music or dance lessons, organized sports - which leave them hardly any time to be themselves.

-BRUNO BETTELHEIM, Austrian child psychologist, writer (1903 - 1990)

What are those traits of childhood behavior that are so valuable yet tend to disappear gradually as human beings grow older? We have only to watch children to see them clearly displayed: Curiosity is one of the most important; imaginativeness; playfulness; open-mindedness; willingness to experiment; flexibility; humor; energy; receptiveness to new ideas, honesty; eagerness to learn; and perhaps the most pervasive and the most valuable of all: the need to love.

Children ask questions endlessly: "Why?" "What

is it?" "What's it for?" "How does it work?" They
watch, and they listen. They want to know
everything about everything. They can keep
themselves busy for hours with the simplest toys,
endowing sticks and stones and featureless objects
with personalities and histories, imagining elaborate
stories about them, building sagas that continue day
after day, month after month. They play games
endlessly, sometimes carefully constructing the rules,
sometimes developing the game as they go along.
They accept changes without defensiveness. When
they try to accomplish something and fail, they are
able to try it another way, and another until they find
a way that works. They laugh - babies smile and
laugh before they can even babble - and children
laugh from sheer exuberance and happiness. Unless
they fear punishment, they tell the truth; they call the
shots as they see them. And they soak up knowledge
and information like sponges; they are learning all
the time; every moment is filled with learning.
    -*ASHLEY MONTAGU, American anthropologist*

My father always said that there are four things a
child needs - plenty of love, nourishing food, regular
sleep, and lots of soap and water - and after those,
what he needs most is some intelligent neglect.
    -*IVY BAKER PRIEST, Treasurer of the U.S.*

Adolescence is a kind of emotional seasickness.
Both are funny, but only in retrospect.
    -*ARTHUR KOESTLER, British writer (1905 - 1983)*

If a child is to keep alive his inborn sense of wonder,
he needs the companionship of at least one adult who

can share it, rediscovering with him the joy, excitement and mystery of the world we live in.

-*RACHEL CARSON, American biologist, writer (1907 - 1964)*

The children who go to bed hungry in a Harlem slum or a West Virginia mining town are not being deprived because no food can be found to give them; they are going to bed hungry because despite all our miracles of invention and production, we have not yet found a way to make the necessities of life available to all of our citizens - including those whose failure is not lack of personal industry or initiative, but only an unwise choice of parents.

-*J. WILLIAM FULBRIGHT, U.S. Senator (1905 - 1995)*

I am not against mothers. I am against the ideology which expects every woman to have children, and I'm against the circumstances under which mothers have to have their chldren.

-*SIMONE DE BEAUVOIR, French novelist, feminist (1908 - 1986)*

Motherhood and homemaking are honorable choices for any woman, provided it is the woman who makes those decisions.

-*MOLLY YARD, American feminist, activist*

The young always have the same problem - how to rebel and conform at the same time. They have now solved this by defying their parents and copying one another.

-*QUENTIN CRISP, English author*

As soon as I stepped out of my mother's womb on to dry land, I realized that I had made a mistake - that I shouldn't have come - but the trouble with children is that they are not returnable.   -*QUENTIN CRISP*

Who of us is mature enough for offspring before the offspring themselves arrive? The value of marriage is not that adults produce children but the children produce adults.

-*PETER DE VRIES, American novelist (1910 - 1993)*

When I can no longer bear to think of the victims of broken homes, I begin to think of the victims of intact ones.   -*PETER DE VRIES*

Youth can measure in only one direction - from things as they are forward to their ideal of what things ought to be. They cannot measure backward, to things as they used to be, because they have not lived long enough, and they cannot measure laterally, to the condition of other societies on this earth, because they have not yet had the opportunity to know them well. Older people must add these two measurements. This is the core reason why the generation gap exists and why it will always exist.

-*ERIC SEVAREID, American journalist, commentator (1912 - 1992)*

If you want your children to keep their feet on the ground put some responsibility of their shoulders.

-*ABIGAIL VAN BUREN, American advice columnist*

Heredity is what sets the parents of a teenager wondering about each other.

-*LAURENCE J. PETER, American educator, author*

A child becomes an adult when he realizes that he has a right not only to be right but also to be wrong.

-*THOMAS SZASZ, American psychiatrist*

We like children who are a little afraid of us, docile, deferential children, though not, of course, if they are so obviously afraid that they threaten our image of ourselves as kind, lovable people whom there is no reason to fear.

*-JOHN HOLT, American educator (1923 - 1985)*

If children live with criticism, they learn to condemn.
If children live with hostility, they learn to fight.
If children live with fear, they learn to be apprehensive.
If children live with jealousy, they learn to feel guilty.
If children live with tolerance, they learn to be patient.
If children live with encouragement, they learn to be confident.
If children live with praise, they learn to be appreciative.
If children live with acceptance, they learn to love.
If children live with approval, they learn to like themselves.
If children live with recognition, they learn it is good to have a goal.
If children live with honesty, they learn what truth is.
If children live with fairness, they learn justice.
If children live with security, they learn to have faith in themselves and those about them.
If children live with friendliness, they learn the world is a nice place in which to live.

*-DOROTHY LAW NOLTE, American writer*

Your success as a family, our success as a society, depends not on what happens at the White House, but on what happens inside your house.

*-BARBARA BUSH, American First Lady*

Parents are only human, and have plenty of problems of their own. And most children can deal with an occasional outburst of anger as long as they have plenty of love and understanding to counter it.

But there are many parents whose negative patterns of behavior are consistent and dominant in a child's life. These are the parents who do the harm.

... When these children [of "toxic parents"] become adults, they continue to bear burdens of guilt and inadequacy, making it extremely difficult for them to develop a positive self-image. The resulting lack of confidence and self-worth can in turn color every aspect of their lives.

By now you may be thinking, "Wait a minute. Almost all the other books and experts say I can't blame anybody else for my problems."

Baloney. Your parents are accountable for what they did. Of course, you are responsible for your adult life, but that life was largely shaped by experiences over which you had no control. The fact is:

You are *not* responsible for what was done to you as a defenseless child!

You *are* responsible for taking positive steps to do something about it now!

*-SUSAN FORWARD, American psychotherapist, author*

I worry about people who get born nowadays because they get born into such tiny families - sometimes into no family at all. When you're the only pea in the pod, your parents are likely to get you confused with the

Hope Diamond.
*-RUSSELL BAKER, American journalist, author, humorist*

It now costs more to amuse a child than it once did to educate his father.
*-HERBERT PROCHNOW, American lawyer, author*

In the family, just where you might expect to be with those most like you, you encounter instead a collection of the strangest folk.

Voltaire supposedly said, "Nothing human is alien to me." Relatives and in-laws belie that. Where else, how else would you ever spend an evening with a man from Orange County who pays dues to the Klan, or with a math professor who interprets signals from outer space, or a junkyard dealer who did time in the state penitentiary. And the manners, the clothes, the bodies! We come to realize that large family affairs, rather than being scenes of convention, are actually performances of high comedy, outrageously funny, which also serve to encourage one's own peculiarities.
*-JAMES HILLMAN, American psychoanalyst, author*

So when people ask me why I write only about dysfunctional families, I say it's because they're more interesting. I could cop Leo Tolstoy's line: "All happy families resemble each other, each unhappy family is unhappy in its own way." But the fact is, I write about dysfunctional families because they are what I see and what I know. All families are dysfunctional in some ways. How can they not be? They are made up of people, each and every one of whom is dysfunctional to a degree. *-JUDITH GUEST*

Happiness is having a large, loving, caring, close-knit family in another city.
-*GEORGE BURNS, American comedian (1896 - 1996)*

Parenting cannot be carried out over the phone, however well meaning and loving the calls may be. It requires physical presence. The notion of "quality time" is a lame excuse for parental absence; it presupposes that bonding and education can take place in brief time bursts, on the run. Quality time occurs withing quantity time. As you spend time with children - fishing, gardening, camping, or "just" eating a meal - there are unpredictable moments when an opening occurs, and education takes hold. As family expert Barbara Dafoe Whitehead puts it: "Maybe there is indeed such a thing as a one-minute manager, but there is no such thing as a one-minute parent."
-*AMITAI ETZIONI, American sociologist*

Gang warfare in the streets, massive drug abuse, a poorly committed work force, and a strong sense of entitlement and a weak sense of responsiblility are, to a large extent, the product of poor parenting. True, economic and social factors also play a role. But a lack of effective parenting is a major cause, and the other factors could be handled more readily if we remained committed to the importance of the upbringing of the young. The fact is, in poor neighborhoods one finds decent and hardworking youngsters right next to anti-social ones. Likewise, in affluent suburbs one finds anti-social youngsters right next to decent, hardworking ones. The difference is often a reflection of the homes they come from. -AMITAI ETZIONE

"Moral intelligence" isn't acquired only by memorization of rules and regulations, by dint of abstract classroom discussion or kitchen compliance. We grow morally as a consequence of learning how to be with others, how to behave in this world, a learning prompted by taking to heart what we have seen and heard. The child is a witness; the child is an ever-attentive witness of grown-up morality - or lack therof; the child looks and looks for cues as to how one ought to behave, and finds them galore as we parents and teachers go about making choices, addressing people, showing in action our rock-bottom assumptions, desires, and values, and therby telling these young observers much more than we may realize.
-ROBERT COLES, American psychiatrist, author

If you bungle raising your children, I don't think whatever else you do well matters very much.
-JACQUELINE KENNEDY ONASSIS, American First Lady (1929 - 1994)

You don't choose your family. They are God's gift to you, as you are to them.
-DESMOND TUTU, South African clergyman

The family is not one of several alternative life-styles; it is not an arena in which rights are negotiated; it is not an old-fashioned barrier to a promiscuous sexlife; it is not a set of cost-benefit calculations. It is a commitment for which there is no feasible substitute. No child ought to be brought into a world where that commitment - from both parents - is absent.

There is no way to prepare for the commitment other than to make it. Living together is not a way of finding out how married life will be, because married life is shaped by the fact that the couple has made a solemn vow before their family and friends that this is for keeps and that any children will be their joint and permanent responsibility. It changes everything.

*-JAMES Q. WILSON, American sociologist, criminologist*

At play and in other realms, fathers tend to stress competition, challenge, initiative, risk taking, and independence. Mothers, as caretakers, stress emotional security and personal safety. On the playground, fathers will try to get the child to swing ever higher, higher than the person on the next swing; while mothers will be cautious, worrying about an accident. It's sometimes said that fathers express more concern for the child's longer-term development, while mothers focus on the child's immediate well-being (which, of course, in its own way has everything to do with a child's long-term well-being).

What is clear is that children have dual needs that must be met. Becoming a mature and competent adult involves the integration of two often-condradictory human desires: for *communion*, or the feeling of being included, connected, and related, and for *agency*, which entails independence, individuality and self-fulfillment. One without the other is a denuded and impaired humanity, an incomplete realization of human potential.

*-DAVID POPENOE, American sociologist, author*

In my many years as a sociologist, I have found few other bodies of evidence that lean so much in one direction as this one: on the whole, two parents - a father and a mother - are better for a child than one parent. There are, to be sure, many factors that complicate this simple proposition. We all know of a two-parent family that is truely dysfunctional - the proverbial family from hell. A child can certainly be raised to a fulfilling adulthood by one loving parent who is wholly devoted to the child's well-being. But such exceptions do not invalidate the rule any more than the fact that some three-pack-a-day smokers live to a ripe old age casts doubt on the dangers of cigarettes. -*DAVID POPENOE*

There are only two lasting bequests we can hope to give our children. One of these is roots, the other, wings.
-*HODDING CARTER, American journalist*

One can't have both a society of equal, gainfully employed men and women and a flourishing family life unless there are radical changes in the organization of work. If we are serious about preserving "family values" we are going to have to abandon our consumerist vision of the good life. It is consumerism that drives the 80-hour work week. When we learn that consumer goods don't make us happy, we can get serious about reconstructing the family. The critical question in America, at the end of the 20th century, is whether consumption or the family will prevail.
-*CHRISTOPHER LASCH, American historian, author (1932 - 1994)*

Historically, the single parent has been the norm in no society, but patriarchal linear life is economically now over. Family values are under attack, not by government programs that discourage family formation (although there are some) and not by media presentations that disparage families (although there are some), but by the economic system itself. It simply won't allow families to exist in the old-fashioned way, with a father who generates most of the earnings and a mother who does most of the nurturing. The one-earner, middle-class family is extinct.
*-LESTER THUROW, American economist*

Your children need your presence more than your presents.
*-JESSE JACKSON, American clergyman, activist*

It is my conviction that the family is God's basic unit in society. God's most important unit in society. No wonder then we are in a holy war for the survival of the family. Before a nation collapses the families of that nation must go down first. What is a local church? Nothing but a congregation of families.
*-JERRY FALWELL, American fundamentalist preacher*

As we all know, virtually every child in America grows up in a family with one or more parents. Parents house children. Parents feed children. Parents clothe children. Parents nurture and protect children. Parents instruct children in everything from using a fork to driving a car. To be sure, there have been vast changes in family life, and, increasingly, parents must depend on teachers, doctors, day-care workers, and technology to help care for and educate their children. Even so, these changes haven't altered one fundamental fact: In American society, parents still bear the primary responsibility for the material and spiritual welfare of children. As our teachers and counselors and politicians keep reminding us, everything begins at home. So, if today's children are in trouble, it's because today's parents are in trouble.

-*BARBARA DAFOE WHITEHEAD, American social historian*

Parenthood changes your view of the culture. Parents are responsible for transmitting values to children, and many parents today report that the culture, particularly the mass media, promotes values that assault and undermine their efforts. As Christopher Lasch puts it, "To see the modern world from the point of view of a parent is to see it in the worst possible light."

In focus groups I've conducted, parents consistently point to a culture that celebrates sex, violence and materialism and call it a hostile force in their lives and lives of their children. This anger at the state of our culture is not confined to prudes and straight arrows. It cuts across traditional ideological lines and seems intrinsically connected to the responsibilities of parenthood. Indeed, it is possible that, in the coming decade, the strongest and most effective moral critique of our culture will be offered not by people who avoided the individualism of an earlier era, but by those who lived it; not by the conservative politicians, but by the former

champions of sex, drugs and rock 'n' roll.
*-BARBARA DAFOE WHITEHEAD*

This is a pervasive phenomenon in American life. It is sort of the defining feature of American family life since the 1970s. It's the common denominator experienced now, this breaking up of families, mainly through divorce, for middle-class people. Politicians have said to me, "Look, I know divorce is a problem, but it is a political loser. I'll talk about illegitimacy, thank you, but not divorce."
*-BARBARA DAFOE WHITEHEAD*

Just for the moment we may still be able to maintain the illusion that divorce and illegitimacy are separate and wholly distinct phenomena. Like the front and back of the bus, illegitimacy for blacks and divorce for whites. For the moment, the illusion is made easier by the fact that unwed motherhood is still relatively rare among white college-educated women. But for the people who make, or fall into, the relevant decisions, divorce and illegitimacy are both distinct entrees into a similar lifestyle: single parenthood. Which is why, despite differences, divorce and illegitimacy are inevitably connected by a deep cultural logic, by prevailing cultural ideas about marriage. How favorably or unfavorably men and women view single parenthood depends on the stories of marriage and family that dominate the culture and the incentives toward marriage, both economic and moral, that are created and sustained by the community.

Are two parents necessary, or simply desirable? Do children need fathers, or can mothers do it all?

How hard is it to be a single mother, anyway? How hard is it to get and stay married, and is the effort worth it?

The answers a community offers to questions like these will shape men's and women's attitudes toward both divorce and unwed motherhood. A society that enthusiastically approves of divorce will make at least one partner happy, and will have difficulty telling unmarried women that it is wrong to have a baby, if doing so will make them happy.

*-MAGGIE GALLAGHER, American writer, journalist*

How well we do is determined not just by our gifts and grit, but also by social background, networks, family connections and - powerfully - by how well our parents did. Life is not merely a footrace, but a relay race. It matters a lot how much headway the previous runner has made when he hands you the baton.

*- WILLIAM RASBERRY, American journalist*

Feeding, cleaning, and dressing a child are not acts of love. They're functions you perform lovingly, and either parent could do them. Women should not feel guilty about wanting to share the work of child care because that's what it is: WORK - repetitive, tedious, often lonely and exhausting.

*-LETTY COTTIN POGREBIN, American journalist*

While everything else in our lives has gotten simpler, speedier, more microwavable and user friendly, child-raising seems to have expanded to fill the time no longer available for it.

*-BARBARA EHRENREICH, American sociologist, author*

I want to have children while my parents are still young enough to take care of them.
-*RITA RUDNER, American comedienne*

Over the past 30 years in the United States, more and more women have begun to work outside the home, and more have divorced. While some commentators conclude that women's work *causes* divorce, my research into changes in the American family suggests something else. Since all wives in the families I studied (over an eight-year period) worked outside the home, the fact that they worked did not account for why some marriages were happy and others were not. What *did* contribute to happiness was the husband's willingness to do the work at home. Whether they were traditional or more egalitarian in their relationship, couples were happier when the man did a sizable share of housework and child care.
-*ARLIE HOCHSCHILD, American sociologist*

Parents are not quite interested in justice, they are interested in quiet.
-*BILL COSBY, American comedian, actor*

The adult world is built on the shifting grounds of friendship and competition. The double message of this society and economy are to get along and get ahead. We want our children to fit in and to stand out. We rarely address the conflict between these goals.
-*ELLEN GOODMAN, American journalist, author*

Americans once expected parents to raise their

children in accordance with the dominant cultural messages. Today they are expected to raise their children in opposition to them.

Once the chorus of cultural values was full of ministers, teachers, neighbors, leaders. They demanded more conformity, but offered more support. Now the messengers are violent cartoon characters, rappers and celebrities selling sneakers. Parents are considered "responsible" only if they are successful in their resistance.

That's what makes child-raising harder. It's not just that American families have less time with their kids; it's that we have to spend more of this time doing battle with our own culture. -ELLEN GOODMAN

We are given children to test us and make us more spiritual.
-GEORGE F. WILL, American columnist, commentator

Reading has always been life unwrapped to me, a way of understanding myself through both the unknown and the everyday. If being a parent consists often of passing along chunks of ourselves to unwitting - often unwilling - recipients, then books are, for me, one of the simplest and most sure-fire ways of doing that. I would be content if my children grew up to be the kind of people who think decorating consists mostly of building bookshelves.
-ANNA QUINDLEN, American journalist, novelist

Writing a book is like rearing children - willpower has very little to do with it. If you have a little baby crying in the middle of the night, and if you depend only on will power to get you out of bed to feed the

the baby, the baby will starve. You do it out of love. Willpower is a weak idea; love is strong. You don't have to scourge yourself with cat-o'-nine-tails to go to the baby. You go to the baby out of love for that particular baby. That's the same way you go to your desk. There's nothing freakish about it. Caring passionately about something isn't against nature, and it isn't against human nature. It's what we're here to do.

*-ANNIE DILLARD, American novelist*

# CHAPTER - 4

# *GOVERNMENT & POLITICS*

\*\*\*

In a country well governed, poverty is
something to be ashamed of.
In a country badly governed, wealth is
something to be ashamed of.
-*CONFUCIUS, Chinese philosopher (551 - 479 B.C.)*

Better to light one candle than curse the darkness.
-*CHINESE PROVERB*

I was really too honest a man to be a politician and
live.
-*SOCRATES, Greek philosopher (c.469 - c.399 B.C.)*

There is a difficulty in apprehending that the true art
of politics is concerned, not with private but with
public good (for public good binds together states,
but private only distracts them); and that both the
public and private good as well of individuals as of
states is greater when the state and not the individual
is first considered. In the second place, although a
person knows in the abstract that this is true, yet if he
be possessed of absolute and irresponsible power, he
will never remain firm in his principles or persist in
regarding the public good as primary in the state, and
private good as secondary. Human nature will

always be drawing him into avarice and selfishness, avoiding pain and pursuing pleasure without any reason, and will bring these to the front, obscuring the juster and better; and so working darkness in his soul will at last fill with evils both him and the whole city.
-PLATO, Greek philosopher (c.428 - c.347 B.C.)

Until philosophers are kings, or the kings and princes of this world have the spirit and power of philosophy, and political greatness and wisdom meet in one, and those commoner natures who pursue either to the exclusion of the other are compelled to stand aside, cities will never have rest from their evils - no, nor the human race, as I believe - and then only will this our state have a possibility of life and behold the light of day. -PLATO

Two requirements of good government: One is the actual obedience of citizens to the laws, the other is the goodness of the laws which they obey.
-ARISTOTLE, Greek philosopher (384 - 322 B.C.)

The forms of government are four - democracy, oligarchy, aristocracy, monarchy. The supreme right to judge and decide always rests, therfore, with either a part or the whole of one or other of these governing powers.

A democracy is a form of government under which the citizens distribute the offices of state among themselves by lot, wheras under oligarchy there is a property qualification, under aristocracy one of education. By education I mean that education which is laid down by the law; for it is those who have been loyal to the national institutions that hold office under an aristocracy. These are bound to be looked upon as 'the best men' and it is from this fact that this form of government has derived its name ('the rule of the best'). Monarchy, as the word implies, is the constitution in which one man has authority over all. There are two forms of monarchy: kingship, which is limited by prescribed conditions, and 'tyranny' which is not limited by anything. *-ARISTOTLE*

The men of old wanting to clarify and diffuse throughout the empire that light which comes from looking straight into the heart and then acting, first set up good government in their own states; wanting good government in their own states, they first established order in their families; wanting good order in their families, they first rectified their hearts.
*-MENCIUS, Chinese philosopher (372 - 289 B.C.)*

We are in bondage to the law in order that we may be free.
*-CICERO, Roman orator, philosopher (106 - 43 B.C.)*

No single type of government lasts very long. This being the case I regard monarchy as the best of the three basic types of government. But a moderate, mixed type of government, combining all three elements, is even better. There should be a monarchical element in the state. The leading citizens ought also to have some power. And the people themselves should have some say in running the affairs of the nation.

This kind of government promotes a high degree of equality - something free men cannot do without for long. Such a constitution also provides stability. The three basic forms of government too easily degenerate into their corresponding perversions: monarchy into despotism, aristocracy into oligarchy and democracy into mob rule or anarchy. These forms often change to new types, but a mixed constitution does not unless grievous errors are made in governing. There appears no reason to change the form of government if all the citizens have a feeling of security. Nor does this form have an opposite perversion into which it can easily slide. -CICERO

However many people a tyrant slaughters he cannot kill his successor.

-SENECA, Roman statesman, philosopher (c.4 B.C. - 65 A.D.)

They are wrong who think that politics is like an ocean voyage or a military campaign, something to be done with some particular end in view, something which leaves off as soon as that end is reached. It is not a public chore, to be got over with. It is a way of life. It is the life of a domesticated political and social creature who is born with a love for public life, with a desire for honor, with a feeling for his fellows; and it lasts as long as need be.

-PLUTARCH, Greek biographer (c.46 - c.120)

This is indeed the true condition of men in public life, who, to gain the vain title of being the people's leaders and governors, are content to make themselves the slaves and followers of all the people's humours and caprices. For as the lookout

men at the ship's prow, though they see what is ahead before the men at the helm, yet constantly look back to the pilots there, and obey the orders they give; so these men, steered, as I may say, by popular applause, though they bear the name of governors, are in reality the mere underlings of the multitude.
-PLUTARCH

If the motions of rulers be constantly opposite and cross to the tempers and inclinations of the people, they will be resented as arbitrary and harsh; as, on the other side, too much deference, or encouragement, as too often it has been, to popular faults and errors, is full of danger and ruinous consequences.  -PLUTARCH

When men are well governed, they neither seek nor desire any other liberty.
- NICCOLO MACHIAVELLI,  Florentine political philosopher (1469 - 1527)

The great majority of mankind are satisfied with appearances, as though they were realities and are often more influenced by the things that *seem* than by those that *are*.  -MACHIAVELLI

It is necessary that the prince should know how to color his nature well, and how to be a hypocrite and dissembler. For men are so simple, and yield so much to immediate necessity, that the deceiver will never lack dupes.  -MACHIAVELLI

It is very easy to accuse a government of imperfection, for all mortal things are full of it.
-MICHEL DE MONTAIGNE,  French moralist, essayist (1533 - 1592)

I will govern according to the common weal, but not according to the common will.

-JAMES I, King of England (1566 - 1625)

The majority is the best way, because it is visible, and has the strength to make itself obeyed. Yet it is the opinion of the least able.

-BLAISE PASCAL, French scientist, philosopher (1623 - 1662)

Justice without force is powerless; force without justice is tyrannical.  -BLAISE PASCAL

Being unable to make what is just strong, we have made what is strong just.  -BLAISE PASCAL

The most tyrannical governments are those which make crimes of opinions, for everyone has an inalienable right to his thoughts.

-BENEDICT SPINOZA, Dutch philosopher (1632 - 1677)

The ultimate aim of government is to free every man from fear, that he may live in all possible security. In fact, the true aim of government is liberty.

-BENEDICT SPINOZA

I easily grant that civil government is the proper remedy for the inconveniences of the state of Nature, which must certainly be great where men may be judges in their own case, since it is easy to be imagined that he who was so unjust as to do his brother an injury will scarce be so just as to condemn himself for it.

-JOHN LOCKE, English philosopher (1632 - 1704)

The great question which, in all ages, has disturbed

mankind, and brought on them the greatest part of their mischiefs, which has ruined cities, depopulated countries, and disordered the peace of the world, has been, not whether there be power in the world, nor whence it came, but who should have it.   *-JOHN LOCKE*

The natural liberty of man is to be free from any superior power on earth, and not to be under the will or legislative authority of man, but to have only the law of nature for his rule. The liberty of man in society is to be under no other legislative power but that established by consent in the commonwealth; nor under the dominion of any will or restraint of any law but what that legislative shall enact according to the trust put in it.   *-JOHN LOCKE*

For law, in its true notion, is not so much the limitation, as the direction of a free and intelligent agent to his proper interest, and prescribes no farther than is for the general good of those under the law.
*-JOHN LOCKE*

If none were to have liberty but those who understood what it is, there would not be many freed men in the world.
*-SIR GEORGE SAVILE, English politician, writer (1633 - 1695)*

Few consider how much we are indebted to government, because few can represent how wretched mankind would be without it.
*-JOSEPH ADDISON, English essayist (1672 - 1719)*

Constant experience shows us that every man invested with power is apt abuse it, and to carry his

authority as far as it will go. To prevent this abuse, it is necessary from the very nature of things that power should be a check to power.
-*BARON DE MONTESQUIEU, French lawyer, philosopher (1689 -1755)*

Liberty is the right to do whatever the law permits.
-*MONTESQUIEU*

Republics come to an end through luxury; monarchies through poverty.  -*MONTESQUIEU*

There has never been a perfect government, because men have passions; and if they did not have passions, there would be no need for government.
-*VOLTAIRE, French author, philosopher (1694 - 1778)*

In general, the art of government consists in taking as much money as possible from one class of citizens to give to the other.  -*VOLTAIRE*

When you assemble a number of men, to have the advantage of their joint wisdom, you inevitably assemble with those men all their prejudices, their passions, their errors of opinion, their local interests, their selfish views. From such an assembly can a perfect production be expected?
-*BEN FRANKLIN, American statesman, writer, scientist (1706 - 1790)*

There is no kind of dishonesty into which otherwise good people more easily and frequently fall than that of defrauding the government.  -*BEN FRANKLIN*

Nature has given women so much power that the law has very wisely given them little.
-*SAMUEL JOHNSON, English lexicographer, writer (1709 - 1784)*

It is universally acknowledged that there is a great
uniformity among the actions of men, in all nations
and ages, and that human nature remains still the
same, in its principles and operations. The same
motives always produce the same actions; the same
events follow from the same causes. Ambition,
avarice, self-love, vanity, friendship, generosity,
public spirit: these passions mixed in various
degrees, and distributed through society, have been,
from the beginning of the world, and still are, the
source of all actions and enterprises which have ever
been observed among mankind.

-*DAVID HUME*, Scottish philosopher (1711 - 1776)

Nothing appears more surprising to those who
consider human affairs with a philosophical eye, than
the easiness with which the many are governed by the
few. -*DAVID HUME*

That government which confines itself to mere
obedience will find difficulty in getting itself
obeyed. If it is good to know how to deal with men
as they are, it is much better to make them what there
is need that they should be. The most absolute
authority is that which penetrates into a man's inmost
being, and concerns itself no less with his will than
with his actions. It is certain that all peoples become
in the long run what the government makes them:
warriors, citizens, men, when it so pleases; or merely
populace and rabble, when it chooses to make them
so. Hence every prince who despises his subjects,
dishoners himself, in confessing that he does not
know how to make them worthy of respect. Make
men, therefore, if you would command men: if you

would have them obedient to the laws, make them love the laws, and then they will need only know what is their duty to do it.

-*JEAN-JACQUES ROUSSEAU, French philosopher (1712 - 1778)*

If life, liberty, and property could be enjoyed in as great perfection in solitude as in society, there would be no need of government.

-*JAMES OTIS, American patriot, writer (1725 - 1783)*

The use of force is temporary. It may subdue for a moment, but it does not remove the necessity of subduing again: and a nation is not governed which is perpetually to be conquered.

-*EDMUND BURKE, British statesman, orator (1729 - 1779)*

The only thing necessary for the triumph of evil is for good men to do nothing.   -*EDMUND BURKE*

Manners are of more importance than laws. Upon them, in a great measure, the laws depend. The law touches us but here and there, and now and then. Manners are what vex or soothe, corrupt or purify, exalt or debase, barbarise or refine us, by a constant, steady, uniform, insensible operation, like that of the air we breathe in. They give their whole form and colour to our lives. According to their quality, they aid morals, they supply them, or they totally destroy them.   -*EDMUND BURKE*

All writers on the science of policy are agreed, and they agree with experience, that all governments must frequently infringe the rules of justice to support themselves; that truth must give way to dissimulation, honesty to convenience, and humanity

itself to the reigning of interest. The whole of this mystery of iniquity is called the reason of state.
*-EDMUND BURKE*

All government - indeed, every human benefit and enjoyment, every virtue and every prudent act - is founded on compromise and barter. *-EDMUND BURKE*

Society cannot exist unless a controlling power upon will and appetite be placed somewhere; and the less of it there is within, the more there must be without. It is ordained in the eternal constitution of things, that men of intemperate minds cannot be free. Their passions forge their fetters. *-EDMUND BURKE*

The basis of our political system is the right of the people to make and to alter their constitutions of government. But the constitution which at any time exists, till changed by an explicit and authentic act of the whole people, is sacredly obligatory upon all. The very idea of the power and right of the people to establish government presupposes the duty of every individual to obey the established government.
*-GEORGE WASHINGTON, 1st President of the United States (1732 - 1799*

Government is not reason, it is not eloquence - it is force. *-GEORGE WASHINGTON*

The spirit of party serves always to distract public councils, and enfeeble the public administration.
*-GEORGE WASHINGTON*

I have always given it as my decided opinion that no nation had a right to intermeddle in the internal concerns of another; that everyone had a right to form and adopt whatever government they liked best to live under themselves. *-GEORGE WASHINGTON*

While all other Sciences have advanced, that of Government is at a stand; little better understood, little better practiced now than 3 or 4 thousand years ago. *-JOHN ADAMS, 2nd President of the United States (1735 - 1826)*

It is agreed that "the end of all government is the good and ease of the people, in a secure enjoyment of their rights without oppression;" but it must be remembered that the rich are *people* as well as the poor; that they have rights as well as others; that they have as clear and as sacred a right to their large property as others have to theirs which is smaller; that oppression of them is as possible and as wicked as to others. *-JOHN ADAMS*

As the happiness of the people is the sole end of government, so the consent of the people is the only foundation of it, in reason, morality, and the natural fitness of things. *-JOHN ADAMS*

The people, when they have been unchecked, have been as unjust, tyrannical, brutal, barbarous, and cruel, as any king or senate possessed of uncontrollable power. The majority has eternally, and without one exception, usurped over the rights of the minority. *-JOHN ADAMS*

No sooner has one Party discovered or invented an amelioration of the condition of man or the order of society, than the opposite Party belies it, misconstrues it, misrepresents it , ridicules it, insults it, and persecutes it. -JOHN ADAMS

Those who expect to reap the blessings of freedom must undergo the fatigue of supporting it.
- THOMAS PAINE, American political philospher, writer (1737 - 1809)

The guilt of a government is the crime of a whole country. -THOMAS PAINE

Administration of justice and of the finances are the two objects which, in a state of peace, comprehend almost all the respective duties of the sovereign and of the people; of the former, to protect the citizens who are obedient to the laws; of the latter, to contribute the share of their property which is required for the expenses of the state.
-EDWARD GIBBON, English historian (1737 - 1794)

We hold these truths to be self-evident; that all men are created equal; that they are endowed by their creator with certain inalienable rights; that among these are life, liberty, and the pursuit of happiness; that to secure these rights, governments are instituted among men, deriving their just powers from the consent of the governed; that whenever any form of government becomes destructive to these ends, it is the right of the people to alter or to abolish it, and to institute new government, laying its foundation on such principles, and organizing its powers in such form, as to them shall seem most likely to effect their safety and happiness.
-DECLARATION OF INDEPENDENCE

Every man wishes to pursue his occupation and to enjoy the fruits of his labours and the produce of his

property in peace and safety, and with the least possible expense. When these things are accomplished, all the objects for which government ought to be established are answered.
— *THOMAS JEFFERSON, 3rd President of the United States (1743 - 1826)*

The basis of our government being the opinion of the people, the very first object should be to keep that right; and were it left to me to decide whether we should have a government without newspapers, or newspapers without a government, I should not hesitiate a moment to prefer the latter. But I should mean that every man should receive those papers, and be capable of reading them.   *-THOMAS JEFFERSON*

The only security of all is in a free press. The force of public opinion cannot be resisted, when permitted freely to be expressed. The agitation it produces must be submitted to. It is necessary, to keep the waters pure.   *-THOMAS JEFERSON*

That government is best which governs the least, because its people discipline themselves.
*-THOMAS JEFFERSON*

The only means to gain one's ends with people are force and cunning. Love also, they say; but that is to wait for sunshine, and life needs every moment.
*-JOHANN WOLFGANG VON GOETHE, German poet, playwright (1749 - 1832)*

To rule is easy, to govern difficult.   *-GOETHE*

Liberty is to faction what air is to fire, an element without which it instantly expires. But it could not be a less folly to abolish liberty, which is essential to political life, because it nourishes faction than it would be to wish the annihilation of air, which is essential to animal life, because it imparts to fire its destructive agency.

-*JAMES MADISON, 4th President of the United States (1751 - 1836)*

If men were angels, no government would be necessary. -*JAMES MADISON*

Justice is the end of government. It is the end of civil society. It ever has been and ever will be pursued until it be obtained, or until liberty be lost in the pursuit. -*JAMES MADISON*

Every nation has the government that it deserves.

-*JOSEPH MARIE MAISTRE, French author (1753 - 1821)*

The science of politics, like most other sciences, has received great improvement. The efficacy of various principles is now well understoood, which were either not known at all, or imperfectly known to the ancients. The regular distribution of power into distinct departments; the introduction of legislative balances and checks; the institution of courts composed of judges holding their offices during good behavior; the representation of the people in the legislature by deputies of their own election: these are wholly new discoveries, or have made their principal progress towards perfection in modern times. They are means, and powerful means, by which the excellences of republican government may be retained and its imperfections lessened or avoided.

-*ALEXANDER HAMILTON, American statesman (1755 - 1804)*

The local interests of a state ought in every case to

give way to the interests of the Union; for when a sacrifice of one or the other is necessary, the former becomes only an apparent, partial interest, and should yield, on the principle that the small good ought never to oppose the great one.
-*ALEXANDER HAMILTON*

In forming a government which is to be administered by men over men the great difficulty lies in this: You must first enable the government to control the governed, and in the next place, oblige it to control itself. -*ALEXANDER HAMILTON*

Society and government are different in themselves, and have different origins. Society is produced by our wants, and government by our wickedness. Society is in every state a blessing; government even it its best state but a necessary evil.
- *WILLIAM GODWIN, English novelist, philosopher (1756 - 1836)*

There are no necessary evils in government. Its evils exist only in its abuses. If it would confine itself to equal protection, and, as Heaven does its rain, shower its favors alike on the high and on the low, the rich and the poor, it would be an unqualified blessing.
- *ANDREW JACKSON, 7th President of the United States (1767 - 1845)*

There are two levers for moving men - interest and fear.
- *NAPOLEON BONAPARTE, Emperor of France (1769 - 1821)*

The science of government is the most abtruse of all sciences; if, indeed, that can be called a science which has but few fixed principles, and practically consists in little more than the exercise of a sound discretion, applied to the exigencies of the state as they arise. It is the science of experiment.

*-WILLIAM JOHNSON, U.S. Supreme Court Justice (1771 - 1834)*

The real object is to vote for the good politician, not for the kind-hearted or agreeable man: mischief is just the same to the country whether I am smiled into a corrupt choice or frowned into a corrupt choice.

*-SYDNEY SMITH, English clergyman, writer (1771 - 1845)*

The three ends which a statesman ought to propose to himself in the government of a nation, are - 1. Security to possessors; 2. Facility to acquirers; and 3. Hope to all.

*-SAMUEL TAYLOR COLERIDGE, English poet (1772 - 1834)*

All legislation, all government, all society is founded upon the principle of mutual concession, politeness, comity, courtesy; upon these everything is based. Let him who elevates himself above humanity, above its weaknesses, its infirmities, its wants, its necessities, say, if he pleases, I will never compromise; but let no one who is not above the frailities of our common nature disdain compromises.

*-HENRY CLAY, American lawyer, statesman (1777 - 1852)*

When a thing ceases to be a subject of controversy, it ceases to be a subject of interest.

*-WILLIAM HAZLITT, English writer (1778 - 1830)*

The office of government is not to confer happiness, but to give men opportunity to work out happiness for themselves.

*-WILLIAM ELLERY CHANNING, American clergyman, writer (1780 - 1842)*

Democracy, as I understand it, requires me to sacrifice myself for the masses, not to them. Who knows not that if you would save the people, you must often oppose them?

-JOHN C. CALHOUN, American lawyer, politician (1782 - 1850)

The Government of the absolute majority instead of the Government of the people is but the Government of the strongest interests; and when not efficiently checked, it is the most tyrannical and oppressive that can be devised.    -JOHN C. CALHOUN

While I trust that liberty and free institutions, as we have experienced them, may ultimately spread over the globe, I am by no means sure that all people are fit for them; nor am I desirous of imposing or forcing our peculiar forms upon any other nation that does not wish to embrace them.

-DANIEL WEBSTER, American lawyer, statesman (1782 - 1852)

Inconsistencies of opinion, arising from changes of circumstances, are often justifiable.    -DANIEL WEBSTER

I do not believe in the collective wisdom of individual ignorance.

-THOMAS CARLYLE, Scottish historian, essayist (1795 - 1881)

Government is emphatically a machine; to the discontented a "taxing machine," to the contented a "machine for securing property."    -THOMAS CARLYLE

An honest politician is one who, when he is bought, will stay bought.

-SIMON CAMERON, Republican boss of Pennsylvania (1799 - 1889)

I hardly know which is the greater pest to society, a paternal government - that is to say a prying, meddlesome government - which intrudes itself into every part of human life, and which thinks it can do everything for everybody better than anybody; or a careless, lounging government, which suffers grievances such as it could at once remove, and to which all complaint and remonstrance has only one answer: "We must let things alone; we must let things take their course; we must let things find their level." There is no more important problem in politics than to ascertain the just mean between these two most pernicious extremes, to draw correctly the line which divides those cases in which it is the duty of the State to interfere from those cases in which it is the duty of the State to abstain from interference.

*- THOMAS B. MACAULAY, English writer, politician (1800 - 1859)*

What are laws but the expression of the opinion of some class which has power over the rest of the community? By what was the world ever governed but by the opinion of some person or persons? By what else can it ever be governed.

*- THOMAS B. MACAULAY*

People say law but they mean wealth.

*- RALPH WALDO EMERSON, American poet, essayist (1803 - 1882)*

Those who stay away from the election think that one vote will do no good; 'Tis but one step more to think one vote will do no harm.   *-EMERSON*

Leave this hypocritical prating about the masses. Masses are rude, lame, unmade, pernicious in their demands and influences, and need not be flattered but to be schooled. I wish not to concede anything to them, but to tame, drill, divide, and break them up, and draw individuals out of them. The worst of charity is that the lives you are asked to preserve are not worth preserving. Masses! The calamity is the masses. I do not wish any mass at all, but honest men only, lovely, sweet, accomplished women only, and no shovel-handed, narrow-minded, gin-drinking million stockingers or lazzeroni at all. If government knew how, I should like to see it check, not multiply the population. When it reaches its true law of action, every man that is born will be hailed as essential. *-RALPH WALDO EMERSON*

The less government we have the better - the fewer laws, and the less confided power. The antidote to this abuse of formal government is the influence of private character, the growth of the individual; the appearance of the principal to supersede the proxy; the appearance of the wise man; of whom the existing government is, it must be owned, but a shabby imitaton. *-RALPH WALDO EMERSON*

Every actual State is corrupt. Good men must not obey the laws too well. What satire on government can equal the severity of censure conveyed in the word *politics* which now for ages has signified *cunning*, intimating that the State is a trick.
*-RALPH WALDO EMERSON*

Foreign policy demands scarcely any of those qualities which are peculiar to democracy; on the contrary it calls for the perfect use of almost all those qualities in which a democracy is deficient. Democracy is favorable to the increase of the internal resources of a state, it diffuses wealth and comfort, and fortifies the respect for law in all classes of society, but it can only with great difficulty regulate the details of an important undertaking, persevere in a fixed design, and work out its execution in spite of serious obstacles. It cannot combine its measures with secrecy or await their consequences with patience. These are qualities which are more characteristic of an individual or an aristocracy.

*-ALEXIS DE TOQUEVILLE, French politician, historian, writer (1805 - 1859)*

As a rule, democracies have very confused or erroneous ideas on external affairs, and generally solve outside questions only for internal reasons.

*-ALEXIS DE TOQUEVILLE*

To commit violent and unjust acts, it is not enough for a government to have the will or even the power; the habits, ideas, and passions of the time must lend themselves to their committal.   *-ALEXIS DE TOQUEVILLE*

One constantly sees a political party exaggerating its feelings in order to embarrass its opponents, and the latter, in order to avoid the trap, pretending to sentiments which they do not feel.   *-TOQUEVILLE*

The deeper we penetrate into the workings of these parties, the more do we perceive that the object of the one is to limit, and that of the other to extend, the popular authority. I do not assert that the ostensible end, or even the secret aim of American parties is to promote the rule of aristocracy or democracy in the country; but I affirm that aristocratic or democratic passions may easily be detected at the bottom of all parties, and that although they escape a superficial observation, they are the main point and the very soul of every faction in the United States.

-*ALEXIS DE TOQUEVILLE*

In politics, again, it is almost a commonplace, that a party of order or stability, and a party of progress or reform, are both necessary elements of a healthy state of political life; until the one or the other shall have so enlarged its mental grasp as to be a party equally of order and of progress, knowing and distinguishing what is fit to be preserved from what ought to be swept away.

-*JOHN STUART MILL*, English philosopher (1806 - 1873)

Over himself, over his own mind and body, the individual is sovereign.     -*JOHN STUART MILL*

How little do politics affect the life, the moral life of a nation. One single good book influences the people a vast deal more.

- *WILLIAM GLADSTONE*, British statesman (1809 - 1898)

This *declared* indifference, but as I must think, covert *real* zeal for the spread of slavery, I can not but hate. I hate it because of the monstrous injustice of slavery itself. I hate it because it deprives our republican example of its influence in the world - enables the enemies of free institutions, with plausibility, to taunt us as hypocrites - causes the real friends of freedom to doubt our sincerity and especially because it forces so many really good men amongst ourselves into an open war with the very fundamental principles of civil liberty - criticizing the Declaration of Independence, and insisting that there is no right principle of action, but *self-interest.*

*-ABRAHAM LINCOLN, 16th President of the United States (1809 - 1865)*

Whenever I see anyone arguing for slavery, I feel a strong impulse to see it tried on him personally.

*-ABRAHAM LINCOLN*

They who deny freedom to others deserve it not for themselves.  *-ABRAHAM LINCOLN*

As I would not be a slave, so I would not be a master. This expresses my idea of democracy.

*-ABRAHAM LINCOLN*

The shepherd drives the wolf from the sheep's throat, for which the sheep thanks the shepherd as his liberator while the wolf denounces him for the same act as the destroyer of liberty.  *-ABRAHAM LINCOLN*

The legitimate object of government is to do for a community of people whatever they need to have done, but cannot do at all in their separate and individual capacities.  *-ABRAHAM LINCOLN*

There are few things wholly evil or wholly good. Almost everything, especially of government policy, is an inseparable compound of the two, so that our best judgement of the preponderance between them is continually demanded.  *-ABRAHAM LINCOLN*

Our government rests on public opinion. Whoever can change public opinion can change the government practically as such. -ABRAHAM LINCOLN

If I were to read, much less answer, all the attacks made on me, this shop might as well be closed for any other business. I do the very best I know how, the very best I can, and I mean to keep doing so until the end. If the end brings me out all right, what is said against me won't amount to anything. If the end brings me out wrong, then angels swearing I was right would make no difference. -ABRAHAM LINCOLN

Nearly all men can stand adversity, but if you want to test a man's character, give him power.
-ABRAHAM LINCOLN

To be governed is to be watched, inspected, spied, directed, law-ridden, regulated, penned up, indoctrinated, preached at, checked, appraised, seized, censured, commanded by beings who have neither title nor knowledge nor virtue.

To be governed is to have every operation, every transaction, every movement noted, registered, counted, rated, stamped, measured, numbered, assessed, licensed, refused, authorized, endorsed, admonished, prevented, reformed, redressed, and corrected.

To be governed is, under pretext of public utility and in the name of the general interest, to be laid under contribution, drilled, fleeced, exploited, monopolized, extorted from, exhausted, hoaxed and robbed; then, upon the slightest resistance, at the first word of complaint, to be repressed, fined, vilified, annoyed, hunted down, pulled about, beaten, disarmed, bound, imprisoned, shot, judged,

condemned, banished, sacrificed, sold, betrayed, and, to crown all, ridiculed, derided, outraged, and dishonored.
*-PIERRE JOSEPH PROUDHON, French socialist (1809 - 1865)*

The difference between a politician and a statesman is: a politician thinks of the next election and a statesman thinks of the next generation.
*-JAMES FREEMAN CLARKE, American clergyman, writer (1810 - 1888)*

You can always get the truth from an American statesman after he has turned seventy or given up hope of the Presidency.
*-WENDELL PHILLIPS, American abolitionist, reformer (1811 - 1884)*

People hardly ever make use of the freedom they have, for example, freedom of thought; instead they demand freedom of speech as a compensation.
*-SÖREN KIERKEGAARD, Dutch philosopher, theologian (1813 - 1855)*

There are a thousand hacking at the branches of evil to one who is striking at the root.
*-HENRY DAVID THOREAU, Americian essayist, naturalist (1817 - 1862)*

Power concedes nothing without a demand. It never did and it never will. Those who want freedom without agitiation are like those who want the ocean without its mighty roar.
*-FREDERICK DOUGLASS, American lecturer, author (c.1817 - 1895)*

The first duty of government is to see that people have food, fuel, and clothes. The second, that they have means of moral and intellectual education.
*-JOHN RUSKIN, English author (1819 - 1900)*

The belief, not only of the socialists but also of those so-called liberals who are diligently preparing the way for them, is that by due skill an ill working humanity may be framed into well-working institutions. It is a delusion. The defective natures of citizens will show themselves in the bad acting of whatever social structure they are arranged into. There is no political alchemy by which you can get golden conduct out of leaden instincts.
-HERBERT SPENCER, English philosopher (1820 - 1903)

Were there no thieves and murderers, prisons would be unnecessary. It is only because tyranny is yet rife in the world that we have armies. Barristers, judges, juries, all the instruments of law, exist simply because knavery exists. Magisterial force is the sequence of social vice, and the policeman is but the complement of the criminal. Therefore it is that we call government "a necessary evil."   -HERBERT SPENCER

Fortunately for themselves and the world, nearly all men are cowards and dare not act on what they believe. Nearly all our disasters come of a few fools having the "courage of their convictions."
-COVENTRY PATMORE, english poet (1823 - 1896)

The masses of men are very difficult to excite on bare grounds of self-interest; most easy if a bold orator tells them confidently they are wronged.
-WALTER BAGEHOT, English economist, journalist (1826 - 1877)

I believe we ought to retain all our liberties. We can't afford to throw them away. They didn't come to us in a night. The trouble with us in America is that

we haven't learned to speak the truth. We have thrown away the most valuable asset we have - the individual right to oppose both flag and country when by one's self we believe them to be in the wrong.
-*MARK TWAIN, American writer, humorist (1835 - 1910)*

Whenever you find yourself on the side of the majority it is time to pause and reflect.   *-MARK TWAIN*

Its name is Public Opinion. It is held in reverence. It settles everything. Some think it is the voice of God.
-*MARK TWAIN*

What makes equality such a difficult business is that we only want it with our superiors.
-*HENRY BECQUE, French dramatist (1837 - 1899)*

He mocks the people who proposes that the Government shall protect the rich and that they in turn will care for the laboring poor.
-*GROVER CLEVELAND, 22nd and 24th President of the United States (1837 - 1908)*

Politics, as a practice, whatever its professions, has always been the systematic organization of hatreds.
-*HENRY ADAMS, American historian (1838 - 1918)*

Modern politics is, at bottom, a struggle not of men but of forces.   *-HENRY ADAMS*

Knowledge of human nature is the beginning and end of political education.   *-HENRY ADAMS*

In a free country more especially, ten men who care are worth a hundred who do not.
-*JAMES BRYCE, British historian, diplomat (1838 - 1922)*

The ordinary American voter does not object to mediocrity. He has a lower conception of the qualities requisite to make a statesman than those who direct public opinion in Europe have. He likes his candidate to be sensible, vigorous, and, above all, what he calls "magnetic," and does not value, because he sees no need for, originality or profundity, a fine culture or a wide knowledge.

-JAMES BRYCE

If the presidential contest may seem to have usually done less for the formation of political thought and diffusion of political knowledge than was to be expected from the immense efforts put forth and the intelligence of the voters addressed, it nevertheless rouses and stirs the public life of the country. One can hardly imagine what the atmosphere of American politics would be without this quadrennial storm sweeping through it to clear away stagnant vapours, and recall to every citizen the sense of his own responsibility for the present welfare and future greatness of his country. Nowhere does government by the people, through the people, for the people, take a more directly impressive and powerfully stimulative form than in the choice of a chief magistrate by 15 millions of citizens voting on one day.   -JAMES BRYCE

Most mistakes in politics arise from the flat and invincible disregard of the plain maxim that it is possible for the same thing to be and not be.

-JOHN MORLEY, English statesman, author (1828 - 1923)

The state, it cannot too often be repeated, does

nothing, and can give nothing, which it does not take from somebody.
-HENRY GEORGE, American economist (1839 - 1897)

Self-interest is not only a legitimate, but a fundamental cause of national policy, one which needs no cloak of hypocrisy. It is vain to expect governments to act continously on any other ground than national interest.
-ALFRED THAYER MAHAN, Americn naval officer, historian (1840 - 1914)

Pretty much all law consists in forbidding men to do some things that they want to do.
-OLIVER WENDELL HOLMES, JR., U.S. Supreme Court Justice (1841 - 1935)

Vote, n. The instrument and symbol of a freeman's power to make a fool of himself and a wreck of his country.
-AMBROSE BIERCE, American journalist, writer (1842 - c.1914)

Conservative, n. A statesman who is enamored of existing evils, as distinguished from a liberal, who wishes to replace them with others. -AMBROSE BIERCE

Politics, n. A strife of interests masquerading as a contest of principles. -AMBROSE BIERCE

Democratic contrivances are quarantine measures against that ancient plague, the lust for power: as such, they are very necessary and very boring.
-FRIEDRICH WILHELM NIETZSCHE, German philosopher, poet (1844 - 1900)

Insanity in individuals is rare - but in groups, parties, nations and epochs, it is the rule. -NIETZSCHE

The real difficulty appears to be that the new

conditions incident to the extraordinary industrial development of the last half-century are continuously and progressively demanding the readjustment of the relations between great bodies of men and the establishment of new legal rights and obligations not contemplated when existing laws were passed or existing limitations upon the powers of government were prescribed in our Constitution.

In place of the old individual independence of life in which every intelligent and healthy citizen was competent to take care of himself and his family, we have come to a high degree of interdependence in which the greater part of our people have to rely for all the necessities of life upon the systematized co-operation of a vast number of other men working through complicated industrial and commercial machinery. ... The relations between the employer and the employed, between owners of aggregated capital and the units of organized labor, between the small producer, the small trader, the consumer, and the great transporting and manufacturing and distributing agencies, all present new questions for the solution of which the old reliance upon the free action of individual wills appears quite inadequate. And in many directions the intervention of that organized control which we call government seems necessary to produce the same result of justice and right conduct which obtained through the attrition of individuals before the new conditions arose.

-ELIHU ROOT, American lawyer, statesman (1845 - 1937)

Those who won our independence believed that the final end of the State was to make men free to develop their faculties; and that in its government the deliberative forces should prevail over the arbitrary. They valued liberty both as an end and as a means. They believed liberty to be the secret of happiness and courage to be the secret of liberty.

*- LOUIS BRANDEIS, U.S. Supreme Court Justice (1856 - 1941)*

The reasonable man adapts himself to the world; the unreasonable one persists in trying to adapt the world to himself. Therfore all progress depends on the unreasonable man.

*- GEORGE BERNARD SHAW, British playwright, critic (1856 - 1950)*

A government that robs Peter to pay Paul can always depend upon the support of Paul.

*- GEORGE BERNARD SHAW*

Power does not corrupt men; fools, however, if they get into a position of power, corrupt power.

*- GEORGE BERNARD SHAW*

Clever and attractive women do not want to vote; they are willing to let men govern as long as they govern men.   *-GEORGE BERNARD SHAW*

A radical is one whom people say "He goes too far." A conservative, on the other hand, is one who "doesn't go far enough." Then there is the reactionary, "one who doesn't go at all." All these terms are more or less objectionable, wherefore we have coined the term "progressive." I should say that a progressive is one who insists upon recognizing new facts as they present themselves - one who adjusts legislation to these new facts.

*- WOODROW WILSON, 28th President of the United States (1856 - 1924)*

I use not only all the brains I have, but all I can borrow.  -*WOODROW WILSON*

Quite as important as legislation, is vigilant oversight of administration.  -*WOODROW WILSON*

There are two ways of exerting one's strength: one is pushing down, the other is pulling up.
-*BOOKER T. WASHINGTON, American educator (1856 - 1915)*

Too many people don't care what happens so long as it doesn't happen to them.
-*WILLIAM HOWARD TAFT, 27th President of the United States (1857 - 1930)*

Constitutions are checks upon the hasty action of the majority. They are the self-imposed restraints of a whole people upon a majority of them to secure sober action and a respect for the rights of the minority.
-*WILLIAM HOWARD TAFT*

No man is above the law and no man is below it; nor do we ask any man's permission when we require him to obey it.
-*THEODORE ROOSEVELT, 26th President of the United States (1858 - 1919)*

A successful politician is he who says what everybody is thinking most often and in the loudest voice.  -*THEODORE ROOSEVELT*

Mankind likes to think in terms of extreme opposites. It is given to formulating its beliefs in terms of *Either-Ors*, between which it recognizes no intermediate possibilities. When forced to recognize that the extremes cannot be acted upon, it is still inclined to hold that they are all right in theory but that when it comes to practical matters circumstances compel us to compromise.

-JOHN DEWEY, American philosopher, educator (1859 - 1952)

Cooperation - called fraternity in the classic French formula - is as much a part of the democratic ideal as is personal initiative. That cultural conditions were allowed to develop (markedly so in the economic phase) which subordinated cooperativeness to liberty and equality serves to explain the decline in the two latter. -JOHN DEWEY

There are two ideas of government. There are those who believe that, if you will only legislate to make the well-to-do prosperous, their prosperity will leak through on those below. The Democratic idea, however, has been that if you legislate to make the masses prosperous, their prosperity will find its way up through every class which rests upon them.

- WILLIAM JENNINGS BRYAN, American politician, fundamentalist (1860 - 1925)

The greater the importance of safeguarding the community from incitements to the overthrow of our institutions by force and violence, the more imperative is the need to preserve inviolate the constitutional rights of free speech, free press and free assembly in order to maintain the opportunity for free political discussion, to the end that government may be responsive to the will of the people and that changes, if desired, may be obtained by peaceful means. Therin lies the security of the Republic, the very foundation of constitutuional government.

-CHARLES EVANS HUGHES, Chief Justice, U.S. Supreme Court (1862 - 1948)

We are under a Constitution, but the Constitution is what the judges say it is.   -CHARLES EVANS HUGHES

We sometimes find ourselves changing our minds without any resistance or heavy emotion, but if we are told that we are wrong we resent the imputation and harden our hearts. We are incredibly heedless in the formation of our beliefs, but find ourselves filled with an illicit passion for them when anyone proposes to rob us of their companionship. It is obviously not the ideas themselves that are dear to us, but our self-esteem which is threatened. We are by nature stubbornly pledged to defend our own from attack, whether it be our person, our family, or our opinion.
-JAMES HARVEY ROBINSON, American historian (1863 - 1936)

If the conscience of an honest man lays down stern rules, so also does the art of politics. At a juncture where no accommodation is possible between the two, the politician may be faced by these alternatives: "Shall I break the rules of my art in order to save my private honor? or shall I break the rules of my conscience in order to fulfill my public trust?"
-FREDERICK SCOTT OLIVER, English writer (1864 - 1934)

Few men are placed in such fortunate circumstances as to be able to gain office, or to keep it for any length of time, without misleading or bamboozling the people.   -FREDERICK SCOTT OLIVER

I listen to one side and they seem right, and then - God! - I talk to the other side and they seem just as right, and here I am where I started. ... God! what a job!

- *WARREN G. HARDING, 29th President of the United States (1865 - 1923)*

My enemies I can handle. It's my friends who keep me walking the floors at night. -*WARREN G. HARDING*

There's just one rule for politicians all over the world: Don't say in Power what you say in Opposition; if you do, you only have to carry out what the other fellows have found impossible.

- *JOHN GALSWORTHY, English novelist, playwright (1867 - 1933)*

The essential nature of a democracy compels it to insist that individual power of all kinds, political, economic, or intellectual, shall not be perversely and irresponsibly exercised.

- *HERBERT CROLY, American writer, editor (1869 - 1930)*

We get the Government we deserve. When we improve, the Government is also bound to improve.

- *MOHANDAS GANDHI, Indian nationalist leader (1869 - 1948)*

The law must be stable, but it must not stand still.

- *ROSCOE POUND, American educator (1870 - 1964)*

The trouble with the world is that the stupid are cocksure and the intelligent full of doubt.

- *BERTRAND RUSSELL, English philosopher (1872 - 1970)*

If all governments taught the same nonsense, the harm would not be so great. Unfortunately, each has its own brand, and the diversity serves to produce hostility between the devotees of different creeds. If there is ever to be peace in the world, governments will have to agree either to inculcate no dogmas, or all to inculcate the same. -*BERTRAND RUSSELL*

Even though counting heads is not an ideal way to govern, at least it is better than breaking them.
-*LEARNED HAND, American jurist (1872 - 1961)*

Our government is a government of political parties under the guiding influence of public opinion. There does not seem to be any other method by which a representative government can function.
-*CALVIN COOLIDGE, 30th President of the United States (1872 - 1933)*

Any party which takes credit for the rain must not be suprised if its opponents blame it for the drought.
-*DWIGHT MORROW, Amrican banker, diplomat (1873 - 1931)*

The most striking defect of our system of government is that it divides political power and therby conceals political responsibility.
-*CARL BECKER, American historian (1873 - 1945)*

Democracy is the worst system devised by the wit of man, except for all the others.
-*WINSTON CHURCHILL, Prime Minister of Great Britain (1874 - 1965)*

Our whole system of self-government will crumble either if officials elect what laws they will enforce or citizens elect what laws they will support. The worst evil of disregard for some law is that it destroys respect for all law. For our citizens to patronize the violation of a particular law on the ground that they are opposed to it is destructive of the very basis of all that protection of life, of homes and property which they rightly claim under other laws. If citizens do

not like a law, their duty as honest men and women is to discourage its violation, their right is openly to work for its repeal.
-*HERBERT HOOVER, 31st President of the United States (1874 - 1964)*

We, through free and universal education, provide the training of the runners; we give to them an equal start, we provide in government the umpire in the race. -*HERBERT HOOVER*

The poor have been rebels but they never have been anarchists; they have more interest than anyone else in there being some decent government; the poor man really has a stake in the country. The rich man hasn't; he can go away to New Guinea in a yacht. The poor have sometimes objected to being governed badly; the rich have always objected to being governed at all.
-*GILBERT KEITH CHESTERTON, English journalist, author (1874 - 1936)*

My country right or wrong is like saying "My mother, drunk or sober." -*GILBERT KEITH CHESTERTON*

The secret of the demagogue is to make himself as stupid as his audience so that they believe they are as clever as he.
-*KARL KRAUS, American satirist, poet (1874 - 1936)*

People vote their resentment, not their appreciation. The average man does not vote *for* anything, but *against* something.
-*WILLIAM MUNRO, American educator, author (1875 - 1957)*

We settle things by a majority vote, and the psychological effect of doing that is to create the impression that the majority is probably right. Of course, on any fine issue the majority is sure to be wrong. Think of taking a majority vote on the best music. Jazz would win over Chopin. Or on the best novel. Many cheap scribbers would win over Tolstoy. Any given day a prizefight will get a bigger crowd, larger gate receipts and wider newspaper publicity than any new revelation of goodness, truth or beauty could hope to achieve in a century.

*-HARRY EMERSON FOSDICK, American clergyman (1878 - 1969)*

The business of government is to keep the government out of business - that is, unless business needs government aid.

*-WILL ROGERS, American actor, humorist (1879 - 1935)*

Politics has got so expensive that it takes lots of money to even get beat with.    *-WILL ROGERS*

Be thankful we're not getting all the government we're paying for.    *-WILL ROGERS*

If you ever injected truth into politics you would have no politics.    *-WILL ROGERS*

The more you read about politics, the more you got to admit that each party is worse than the other.

*-WILL ROGERS*

A politician is nothing but a local bandit sent to Washington to raid headquarters.    *-WILL ROGERS*

A flock of Democrats will replace a mess of Republicans, but it won't mean a thing; they will go in like all the rest of 'em, go in on promises and come out on alibis.   -*WILL ROGERS*

I really can't see any advantage of having one of your own party in as president.  I would rather be able to criticize a man, than have to apologize for him.
-*WILL ROGERS*

The short memories of American voters is what keeps our politicians in office.   -*WILL ROGERS*

We Americans generally do the right thing after first exhausting every other available alternative.
-*WILL ROGERS*

I don't make jokes - I just watch the government and report the facts.   -*WILL ROGERS*

No other factor in history, not even religion, has produced so many wars as has the clash of national egotisms sanctified by the name of patriotism.
-*PRESERVED SMITH, American historian (1880 - 1941)*

When a man you like switches from what he said a year ago, or a few years ago, he is a broad-minded person who has courage enough to change his mind with changing conditions.  When a man you don't like does it, he is a liar who has broken his promises.
-*FRANKLIN P. ADAMS, American journalist, humorist (1881 - 1960)*

Government has a final responsibility for the welfare of its citizens.  If private cooperative effort fails to provide work for willing hands and relief for the unfortunate, those suffering hardship through no fault of their own have a right to call upon the government for aid.  And a government worthy of the

name must make a fitting response.
-*FRANKLIN D. ROOSEVELT,* 32nd President of the United States (1882 - 1945)

The moment a mere numerical superiority by either states or voters in this country proceeds to ignore the needs and desires of the minority, and for their own selfish purpose or advancement, hamper or oppress that minority, or debar them in any way from equal privileges and equal rights - that moment will mark the failure of our constitutional system.
-*FRANKLIN D. ROOSEVELT*

Governments can err. Presidents do make mistakes, but the immortal Dante tells us that divine justice weighs the sins of the cold-blooded and the sins of the warm-hearted in different scales. Better the occasional faults of a Government that lives in a spirit of charity than the consistent omissions of a Government frozen in the ice of its own indifference.
-*FRANKLIN D. ROOSEVELT*

Let us never forget that government is ourselves and not an alien power over us. The ultimate rulers of our democracy are not a President and senators and congressmen and government officials, but the voters of this country. -*FRANKLIN D. ROOSEVELT*

Government is itself an art, one of the subtlest of the arts. It is neither business, nor technology, nor applied science. It is the art of making men live together in peace and with reasonable happiness. And that is why the art of governing has been achieved best by men to whom governing is itself a profession. One of the shallowest disdains is the sneer against the professional politician. The invidious implication of the phrase is, of course, against those who pursue self-interest through politics. But too prevalently the baby is thrown out with the bath. We forget that the most successful statesmen have been professionals. Walpole, Pitt, Gladstone, Disraeli, and Asquith were professional politicians. Beveridge's *Life of Abraham Lincoln* serves as a reminder that Lincoln was a professional politician. Politics was Roosevelt's profession; Wilson was all his life, at least preoccupied with politics; and Calvin Coolidge, though nominally a lawyer, has had no profession except politics.

*-FELIX FRANKFURTER, U.S. Supreme Court Justice (1882 - 1965)*

A politician is a man who understands government and it takes a politician to run a government. A statesman is a politician who's been dead 10 or 15 years.

*-HARRY TRUMAN, 33rd President of the United States (1884 - 1972)*

Well all the President is, is a glorified public relations man who spends his time flattering, kissing, and kicking people to get them to do what they are supposed to do anyway.    *-HARRY TRUMAN*

The creation of constitutional government is a most significant mark of the distrust of human beings in human nature. It signalizes a profound conviction, born of experience, that human beings vested with authority must be restrained by something more potent than their own discretion.

*-RAYMOND MOLEY, American journalist, educator (1886 - 1975)*

In politics, where immediate success is attained by saying what people can be made to believe, rather than what is demonstrably true, accent is generally placed on the desirable rather than on the possible.

-RAYMOND MOLEY

Politics is the science of who gets what, when, and why.

-SYDNEY HILLMAN, American labor leader (1887 - 1946)

The form of government is after all a means to an end; even freedom itself is a means, the end being human well-being, human growth, the ending of poverty and disease and suffering, and the opportunity for everyone to live the "good life," physically and mentally.

-JAWAHARLAL NEHRU, Indian nationalist, Prime Minister (1889 - 1964)

The public interest may be presumed to be what men would choose if they saw clearly, thought rationally, and acted disinterestedly and benevolently.

- WALTER LIPPMANN, American writer, editor (1889 - 1974)

It is perfectly true that the government is best which governs least. It is equally true that the government is best which provides the most.      -WALTER LIPPMANN

Wheras each man claims his freedom as a matter of right, the freedom he accords to other men is a matter of toleration.      -WALTER LIPPMANN

If you wish the sympathy of broad masses then you must tell them the crudest and most stupid things.

-ADOLF HITLER, German Chancellor and Führer (1889 - 1945)

In order to become the master, the politician poses as the servant.
-*CHARLES DE GAULLE*, President of France (1890 - 1970)

Since a politician never believes what he says, he is always astonished when others do. -*CHARLES DE GAULLE*

To govern is always to choose among disadvantages.
-*CHARLES DE GAULLE*

How can you govern a country with two hundred and forty-six varieties of cheese. -*CHARLES DE GAULLE*

The middle of the road is all of the usable surface. The extremes, right and left, are in the gutters.
-*DWIGHT D. EISENHOWER*, 34th President of the United States (1890 - 1969)

In America you can go on the air and kid the politicians, and the politicians can go on the air and kid the people.
-*GROUCHO MARX*, American comedian, actor (1890 - 1977)

When the weak or oppressed assert the rights that have been so long denied them, those in power inevitably resist on the basis of the necessity for tranquility.
-*EARL WARREN*, Chief Justice of the U.S. Supreme Court (1891 - 1974)

Man's capacity for justice makes democracy possible, but man's inclination to injustice makes democracy necessary.
-*REINHOLD NIEBUHR*, American theologian (1892 - 1971)

The sad duty of politics is to establish justice in a sinful world. -*REINHOLD NIEBUHR*

No man has a right in America to treat any other man "tolerantly" for tolerance is the assumption of superiority. Our liberties are equal rights of every citizen.
- WENDELL WILLKIE, American politician (1892 - 1944)

It is not the function of our Government to keep the citizen from falling into error; it is the function of the citizen to keep the Government from falling into error.
- ROBERT JACKSON, U.S. Supreme Court Justice (1892 - 1954)

A revolution does not march a straight line. It wanders where it can, retreats before superior forces, advances wherever it has room, attacks whenever the enemy retreats or bluffs and, above all, is possessed of enormous patience.
- MAO TSE-TUNG, Chariman of Chinese Communist Party (1893 - 1976)

Every Communist must grasp the truth: "Political power grows out of the barrel of a gun."
- MAO TSE-TUNG

Politics is war without bloodshed, and war is politics with blood.    -MAO TSE-TUNG

Of all forms of government and society, those of free men and women are in many respects the most brittle. They give the fullest freedom for activities of private persons and groups who often identify their own interests, essentially selfish, with the general welfare.
- DOROTHY THOMPSON, American journalist, author (1894 - 1961)

Politicians are the same all over. They promise to

build a bridge even where there is no river.
- *NIKITA KHRUSHCHEV,* Premier of Soviet Union (1894 - 1971)

At home, you always have to be a politician; when you're abroad, you almost feel yourself a statesman.
- *HAROLD MACMILLAN,* British Prime Minister (1894 - 1986)

One of the greatest disasters that happened to modern civilization was for democracy to inscribe "liberty" on its banners instead of "justice". Because "liberty" was considered the ideal, it was not long until some men interpreted it as meaning "freedom from justice", then when religion and decent government attempted to bring them back to justice, organized into "freedom groups" and protested that their constitutional and natural rights were being violated.

The industrial and social unjustice of our era is the tragic aftermath of democracy's overemphasis on freedom as the "right to do whatever you please." No, freedom means the right to do what you *ought*, and *ought* implies law, and law implies justice, and justice implies God.
- *FULTON J. SHEEN,* American prelate (1895 - 1979)

Our government wasn't created to be efficient. It was created to preserve the individual.
- *SAM ERVIN,* U.S. Senator (1896 - 1985)

I am a man of fixed and unbending principles, the first of which is to be flexible at all times.
- *EVERETT MCKINLEY DIRKSEN,* U.S. Senator (1896 - 1969)

The notion that the sole concern of a free society is the limitation of governmental authority and that government is best which governs least is certainly archaic. Our object today should not be to weaken government in competition with other centers of power, but rather to strengthen it as the agency charged with responsibility for the common good. That government is best which governs best.

*-ROBERT MAYNARD HUTCHINS, American educator (1899 - 1977)*

Nowhere are prejudices more mistaken for truth, passion for reason, and invective for documentation than in politics. That is a realm, peopled only by villains or heroes, in which everything is black or white and gray is a forbidden color.

*-JOHN MASON BROWN, American drama critic, author (1900 - 1969)*

Never doubt that a small group of committed citizens can change the world. Indeed, it's the only thing that ever has.

*-MARGARET MEAD, American anthropologist (1901 - 1978)*

Fundamentally, liberalism is an attitude. The chief characteristic being human sympathy, a receptivity to change, and a willingness to follow reason rather than fixed ideas.

*-CHESTER BOWLES, American politician, diplomat (1901 - 1986)*

In a society in which there is no law, and in theory no compulsion, the only arbiter of behavior is public opinion. But public opinion, because of the tremendous urge to conformity in gregarious animals, is less tolerant than any system of law.

*-GEORGE ORWELL, English novelist, essayist (1903 - 1950)*

We must not confuse dissent with disloyalty.

*-EDWARD R. MURROW, American journalist, commentator (1908 - 1965)*

Law cannot stand aside from the social changes around it.
*-WILLIAM J. BRENNAN, U.S. Supreme Court Justice (1906 - 1997)*

The American experiment (or some of its imitations) with all its bugs, corruption and ineptitude, its senatorial rhetoric, and back-alley violence, is the only workable form of government not only for men who want to be free but for all men, because it is endowed with self-adjusting mechanisms which rigid regimes lack.
*-LUIGI BARZINI, Italian journalist (1908 - 1984)*

Politics is the life blood of democracy. To call politics "dirty" is to call democracy "dirty". ... Politics, of course, requires sweat, work, combat, and organization. But these should not be ugly words for any free people.
*-NELSON ROCKEFELLER, American politician (1908 - 1979)*

I would remind you that extremism in the defense of liberty is no vice. And let me remind you also that moderation in the pursuit of justice is no virtue.
*-BARRY GOLDWATER, U.S. Senator (1909 - 1998)*

If I believe in something, I will fight for it with all I have. But I do not demand all or nothing. I would rather get something than nothing. Professional liberals want the fiery debate. They glory in defeat. The hardest job for a politician today is to have the courage to be a moderate. It's easy to take an extreme position.
*-HUBERT HUMPHREY, U.S. Senator (1911 - 1978)*

The story of man is the history, first, of the

acceptance and imposition of restraints necessary to permit communal life; and second, of the emancipation of the individual within that system of necessary restraints.

-*ABE FORTAS, U.S. Supreme Court Justice (1910 - 1982)*

Economic freedom is an essential requisite for political freedom. By enabling people to cooperate with one another without coercion or central direction, it reduces the area over which political power is exercised.

-*MILTON FRIEDMAN, American economist*

Newspapers, television networks, and magazines have sometimes been outrageously abusive, untruthful, arrogant and hypocritical. But it hardly follows that elimination of a strong and independent press is the way to eliminate abusiveness, untruth, arrogance, or hypocrisy from government itself.

-*POTTER STEWART, U.S. Supreme Court Justice*

The best time to listen to a politician is when he's on a stump on a street corner in the rain late at night when he's exhausted. Then he doesn't lie.

-*THEODORE H. WHITE, American author (1915 - 1986)*

The hardest thing about any political campaign is how to win without proving that you are unworthy of winning.

-*ADLAI STEVENSON, American statesman, politician (1900 - 1965)*

I am not even sure what it means when one says that he is a conservative in fiscal affairs and a liberal in human affairs. I assume what it means is that you will strongly recommend the building of a great

many schools to accomodate the needs of our children, but not provide the money.
*-ADLAI STEVENSON*

Socialism is the public ownership of the means of production, and no one is proposing that. But as we use the word, it seems to be any government authority we do not like. Of course, things we like - tariffs, subsidies, mail concessions, support prices, tax write-offs, depletion allowances and government aids to particular groups - are rarely denounced as "socialism" except perhaps by the groups competitors. *-ADLAI STEVENSON*

After lots of people who go into politics have been in it for a while they find that to stay in politics they have to make all sorts of compromises to satisfy their supporters and that it becomes awfully important for them to keep their jobs because they have nowhere else to go. *-ADLAI STEVENSON*

Those who corrupt the public mind are just as evil as those who steal from the public purse.
*-ADLAI STEVENSON*

Thinking implies disagreement; and disagreement implies nonconformity; and nonconformity implies heresy; and heresy implies disloyalty - so, obviously, thinking must be stopped. *-ADLAI STEVENSON*

Let's talk sense to the American people. Let's tell them the truth, that there are no gains without pains.
*-ADLAI STEVENSON*

It seems to me that goverment is like a pump, and

what it pumps up is just what we are, a fair sample of the intellect, the ethics and the morals of the people, no better, no worse. *-ADLAI STEVENSON*

The know-nothing crusade against government springs from a conviction that, if we get government off our backs, our problems will solve themselves. But, far from solving problems, the old unregulated *laissez-faire* economy of the Nineteenth Century generated the problems that produced class war and the *Communist Manifesto.* What rescued capitalism from Marxist prophecy in the Twentieth Century was the work of reformers like the two Roosevelts who used the national government to humanize the industrial order, to cushion the operations of the economic system, to strengthen the bargaining position of workers and farmers and consumers, to reduce the economic gap between the classes, to ensure against recurrent depression by built-in economic stabilizers; above all, to combine individual opportunity with social responsibility.
*-ARTHUR SCHLESINGER JR., American historian*

In the United States the difficulties are not a Minotaur or a dragon - not imprisonment, hard labor, death, government harassment and censorship - but greed, boredom, sloppiness, indifference. Not the acts of a mighty all-pervading repressive government, but the failure of a listless public to make use of the freedom that is its birthright.
*-ALEKSANDR SOLZHENITSYN, Russian novelist*

At this juncture in our history the American electorate appears too debased to give rise to great and effective leaders or to sustain and support them. The people corrupt and debase their leaders in the process of electing them, then their leaders corrupt and debase the people to gain their continuing approval. It is a continous and ultimately ruinous cycle from which there is no present prospect of escape and which emphasizes at every turn the petty, the commonplace and the mundane.

*-HARRY M. CAUDILL, American attorney, writer (1922 - 1990)*

A foolish American myth has it that the rich and super-rich are entrepreneurial Daniel Boones who decry the restraints of government and, as rugged individualists, fare forth to wrest fame and fortune from other like-minded souls. With some notable exceptions nothing could be further from the truth. In the main the rich are the clever and adroit who understand the purposes and functions of government and bend it to their purposes. Government becomes a device which they use to expand their fortunes, then hide behind to make certain their gains remain intact.

*-HARRY M. CAUDILL*

The day before my inauguration President Eisenhower told me, "You'll find that no easy problems ever come to the President of the United States. If they are easy to solve, somebody else has solved them."

*-JOHN F. KENNEDY, 35th President of the United States (1917 - 1963)*

Mothers all want their sons to grow up to be President, but they don't want them to become politicians in the process.     *-JOHN F. KENNEDY*

Liberty without learning is always in peril, and learning without liberty is always in vain.
*-JOHN F. KENNEDY*

John Stuart Mill suggested three possibilities to consider when deciding if men should have freedom of opinion and expression. First, the opinion in question may be true, in which case it is plainly right that it should be published. Second, the opinion may be false; it would still be good for it to be published, because truth gains vigor from being challenged and vindicated. (A true belief that is never challenged becomes a dead maxim, which everyone repeats and nobody thinks about.) Third, the opinion may be partly true and partly false. Again Mill argued for expression, on the ground that the exercise of disentangling the false from the true would help to correct errors.

Since these exhaust the possibilities, Mill concluded, it must always be right to grant liberty of opinion and expression.
*-MAURICE CRANSTON, English philosopher, author (1920 - 1993)*

The tenets of my own beliefs.

First, I believe every American has something to say and, under our system, a right to an audience.

Second, I believe there is always a national answer to each national problem, and, believing this, I do not believe that there are necessarily two sides to every question.

Third, I regard achievement of the full potential of our resources - physical, human, and otherwise - to be the highest purpose of the governmental policies next to the protection of those rights we regard as inalienable.

Fourth, I regard waste as the continuing enemy of our society and the prevention of waste - waste of resources, waste of lives, or waste of opportunity - to be the most dynamic of the responsibilities of our government.
*-LYNDON JOHNSON, 36th President of the United States (1908 - 1973)*

There are no problems we cannot solve together, and very few that we can solve by ourselves.
*-LYNDON JOHNSON*

I know I've got heart big enough to be President. I know I've got guts enough to be President. But I wonder whether I've got intelligence and ability to be President - I wonder if any man does.
*-LYNDON JOHNSON*

I have a theory that in the United States those who seek the Presidency never win it. Circumstances rather than a man's ambition determine the results. If he is the right man for the right time, he will be chosen.
*-RICHARD NIXON, 37th President of the United States (1913 - 1994)*

I have seen it happen more often than not in government that when one asks for choices, one is always given three: two absurd ones and the preferred one. And the experienced bureaucrat can usually tell the preferred one because it is almost always the one typed in the middle.
*-HENRY KISSENGER, American statesman*

Idealism is fine, but as it approaches reality the cost

becomes prohibitive.
-*WILLIAM F. BUCKLEY, JR.,* American journalist, author

There is one right I would not grant anyone. And that is the right to be indifferent.
-*ELIE WIESEL,* American author

It may be true that the law cannot make a man love me, but it can keep him from lynching me, and I think that's pretty important.
-*MARTIN LUTHER KING, JR.,* American clergyman, activist (1929 - 1968)

In all these years in the United States, I have never gotten used to the fact that Americans can't seem to find a middle ground between superficial contact and angry confrontation. Community, which we are trying to build, both creates and benefits from dialogue, in which you open up to others, get upset, work things out, and continue together.
-*AMITAI ETZIONI,* American sociologist

The experience of democracy is like the experience of life itself - always changing, infinite in its variety, sometimes turbulent and all the more valuable for having been tested by adversity.
-*JIMMY CARTER,* 39th President of the United States

A simple and a proper function of government is just to make it easy for us to do good and difficult for us to do wrong.   -*JIMMY CARTER*

America did not invent human rights. In a very real sense, it is the other way around. Human rights invented America.   -*JIMMY CARTER*

I'm sure everyone feels sorry for the individual who has fallen by the wayside or who can't keep up in our competitive society, but my own compassion goes beyond that to those millions of unsung men and women who get up every morning, send the kids to school, go to work, try to keep up the payments on their house, pay exorbitant taxes to make possible compassion for the less fortunate, and as a result have to sacrifice many of their own desires and dreams and hopes. Government owes them something better than always finding a new way to make them share the fruit of their toils with others.

*-RONALD REAGAN, 40th President of the United States*

For many years now, you and I have been shushed like children and told there are no simple answers to the complex problems that are beyond our comprehension. Well, the truth is there are simple answers. There are just not easy ones.

*-RONALD REAGAN*

Government exists to protect us from each other. Where Government has gone beyond its limits is in deciding to protect us from ourselves.

*-RONALD REAGAN*

Government exists to protect rights which are ours from birth; the right to life, liberty, and the pursuit of happiness. A man may choose to sit and fish instead of working - that's his pursuit of happiness. He does not have the right to force his neighbors to support him in his pursuit because that interferes with their pursuit of happiness.    *-RONALD REAGAN*

Politics I supposed to be the second-oldest profession. I have come to realize that it bears a very close resemblance to the first. -*RONALD REAGAN*

A government is not legitimate merely because it exists.
-*JEANNE KIRKPATRICK, American politician, diplomat*

Of course it's the same old story. Truth usually is the same old story.
-*MARGARET THATCHER, British Prime Minister*

The reason I am in politics is because I believe in certain things and try to put them into practice.
-*MARGARET THATCHER*

In the last century, when Marx wrote, and continuing on into this century and the years of the Great Depression, the survival of capitalism in its original and idealogically exact form was very much in doubt. The distribution of power and income between employer and employed was highly unequal. Workers, when unneeded, were discarded without income. There was cruel exploitation of women and children.

Most threatening of all, as Marx foresaw, were the recurring economic crises or depressions that swept millions into unemployment and deprivation. From all this came anger and alienation and, for many, the strong feeling, perhaps the near certainty, that the system could not survive.

The system did survive, however, because the welfare state mitigated many of the hardships and the cruelties of pure capitalism. Also, trade unions were legitimized and soon began to exercise countervailing power. And the Keynesian revolution gave to the state the responsibility - however imperfectly discharged - of smoothing out the business cycle and limiting the associated hardship and despair. The prevention of mass unemployment and the assurance of economic growth became the prime tests of government competence.

*-JOHN KENNETH GALBRAITH, American economist*

We have a lot of well-off people whose personal comfort is threatened by government action. I would hope that there were a few people whose compassion and sympathies would extend to the unfortunate and who would be willing to accept affirmative government and what it can do for those who are less fortunately situated. Once the great dialectic was capital versus labor. Now it's the conflict between the comfortable and the deprived. And the comfortable see government as the threat because it is the only hope for the deprived.

*-JOHN KENNETH GALBRAITH*

A basic viewpoint of comfortably situated Americans is their highly selective view of government. Broadly, the state is seen as a burden; no political slogan of modern times has been so often reiterated and so warmly applauded as the call to "get government off the backs of the people."

Yet, unfortunately, the services these taxes pay for are elemental to the lives of the poor - and increasingly the poor alone.

In the United States, as in other industrial lands, the poorest people must rely on the government for shelter, health care, food and education.

The poor also need public parks and recreational facilities; in affluent areas these are less important because of private yards, health clubs, and country clubs. The poor need public libraries; the more fortunate can buy magazines and books. Many of the poor live in the inner cities, where police presence is necessary every day; in the suburbs such protection is of less urgency. For those at yet higher levels of income, there are private security guards, the number of whom now exceeds the number of publicly employed police officers in the United States.

*-JOHN KENNETH GALBRAITH*

All successful revolutions are the kicking in of a rotten door.     *-JOHN KENNETH GALBRAITH*

Ninety percent of politics is deciding whom to blame. ...

From King George to "that man" (FDR) to our own era's Newt Gingrich, there have always been plenty of individuals in high places to blame not only for their own indisputable faults, but also for just about everything else. But the far more common phenomenon has been blame of groups - real and unreal, seen and unseen - for whatever is ailing the electorate. Classically these malign forces are believed to be vast, intricately structured, enormously powerful and corrupt and greedy beyond describing. All are accussed of getting something they don't deserve at the expense of those who do. Publics rely on such assumptions to explain their own failures and miseries. Politicians rely on them to mobilize the angry publics who will then catapult them into office. Thus throughout our history we have had surges of well organized political hatred of Catholic and Jews and immigrants; we have heard about the "yellow peril" and the "welfare queens" who were threatening our economic well-being; we have said the whole damn thing was the fault of the banks and the economic royalists and the Eastern establishment and the military industrial complex and liberal elites, and, most recently incorporating many of the above culprits in one category, "Washington."

*-MEG GREENFIELD, American journalist, columnist. In* Newsweek

We believe that while survival of the fittest may be a good working description of the process of evolution, a government of humans should elevate itself to a higher order, one which fills the gaps left by chance or a wisdom we don't understand.

*-MARIO CUOMO, American politician*

So much of what goes on in politics these days is what I refer to as the "war of the poses." The slogans, the labels, the simplistics, the misdirection, the inappropriateness, the irrelevance, the caricaturing, the posturing. It's exasperating.

Our system requires that the most exquisitely complex issues be discussed in a way the voters understand. But the voters are often too distracted with their own homes, their own children, and their own ambitions to make subtle judgements. They make gross ones. So, politicians do everything in hyperbole, simplistics, cartooning. We've lost our subtlety. *-MARIO CUOMO*

You campaign in poetry. You govern in prose.
-*MARIO CUOMO*

Let us begin with a simple proposition: What democracy requires is public debate, not information. Of course it needs information too, but the kind of information it needs can be generated only by vigorous popular debate. We do not know what we need to know until we ask the right questions, and we can identify the right questions only by subjecting our own ideas about the world to the test of public controversy. Information, usually seen as the precondition of debate, is better understood as its by-product. When we get into arguments that focus and fully engage our attention, we become avid seekers of relevant information. Otherwise, we take in information passively - if we take it in at all.
-*CHRISTOPHER LASCH, American historian, author (1932 - 1994)*

Government is the art of trying to solve problems. Politics is the art of trying to attain power. The two meet sometimes, but not often.
-*BILL MOYERS, American journalist, author*

The central conservative truth is that it is culture, not politics, that determines the success of a society. The central liberal truth is that politics can change a culture and save it from itself.
-*DANIEL PATRICK MOYNIHAN, U.S. Senator*

Responding to public opinion in a democracy is no disgrace - FDR was a master of it. He probably had a better grasp of public opinion than any other president before or since. His habits of reading, listening, consulting, and yes, even studying public opinion polls, were not a means of deciding which way to veer but of discovering how much and what kind of persuasion was needed to bring the people along. Roosevelt believed that the relationship between the president and the people was direct but not reciprocal.

*-CAROL GELDERMAN, American educator, writer*

In Washington the trick is to sustain the illusion of social change while preserving the freeze frame of the status quo, and "the true business of government," notwithstanding the earnest rhetoric that decorates the nation's op-ed pages, is the achieving of a perfect state of inaction. Congress warily avoids solutions to "real problems" because solutions invariably mean that somebody has to lose something or give something up; solutions imply change, and change is unacceptable because change translates into resentment, and resentment loses votes.

*-LEWIS LAPHAM, American writer, editor. In Harper's Magazine*

Democracy was made for open country and public spaces in which people spoke to one another face to face. Understood as a means and not an end, democratic government defends the future against the past, allowing its citizens the liberty to think and make and build. But if we wish to live in so generous a state of freedom, we must accustom ourselves to the shadows on the walls and the wind in the trees. The sense of uncertainty is the cost of doing business. *-LEWIS LAPHAM*

Society cannot be run by authority alone. What

we are really facing is a crisis of values. There has to be an inner compass that guides people. And, of course, there must also be hope. The responsiblity of government is to give to people the hope that life can be better, that education can proceed, that there will be a job, that there will be a chance to climb that ladder we call the American Dream. The government can help provide the environment of hope, the education, housing and jobs, with the help of the private sector. But, ultimately, the Judeo-Christian teaching of personal responsibility is the crux of the matter.

-JACK KEMP, American politician

Modern government - spending more than it taxes, subsidizing and regulating and conferring countless other blessings - is a mighty engine for the stimulation of consumption. Every government benefit creates a constituency for the expansion of the benefit, so the servile state inflames more appetites than it slakes. It has fostered a perverse entrepreneurship, the manipulation of government - public power - for private purposes. It has eroded society's disciplining sense of the true costs of things.

-GEORGE F. WILL, American newspaper columnist, commentator

Both sides in the war over middle-class morality have to recognize that politics is a two-way street. Liberals cannot expect government to be in the business of helping people without recognizing that the beneficiaries have an obligation to behave responsibly. Conservatives cannot go around telling people how to behave if they are unwilling to make the plight of the unfortunate their business. Liberals are surely correct when they remind us that without rights we lose our freedom. But conservatives are also correct when they point out that without obligations, we have no rights. Thinking about politics as the art of balancing rights and obligations does not tell us what to do in situations of moral complexity, but it does at least force us to consider the positions of those with whom we disagree.

-*ALAN WOLFE, American sociologist*

Ever since the eclipse of our native cultures, the dominant view has been that we should cultivate the self rather than the community; that we should look to the individual as the source of hope and center of value, while expecting hindrance and harm from society. We have understood freedom for the most part negatively rather than positively, as release from constraints rather than as a condition for making a decent life in common. Hands off, we say; give me elbow room; good fences make good neighbors; my home is my castle; don't tread on me. I'm looking out for number one, we say; I'm doing my own thing. We have a Bill of Rights, which protects each of us from a bullying society, but no Bill of Responsibilities, which would oblige us to answer the needs of others.

-*SCOTT RUSSELL SANDERS, American novelist, esssayist*

What is the essence of America? Finding and maintaining that perfect, delicate balance between freedom "to" and freedom "from."

-*MARILYN VOS SAVANT, American writer, columnist*

America is not like a blanket - one piece of unbroken

cloth, the same color, the same texture, the same size. America is more like a quilt - many patches, many pieces, many colors, many sizes, all woven and held together by a common thread.
-*JESSE JACKSON, American clergyman, activist*

Democrats are the party that says government can make you richer, smarter, taller and get the chickweed out of your lawn. Republicans are the party that says government doesn't work, and then they get elected to prove it.
-*P.J. O'ROURKE, American editor, author, humorist*

I'm a registered Republican and consider socialism a violation of the American principle that you shouldn't stick your nose in other people's business except to make a buck.   -*P.J. O'ROURKE*

There is only one basic human right, the right to do as you please unless it causes others harm. With it comes the only basic human duty, the duty to take the consequences.   -*P.J. O'ROURKE*

For more than a quarter century, the Freedom of Information Act has played a unique role in strengthening our democratic form of government. The statute was enacted based on the fundamental principle that an informed citizenry is essential to the democratic process and that the more the American people know about their government the better they will be governed.
-*BILL CLINTON, 42nd President of the United States*

I have bent over backwards as a Governor and as a President to respect the religious convictions of all

Americans. I have strong religious convictions myself. But that is very different from what is going on when people come into the system, and they say that anybody who doesn't agree with them is Godless; anyone who doesn't agree with them is not a good Christian; anyone who doesn't agree with them is fair game for any wild charge, no matter how false - for any kind of personal, demeaning attack.
-*BILL CLINTON*

To renew America we must be bold. We must do what no generation has had to do before. We must invest more in our own people - in their jobs and in their future - and at the same time cut our massive debt. And we must do so in a world in which we must compete for every opportunity. It will not be easy. It will require sacrifice. But it can be done and done fairly. Not choosing sacrifice for its own sake, but for our own sake. We must provide for our nation the way a family provides for its children.

Our founders saw themselves in the light of posterity. We can do no less. Anyone who has ever watched a child's eyes wander into sleep knows what posterity is. Posterity is the world to come; the world for whom we hold our ideals, from whom we have borrowed our planet and to whom we bear sacred responsibility. We must do what America does best: offer more opportunity to all and demand more responsibility from all.   -*BILL CLINTON*

The era of big government is over.   -*BILL CLINTON*

If the era of big government is over, the era of big

citizens better begin.
-*HARRIS WOFFORD, American educator, writer, politician*

If we insist that public life be reserved for those whose personal history is pristine, we are not going to get paragons of virtue running our affairs. We will get the very rich, who contract out the messy things in life; the very dull, who have nothing to hide and nothing to show; and the very devious, expert at covering their tracks and ambitious enough to risk their discovery.
-*CHARLES KRAUTHAMMER, American psychiatrist, editor, columnist*

One of my black friends believes there is a special place in hell for black folks who rip off anti-poverty programs or cheat on affirmative action for their own advantage. Personally, I don't think black folks are that special. Doctors who rip off Medicaid, farmers who rip off the subsidy programs and defense contractors who rip off the Pentagon all cost us a lot more money. That's why I believe in Perpetual Reform. In my observation, no matter how we fix the laws to get a level playing field, within 10 years, some set of SOBs will have figured out how to take special advantage of them - usually those with the most money already. So we just have to keep fixing them.
-*MOLLY IVINS, American newspaper columnist, author*

The democratic alternatives to conservatism - New Dealism and social democracy - have endured despite numerous practical difficulties and intellectual inconsistencies because majorities in most free electorates simply do not accept that market outcomes are automatically blessed. Free markets are useful and practical but not sanctified. If the market does not make health care affordable or available to all, voters will eventually come around to demanding it from government. That is why Medicare passed. It's also why polls show that despite President Clinton's problems on health care, most Americans favor government action to guarantee coverage for everyone. Voters may criticize government in the abstract, but they will turn to it to keep the air and water clean, the streets safe, and poor children fed.

Similarly, people value the communities that traditional conservatives so extol, but they also recognize that such communities can be disrupted or destroyed by economic change. So, in the name of conservative values, those who treasure these communities often turn to the state for protection or relief. What the moderate Left has always understood - and what conservatives usually try to deny - is that capitalism, in effect, socializes its problems. The state steps in to resolve difficulties that capitalism can't. Where there is no money to be made, capitalism moves on. Government necessarily cleans up after it.

*-E.J. DIONNE, American journalist, author*

Democratic politics is supposed to be about making public arguments and persuading fellow citizens. Instead, it has become an elaborate insider industry in which those skilled at fund-raising, polling, media relations, and advertising have the upper hand.

*-E.J. DIONNE*

The fact of the matter is every Senator knows this system stinks. Every Senator who participates in it knows this system stinks. And the American people are right when they mistrust this system, where what matters most in seeking public office is not integrity, not ability, not judgement, not reason, not responsibility, not experience, not intelligence, but money. We could have a candidate of the highest integrity, highest intelligence, the most vast experience, who can be overwhelmed by a tide of money by someone who has none of them. Money dominates this system. Money infuses this system. Money *is* the system.

*-GEORGE MITCHELL, U.S. Senator*

George Washington might have been puzzled by the populism, real and phony, of modern campaigning. Pat Buchanan talking about peasants and pitchforks. Lamar Alexander wearing a plaid shirt. Bill Clinton running as the Man from Hope. Washington dealt courteously with all classes of people, and as president, he held a weekly reception, from 3 to 4 on Tuesday afternoons, when anyone might show up for an hour and greet him. But he never forgot that he was a Virginia gentleman, and he dressed and acted the part, paying careful attention to his clothes, his carriage, and the ornaments on his dinner table. He did not feel compelled to impersonate the average man in order to lead or inspire him.

*-RICHARD BROOKHISER, American writer, editor*

The term Rule of Law, like the phrases "Love of God" and "Brotherhood Of Man," is a short and simple expression of one of the few most sublime

concepts that the mind and spirit of man has yet achieved.
-*GEORGE H. BOLDT, American jurist*

In the West for almost a century, democracy has meant "liberal democracy" - a political system marked by free and fair elections as well as by the rule of law, a separation of powers, and the protection of basic liberties of speech, assembly, religion and property. This "constitutional liberalism" is not about the procedures for electing government, but about protecting an individual's autonomy and dignity against coercion by state, church or society. It is *liberal* because it draws on the philosophy, beginning with the Greeks, that emphasizes liberty. It is *constitutional* because it rests on the tradition, beginning with the Romans, of the rule of law.
- *FAREED ZAKARIA, writer, editor. In* Foreign Affairs.

America's citizens want their elected officials to use common sense for the common good, but too often those voices are drowned out by the extremes in both parties who are usually wrong but never in doubt.
-*SAM NUNN, U.S. Senator*

We are not a cynical people. The will to believe lingers on. We like to think that heroes can emerge from obscurity, as they sometimes do; that elections do matter, even though the process is at least part hokum; that through politics we can change our society and maybe even find a cause to believe in.
-*RONALD STEEL, American writer*

# CHAPTER - 5

# *EDUCATION*

## ***

If I am walking with two other men each of them will serve as my teacher. I will pick out the good points of the one and imitate them, and the bad points of the other and correct them in myself.
*-CONFUCIUS, Chinese philosopher (551 - 479 B.C.)*

I hear and I forget. I see and I remember. I do and I understand.
*-CHINESE PROVERB*

Memory is the mother of all wisdom.
*-AESCHYLUS, Greek playwright (525 - 456 B.C.)*

The beginning of wisdom is the definition of terms.
*-SOCRATES, Greek philosopher (c.469 - c.399 B.C.)*

Whom, then, do I call educated? First, those who mangage well the circumstances which they encounter day by day and who possess a judgement which is accurate in meeting occasions as they arise and rarely miss the expedient course of action; next, those who are decent and honorable in their intercourse with all men, bearing easily and goodnaturedly what is unpleasant or offensive in others, and being themselves as agreeable and reasonable to their associates as it is humanly possible to be; furthermore, those who hold their pleasures always under control and are not unduly overcome by their misfortunes, bearing up under them bravely and in a manner worthy of our common nature; finally, and most important of all, those who are not spoiled by their successes and who do not desert their true selves, but hold their ground steadfastly as wise and soberminded men, rejoicing no more in the good things which have come to them through chance than in those which through their own nature and intelligence are theirs since birth. Those who have a character which is in accord, not with one of these things, but with all of them - those I maintain are educated and whole men, possessed of all the virtues of a man.

-*ISOCRATES, Athenian orator (436 - 338 B.C.)*

By education, then, I mean goodness in the term in which it is first acquired by a child ... the rightly disciplined state of pleasures and pains wherby a man from his first beginnings on will abhor what he should abhor and relish what he should relish.

-*PLATO, Greek philosopher (c.428 - c.347 B.C.)*

The direction in which education starts a man will determine his future life.    -*PLATO*

But if you ask what is the good of education in general, the answer is easy; that education makes good men, and that good men act nobly.    -*PLATO*

Knowledge which is acquired under compulsion has no hold on the mind. Therfore do not use compulsion, but let early education be rather a sort of amusement; this will better enable you to find out the natural bent of the child.  *-PLATO*

They who educate children well, are more to be honored than they who produce them; for these only gave them life, those the art of living well.
*-ARISTOTLE, Greek philosopher (384 - 322 B.C.)*

The legislator should direct his attention above all to the education of youth; for the neglect of education does harm to the constitution. The citizen should be moulded to suit the form of government under which he lives. For each government has a peculiar character which originally formed and which continues to preserve it. The character of democracy creates democracy, and the character of oligarchy creates oligarchy; and always the better the character, the better the government.  *-ARISTOTLE*

All who have meditated on the art of governing mankind have been convinced that the fate of empires depends on the education of youth.
Educated men are as much superior to uneducated men as the living are to the dead.  *-ARISTOTLE*

Education is the best provision for old age.
*-ARISTOTLE*

We cannot learn without pain.  *-ARISTOTLE*

It is only the ignorant who despise education.
*-PUBLILIUS SYRUS, Latin writer, actor (1st century B.C.)*

A father should, as soon as his son is born,

conceive the greatest possible hopes for the child's future. He will therby grow the more solicitous about his improvement from the very beginning. For it is an assertion without foundation that claims that "to very few people is granted the faculty of comprehending what is imparted to them, and that most, through dullness of understanding, lose their labour and their time." On the contrary, you will find that the greater number of men are both ready in apprehending and quick in learning, since such a faculty is natural to man. As birds are born to fly, horses to run, and wild beasts to show fierceness, so to us peculiarly belong activity and sagacity of understanding.

Therfore, the mind is considered to be a gift from heaven. Dull and unteachable persons are no more produced in the course of nature than are persons marked by deformity or monstrosity. Such are certainly few. A simple proof of this assertion is that among boys, most of them show good promise. And if it turns out that this promise never materializes, it is not usually for lack of latent ability, but because care was never taken in nurturing it. You may respond that some surpass others in ability. I grant this to be true, in that some accomplish more and others less. But there is no one who does not gain by some studying.

-*QUINTILIAN, Roman rhetorician (c.35 - c.99)*

The very spring and root of honesty and virtue lie in good education.

-*PLUTARCH, Greek biographer (c.46 - c.120)*

We must not believe the many, who say that free

persons only ought to be educated, but we should rather believe the philosophers, who say that the educated only are free.
-*EPICTETUS, Greek philosopher (55 - 135)*

Free curiosity is of more value than harsh discipline.
-*ST. AUGUSTINE, Church father, philosopher (354 - 430)*

The world is a book, and those who do not travel read only one page. -*ST. AUGUSTINE*

The prosperity of a country depends, not on the abundance of its revenues, nor on the strength of its fortifications, nor on the beauty of its public buildings; but it consists in the number of its cultivated citizens, in its men of education, enlightenment and character.
-*MARTIN LUTHER, German religious reformer (1483 - 1546)*

We can be knowledgeable with other men's knowledge, but we cannot be wise with other men's wisdom.
-*MICHEL DE MONTAIGNE, French moralist, essayist (1533 - 1592)*

By education most have been misled;
So they believe, because they were so bred.
The priest continues what the nurse began,
And thus the child imposes on the man.
-*JOHN DRYDEN, English poet, critic (1631 - 1700)*

Those who have read of everything are thought to understand everything too; but it is not always so - reading furnishes the mind only with the materials of knowledge; it is thinking that makes what is read ours. We are of the ruminating kind, and it is not

enough to cram ourselves with a great load of collections; unless we chew them over again, they will not give us strength and nourishment.
-JOHN LOCKE, English philosopher (1632 - 1704)

A sound mind in a sound body is a short but full description of a happy state in this world. He that has these two has little more to wish for; and he that wants either of them will be but little the better for anything else. Men's happiness or misery is most part of their own making. He whose mind directs not wisely will never take the right way; and he whose body is crazy and feeble will never be able to advance in it. I confess there are some men's constitutions of body and mind so vigorous and well framed by nature that they need not much assistance from others; but by the strength of their natural genius they are from their cradles carried towards what is excellent; and by the privilege of their happy constitutions are able to do wonders. But examples of this kind are but few; and I think I may say that of all the men we meet with, nine parts of ten are what they are, good or evil, useful or not, by their education. 'Tis that which makes the great difference in mankind.    -JOHN LOCKE

Our delight in any particular study, art, or science rises and improves in proportion to the application which we bestow upon it. Thus what was at first an exercise becomes at length an entertainment.
-JOSEPH ADDISON, English essayist (1672 - 1719)

Learning is acquired by reading books; but the much more necessary learning, the knowledge of the world, is only to be acquired by reading men, and studying all the various editions of them.

-*LORD CHESTERFIELD, English statesman, scholar (1694 - 1773)*

General virtue is more probably to be expected and obtained from the *education* of youth than from the *exhortation* of adult persons; bad habits, and vices of the mind being, like diseases of the body, more easily prevented than cured.

-*BEN FRANKLIN, American statesman, writer, inventor (1706 - 1790)*

If a man empties his purse into his head, no man can take it away from him. An investment in knowledge always pays the best interest.   -*BEN FRANKLIN*

Be not too hasty to trust or to admire the teachers of morality: they discourse like angels but they live like men.

-*SAMUEL JOHNSON, English lexicographer, writer (1709 - 1784)*

The only end of writing is to enable the readers better to enjoy life or better to endure it.

-*SAMUEL JOHNSON*

From the first moment of life, men ought to begin learning to deserve to live; and, as at the instant of birth we partake of the rights of citizenship, that instant ought to be the beginning of the exercise of our duty. If there are laws for the age of maturity, there ought to laws for infancy, teaching obedience to others; and as the reason each man is not left to be the sole arbiter of his duties, government ought the less indiscriminately to abandon to the intelligence and prejudices of fathers the education of their children, as that education is of still greater importance to the State than to the fathers; for, according to the course of nature the death of the father often deprives him of the final fruits of education; but his country sooner or later perceives its effects. Families dissolve, but the State remains.

-JEAN-JACQUES ROUSSEAU, French philosopher (1712 - 1778)

A man without the proper use of the intellectual faculties of a man, is, if possible, more contemptible than even a coward, and seems to be mutilated and deformed in a still more essential part of the character of human nature. Though the state was to derive no advantage from the instruction of the inferior ranks of people, it would still deserve its attention that they should not be altogether uninstructed. The state, however, derives no small advantage from their instruction. The more they are instructed the less liable they are to the delusions of enthusiasm and superstition, which, among ignorant nations, frequently occasion the most dreadful disorders.

An instructed and intelligent people, besides, are always more decent and orderly than an ignorant and stupid one. They feel themselves, each individually, more respectable and more likely to obtain the respect of their lawful superiors, and they are therfore more disposed to respect those superiors. They are more disposed to examine, and more capable of seeing through, the interested complaints of faction and sedition, and they are, upon that account, less apt to be misled into any wanton or unnecessary opposition to the measures of government. In free countries, where the safety of government depends very much upon the favourable judgement which the people may form of its conduct, it must surely be of the highest importance that they should not be disposed to judge rashly or capriciously concerning it.

*-ADAM SMITH, Scottish economist (1723 - 1790)*

Facts are stubborn things; and whatever may be our wishes, our inclinations, or the dictates of our passions, they cannot alter the state of facts and evidence.

*-JOHN ADAMS, 2nd President of the United States (1735 - 1826)*

The most important bill in our whole code is that for the diffusion of knowledge among the people. No other sure foundation can be devised, for the preservation of freedom and happiness.

*-THOMAS JEFFERSON, 3rd President of the United States (1743 - 1826)*

If a nation expects to be ignorant and free, in a state of civilization, it expects what never was and never will be. *-THOMAS JEFFERSON*

Ignorance is preferable to error; and he is less remote from the truth who believes nothing, than he who believes what is wrong. *-THOMAS JEFFERSON*

There is but one method of preventing crimes, and of rendering a republican form of government durable, and that is by disseminating the seeds of virtue and knowledge through every part of the state by means of proper places and modes of education, and this can be done effectively only by the interference and aid of the Legislature.

*-BENJAMIN RUSH, American physician, political leader (1745 - 1813)*

It is easy to learn something about everything, but difficult to learn everything about anything.
-*NATHANIEL EMMONS, American theologian (1745 - 1840)*

Treat people as if they were what they ought to be and you help them to become what they are capable of being.
-*JOHANN WOLFGANG VON GOETHE, German poet, playwright (1749 - 1832)*

It is better to debate a question without settling it than to settle a question without debating it.
-*JOSEPH JOUBERT, French moralist, essayist (1754 - 1824)*

To teach is to learn twice.  -*JOSEPH JOUBERT*

Education should be gentle and stern, not cold and lax.  -*JOSEPH JOUBERT*

In later life as in earlier, only a few persons influence the formation of character; the multitude pass us by like a distant army. One friend, one teacher, one beloved, one club, one dining table, one work table, are the means by which his nation and the spirit of his nation affect the individual.
-*JEAN PAUL RICHTER, German novelist (1763 - 1825)*

Never try to reason the prejudice out of a man. It was not reasoned into him, and cannot be reasoned out.
-*SYDNEY SMITH, English clergyman, writer (1771 - 1845)*

Education makes a people easy to lead, but difficult to drive; easy to govern, but impossible to enslave.
-*HENRY PETER, LORD BROUGHAM, British jurist, politician (1778 - 1868)*

If there were no falsehoods in the world, there would

be no doubt; if there were no doubt, there would be no inquiry; if no inquiry, no wisdom, no knowledge, no genius.

*- WALTER LANDOR, English writer (1775 - 1864)*

Knowledge acquired by labor becomes a possession - a property entirely our own. A greater vividness and permanency of impression is secured, and facts thus acquired become registered in the mind in a way that mere imparted information can never produce.

*- THOMAS CARLYLE, Scottish essayist, historian (1795 - 1881)*

A human being is not, in any proper sense, a human being till he is educated.

*- HORACE MANN, American educator (1796 - 1859)*

Education, beyond all other devices of human origin, is a great equalizer of the conditions of men - the balance wheel of the social machinery. *-HORACE MANN*

Republics, one after another, have perished from a want of intelligence and virtue in the masses of the people. ... If we do not prepare children to become good citizens; if we do not develop their capacities, if we do not enrich their minds with knowledge, imbue their hearts with love of truth and duty, and a reverence for all things sacred and holy, then our republic must go down to destruction, as others have gone before it; and mankind must sweep through another vast cycle of sin and suffering, before the dawn of a better era can arise upon the world.

*-HORACE MANN*

Schoolhouses are the republican line of fortifications. *-HORACE MANN*

Education in its widest sense includes everything that exerts a formative influence, and causes a young person to be, at a given point, what he is.
*-MARK HOPKINS, American educator, author (1802 - 1887)*

Every human being has four hungers; the hunger of the loins, the hunger of the belly, the hunger of the mind, the hunger of the soul. You can get by a long time on the loins and the belly, but there is a good deal of evidence that even the meanest of men eventually crave something for the mind and soul.
*-JAMES WEBB, American journalist, diplomat (1802 - 1884)*

Our knowledge is the amassed thought and experience of innumerable minds; our language, our science, our religion, our opinions, our fancies we inherited.
*-RALPH WALDO EMERSON, American essayist, poet (1803 - 1882)*

Great men are they who see that spiritual is stronger than any material force, that thoughts rule the world.
*-RALPH WALDO EMERSON*

The more extensive a man's knowledge of what has been done, the greater will be his power of knowing what to do.
*-BENJAMIN DISRAELI, British Prime Minister, author (1804 - 1881)*

Seeing much, suffering much, and studying much, are the three pillars of learning.     *-BENJAMIN DISRAELI*

Men are men before they are lawyers, or physicians, or merchants, or manufacturers; and if you make them capable and sensible men, they will make themselves capable and sensible lawyers or physicians. What professional men should carry away with them from a University, is not professional knowledge, but that which should direct the use of the professional knowledge, and bring the light of general culture to illuminate the technicalities of a special pursuit. Men may be competent lawyers without general education, but it depends on general education to make them philosophic lawyers - who demand, and are capable of apprehending, principles, instead of merely cramming their memory with details. And so of all useful pursuits, mechanical included. Education makes a man a more intelligent shoemaker, if that be his occupation, but not by teaching him how to make shoes; it does so by the mental exercise it gives, and the habits it impresses.

*-JOHN STUART MILL, English philosopher, (1806 - 1873)*

It has often been said, and requires to be repeated still oftener, that books and discourses alone are not education; that life is a problem, not a theorem; that action can only be learned in action. A child learns to write its name only by a succcession of trials; and is a man to be taught to use his mind and guide his conduct by mere precept? What can be learned in schools is important, but not all important. The main branch of the education of human beings is their habitual employment, which must be either their individual vocation or some matter of general concern, in which they are called to take a part.

The private money-getting occupation of almost everyone is more or less a mechanical routine; it brings but few of his faculties into action, while its exclusive pursuit tends to fasten his attention and interest exclusively upon himself, and upon his family as an appendage of himself - making him indifferent to the public, to the more generous objects and the nobler interests, and in his inordinate regard for his personal comforts, selfish and cowardly.

Balance these tendencies by contrary ones; give him something to do for the public, whether as a vestryman, a juryman, or an elector; and in that degree, his ideas and feelings are taken out of his narrow circle. He becomes acquainted with more varied business and a larger range of considerations. He is made to feel that besides the interests which separate him from his fellow citizens, he has interests which connect him with them; that not only the common good is his good but that it partly depends upon his exertions. Whatever might be the case in some other constitutions of society, the spirit of a commercial people will be, we are persuaded, essentially mean and slavish wherever public spirit is not cultivated by an extensive participation of the people in the business of government in detail; nor will the desirability of a general diffusion of intelligence among either the middle or lower classes be realized, but by a corresponding dissemination of public functions, and a voice in public affairs.

-*JOHN STUART MILL*

The strongest foundation for any belief is a standing invitation to prove it wrong.     -*JOHN STUART MILL*

The great end of education is to discipline rather than to furnish the mind; to train it to the use of its own powers, rather than fill it with the accumulation of others.

-*TYRON EDWARDS, American clergyman, author (1809 - 1894)*

Education is the knowledge of how to use the whole of oneself. Many men use but one or two faculties out of the score with which they are endowed. A man is educated who knows how to make a tool of every faculty - how to open it, how to keep it sharp, and how to apply it to all practical purposes.

-*HENRY WARD BEECHER, American cleric, writer (1813 - 1887)*

What does education often do? It makes a straight-cut ditch of a free, meandering brook.

-*HENRY DAVID THOREAU, American essayist, naturalist (1817 - 1862)*

What the first philosopher taught the last will have to repeat.    -*HENRY DAVID THOREAU*

As scarce as truth is, the supply has always been in excess of the demand.

-*JOSH BILLINGS, American writer, humorist (1818 - 1885)*

Solitude is as needful to the imagination as society is wholesome for the character.

-*JAMES RUSSELL LOWELL, American writer, diplomat (1819 - 1891)*

It was in making education not only common to all, but in some sense compulsory on all, that the destiny of the free republics of America was practically settled.    -*JAMES RUSSELL LOWELL*

Education is the leading of human souls to what is best, and making what is best out of them; and these two objects are always attainable together, and by the same means. The training which makes men happiest in themselves also makes them most serviceable to others.

-*JOHN RUSKIN, English author (1819 - 1900)*

Education does not mean teaching people what they do not know. It means teaching them to behave as they do not behave. It is not teaching the youth the shapes of letters and the tricks of numbers, and then leaving them to turn their arithmetic to roguery, and their literature to lust. It means, on the contrary, training them into the perfect exercise and kingly continence of their bodies and souls. It is painful, continual and difficult work, to be done by kindness, by watching, by warning, by precept and by praise, but above all - by example. -*JOHN RUSKIN*

Even when we fancy that we have grown wiser, it may be only that new prejudices have displaced old ones.

-*CHRISTIAN NESTELL BOVEE, American writer (1820 - 1904)*

The sure foundations of the State are laid in knowledge, not in ignorance; and every sneer at education, at culture, and at book-learning, which is the recorded wisdom of the experience of mankind, is the demagogue's sneer at intelligent liberty, inviting national degeneracy and ruin.

-*GEORGE CURTIS, American author (1824 - 1892)*

"Learn what is true in order to do what is right" is the summing up of the whole duty of man.

-*THOMAS HUXLEY, English biologist, writer (1825 - 1895)*

Perhaps the most valuable result of all education is

the ability to make yourself do the thing you have to do, when it ought to be done, whether you like it or not; it is the first lesson that ought to be learned; and however early a man's training begins, it is probably the last lesson that he learns thoroughly.

*-THOMAS HUXLEY*

Education is the instruction of the intellect in the laws of Nature, under which name I include not merely things and their forces, but men and their ways; and the fashioning of the affections and of the will into an earnest desire to move in harmony with these laws.   *-THOMAS HUXLEY*

When I was a boy on the Mississippi River there was a proposition in a township there to discontinue public schools because they were too expensive. An old farmer spoke up and said if they stopped the schools they would not save anything, because every time a school was closed a jail had to be built.

*-MARK TWAIN, American writer, humorist (1835 - 1910)*

The man who does not read good books has no advantage over the man who can't read them.

*-MARK TWAIN*

Travel is fatal to prejudice, bigotry, and narrowmindedness, and many of our people need it sorely on these accounts. Broad, wholesome, charitable views of men and things cannot be acquired by vegetating in one little corner of the earth all one's lifetime.   *-MARK TWAIN*

Education in the long run is an affair that works itself out between the individual student and his opportunities. Methods, of which we talk so much, play but a minor part. Offer the opportunities, leave the student to his natural reaction on them, and he will work out his personal destiny, be it a high one or a low one.

-WILLIAM JAMES, American philosopher, psychologist (1842 - 1910)

The sin of "Science" is to attain conceptions so adequate and exact that we shall never need to change them. There is an everlasting struggle in every mind between the tendency to keep unchanged and the tendency to renovate its ideas. Our education is a ceaseless compromise between the conservative and the progressive factors.   -WILLIAM JAMES

A teacher affects eternity; he can never tell where his influence stops.

-HENRY ADAMS, American historian (1838 - 1918)

The advice of their elders to young men is very apt to be as unreal as a list of the hundred best books.

-OLIVER WENDELL HOLMES, JR., U.S. Supreme Court Justice (1841 - 1935)

It is human nature to think wisely and act foolishy.

-ANATOLE FRANCE, French author (1844 - 1924)

The surest way to corrupt a youth is to instruct him to hold in higher esteem those who think alike than those who think differently.

-FRIEDRICH WILHELM NIETZCHE, German philosopher (1844 - 1900)

The sounder your argument, the more satisfaction you get out of it.

-ESGAR WATSON HOWE, American journalist, editor (1853 - 1937)

The problem of education is twofold: first to know, and then to utter. Everyone who lives any semblance of an inner life thinks more nobly and profoundly than he speaks.

*- ROBERT LOUIS STEVENSON, Scottish novelist, poet (1850 - 1894)*

Every man is a damn fool for at least five minutes every day; wisdom consists in not exceeding the limit.

*- ELBERT HUBBARD, American writer, publisher (1856 - 1915)*

Few people think more than two or three times a year; I have made an international reputation for myself by thinking once or twice a week.

*- GEORGE BERNARD SHAW, British playwright, critic (1856 - 1950)*

To think is to differ.

*- CLARENCE DARROW, American lawyer (1857 - 1938)*

True education makes for inequality; the inequality of individuality, the inequality of success; the glorious inequality of talent, of genius; for inequality, not mediocrity, individual superiority, not standardization, is the measure of the progress of the world.

*- FELIX E. SCHELLING, American educator (1858 - 1945)*

A man who has never gone to school may steal from a freight car; but if he has a university education, he may steal the whole railroad.

*- THEODORE ROOSEVELT, 26th President of the United States (1858 - 1919)*

The devotion of democracy to education is a familiar fact. The superficial explanation is that a government resting upon popular suffrage cannot be successful unless those who elect and obey their governors are educated. Since a democratic society repudiates the principle of external authority, it must find a substitute in voluntary disposition and interest; these can be created only by education.

-*JOHN DEWEY, American philosopher, educator (1859 - 1952)*

Culture is activity of thought, and receptiveness to beauty and humane feeling. Scraps of information have nothing to do with it. A merely well-informed man is the most useless bore on God's earth. What we should aim at producing is men who possess both culture and expert knowledge in some special direction. Their expert knowledge will give them the ground to start from, and their culture will lead them as deep as philosophy and as high as art. We have to remember that the valuable intellectual development is self-development, and that it mostly takes place between the ages of sixteen and thirty. As to training, the most important part is given by mothers before the age of twelve.

-*ALFRED NORTH WHITEHEAD, English philosopher (1861 - 1947)*

A new idea is delicate. It can be killed by a sneer or a yawn; it can be stabbed to death by a quip and worried to death by a frown on the right man's brow.

-*CHARLES BROWER, American explorer (1862 - 1950)*

The great difficulty in education is to get experience out of ideas.

-*GEORGE SANTAYANA, American philosopher, poet (1863 - 1952)*

Almost every wise saying has an opposite one, no less wise, to balance it.    -*GEORGE SANTAYANA*

If you think education is expensive - try ignorance.
*-DEREK BOK, American editor (1863 - 1930)*

Anyone who stops learning is old, whether at twenty or eighty. Anyone who keeps learning stays young. The greatest thing in life is to keep your mind young.
*-HENRY FORD, American industrialist (1863 - 1947)*

Education is not the filling of a pail, but the lighting of a fire.
*-WILLIAM BUTLER YEATS, Irish poet, playwright (1865 - 1939)*

Human history becomes more and more a race between education and catastrophe.
*-H.G. WELLS, English novelist, historian (1866 - 1946)*

Nothing in life is to be feared, it is only to be understood.
*-MARIE CURIE, French chemist (1867 - 1934)*

Education is a state-controlled manufactory of echoes.
*-NORMAN DOUGLASS, English author (1868 - 1952)*

Education and work are the levers to uplift a people. Work alone will not do it unless inspired by the right ideals and guided by intelligence. Education must not simply teach work - it must teach life.
*-W.E.B. DU BOIS, American writer, educator (1868 - 1963)*

The liberty of the child should have as its *limit* the collective interest; as its form, what we universally consider good breeding. We must therfore check in the child whatever offends or annoys others, or whatever tends toward rough or ill-bred acts. But all the rest - every manifestation having a useful scope, whatever it be, and under whatever form it expresses itself - must not only be permitted, but must be observed by the teacher.

*-MARIA MONTESSORI, Italian educator (1870 - 1952)*

Establishing lasting peace is the work of education; all politics can do is keep us out of war.

*-MARIA MONTESSORI*

There is no school equal to a decent home, and no teachers equal to honest virtuous parents.

*-MOHANDAS GANDHI, Indian nationalist leader (1869 - 1948)*

Every man has a right to his opinion, but no man has a right to be wrong in his facts.

*-BERNARD BARUCH, American businessman, diplomat (1870 - 1965)*

The fact that an opinion has been widely held is no evidence whatever that it is not utterly absurd; indeed in view of the silliness of the majority of mankind, a widespread belief is more likely to be foolish than sensible.

*-BERTRAND RUSSELL, English philosopher (1872 - 1970)*

The more purely intellectual aim of education should be the endeavor to make us see and imagine the world in an objective manner as far as possible as it really is in itself, and not merely through the distorting medium of personal desires.

*-BERTRAND RUSSELL*

Education is, as a rule, the strongest force on the side of what exists and against fundamental change; threatened institutions, while they are still powerful, possess themselves of the educational machine, and instill a respect for their own excellence into the malleable minds of the young. Reformers retort by trying to oust their opponents from their position of vantage. The children themselves are not considered by either party; they are merely so much material, to be recruited into one army or the other.

If the children themselves were considered, education would not aim at making them belong to this party or that, but at enabling them to choose intelligently between the parties; it would aim at making them able to think, not at making them think what their teachers think. Education as a political weapon could not exist if we respected the rights of children. If we respected the rights of children, we should educate them so as to give them the knowledge and the mental habits required for forming independent opinions; but education as a political institution endeavors to form habits and to circumscribe knowledge in such a way as to make one set of opinions inevitable.

*-BERTRAND RUSSELL*

Half the world is composed of people who have something to say and can't, and the other half who have nothing to say and keep on saying it.

*-ROBERT FROST, American poet (1874 - 1963)*

Education is the ability to listen to almost anything without losing your temper or your self-confidence.

*-ROBERT FROST*

A university studies politics, but it will not advocate facism or communism. A university studies military tactics, but it will not promote war. A university studies peace, but it will not organize crusades of pacifism. It will study every question that effects human welfare, but it will not carry a banner in a crusade for anything except freedom of learning.

*-LOTUS DELAT COFFMAN, American educator (1875 - 1938)*

It is a great nuisance that knowledge can be acquired only by hard work.

*- W. SOMERSET MAUGHAM, English novelist, playwright (1874 - 1965)*

I respect faith, but doubt is what gets you an education.

*- WILSON MIZNER, American playwright, screenwriter (1876 - 1933)*

Education has produced a vast population able to read but unable to distinguish what is worth reading.

*- GEORGE MACAULAY TREVELYAN, English historian (1876 - 1962)*

I suggest that the only books that influence us are those for which we are ready, and which have gone a little farther down our particular path than we have yet got ourselves.

*-E.M. FORSTER, English novelist (1879 - 1970)*

Education is a weapon, whose effects depend on who holds it in his hands and at whom it is aimed.

*-JOSEPH STALIN, Soviet political leader (1879 - 1953)*

Everybody is ignorant, only on different subjects.

*- WILL ROGERS, American actor, humorist (1879 - 1935)*

The important thing is not to stop questioning. Curiosity has its own reason for existing. One cannot help but be in awe when he contemplates the mysteries of eternity, of life, of the marvelous structures of reality. It is enough if one merely tries to comprehend a little of this mystery every day. Never lose a holy curiosity.

*-ALBERT EINSTEIN, American physicist (1879 -1955)*

When I examine myself and my methods of thought, I come close to the conclusion that the gift of fantasy has meant more to me than my talent for absorbing positive knowledge. *-ALBERT EINSTEIN*

It is essential that the student acquire an understanding of and a lively feeling for values. He must acquire a vivid sense of the beautiful and of the morally good. Otherwise he - with his specialized knowledge - more closely resembles a well-trained dog than a harmoniously developed person.

*-ALBERT EINSTEIN*

The crippling of individuals I consider the worst evil of capitalism. Our whole educational system suffers from this evil. An exaggerated competitive attitude is inculcated into the student, who is trained to worship acquisitive success as a preparation for his future career. *-ALBERT EINSTEIN*

By academic freedom I understand the right to search for truth and to publish and teach what one holds to be true. This right implies also a duty: one must not conceal any part of what one has recognized to be true. *-ALBERT EINSTEIN*

Truth is what stands the test of experience.
*-ALBERT EINSTEIN*

The object of the university is not to make ideas safe for students but to make students safe for ideas.
-*ALBERT EINSTEIN*

The man who strives to educate himself - and no one else can educate him - must win a certain victory over his own nature. He must learn to smile at his dear idols, analyze his every prejudice, scrap if necessary his fondest and most consoling belief, question his presuppositions, and take his chances with the truth.
-*EVERETT DEAN MARTIN, American educator (1880 - 1941)*

The trouble about man is twofold. He cannot learn truths which are too complicated; he forgets truths which are too simple.
-*REBECCA WEST, British novelist, critic, actress (1882 - 1983)*

Wisdom too often never comes, and so one ought not to reject it merely because it comes late.
-*FELIX FRANKFURTER, U.S. Supreme Court Justice (1882 - 1965)*

Sixty years ago I knew everything; now I know nothing; education is a progressive discovery of our own ignorance.
-*WILL DURANT, American historian, (1885 - 1981)*

To admit authorities, however heavily furred and gowned, into our libraries and let them tell us how to read, what to read, what value to place upon what we read, is to destroy the spirit of freedom which is the breath of those sanctuaries. Everywhere else we may be bound by laws and conventions - there we have none.
-*VIRGINIA WOOLF, British writer (1882 - 1941)*

With the stones we cast at them, geniuses build new roads for us.

-*PAUL ELDRIDGE,  American educator, novelist*

A guidance counselor who has made a fetish of security, or who has unwittingly surrendered his thinking to economic determinism, may steer a youth away from his dream of becoming a poet, an artist, a musician, or any other of thousands of things, because it offers no security, it does not pay well, there are no vacancies, it has no "future." Among all the tragic consequences of depression and war, this suppression of personal self-expression through one's life work is among the most poignant.

-*HENRY WRISTON, American educator (1889 - 1978)*

There are only two ways to be quite unprejudiced and impartial. One is to be completely ignorant. The other is to be completely indifferent. Bias and prejudice are attitudes to be kept in hand, not attitudes to be avoided.

-*CHARLES P CURTIS, American lawyer, writer (1891 - 1959)*

The dissenter is every human being at those moments of his life when he resigns momentarily from the herd and thinks for himself.

-*ARCHIBALD MACLEISH, American poet, essayist (1892 - 1982)*

The advantage of a classical education is that it enables you to despise the wealth which it prevents you from achieving.

-*RUSSELL GREEN, English author*

Those who worry about radicalism in our schools and colleges are often either reactionaries who themselves do not bear allegiance to the traditional American principles, or defeatists who despair of the success of our own philosophy in an open competition.

*-JAMES BRYANT CONANT, American educator (1893 - 1978)*

Most ignorance is vincible ignorance. We don't know because we don't want to know.

*-ALDOUS HUXLEY, English author (1894 - 1963)*

Every man who knows how to read has it in his power to magnify himself, to multiply the ways in which he exists, to make his life full, significant and interesting. *-ALDOUS HUXLEY*

A liberal education frees a man from the prison house of his class, race, time, place, background, family, and even his nation.

*-ROBERT MAYNARD HUTCHINS, American educator (1899 - 1977)*

The faith rests on the proposition that man is a political animal, that participation in political decisions is necessary to his fulfillment and happiness, that all men can and must be sufficiently educated and informed to take part in making these decisions, that protection against arbitrary power, though indispensable, is insufficient to make either free individuals or a free society, that such a society must make positive provisions for its development into a community learning together; for this is what political participation, government by consent, and the civilization of the dialogue all add up to.

*-ROBERT MAYNARD HUTCHINS*

Why is it that the boy or girl who on June 15 receives

his degree, eager, enthusiastic, outspoken, idealistic, reflective, and independent, is on the following Sept. 15, or even June 16, dull, uninspiring, shifty, pliable and attired in a double breasted blue serge suit?  The answer must lie in the relative weakness of the higher education, compared with the forces that make everybody think and act like everybody else.
-*ROBERT MAYNARD HUTCHINS*

We can put television in its proper light by supposing that Gutenberg's great invention had been directed at printing only comic books.    -*ROBERT MAYNARD HUTCHINS*

If our freedom means ease alone, if it means shirking the hard disciplines of learning, if it means evading the rigors and rewards of creative activity, if it means more expenditure on advertising than education, if it means in the  schools the steady cult of the trivial and the mediocre, if it means - worst of all - indifference, or even contempt for all but athletic excellence, we may keep for a time the forms of free society, but its spirit will be dead.
-*ADLAI STEVENSON, American statesman, politician (1900 - 1965)*

We must recover the element of quality in our traditional pursuit of equality.  We must not, in opening our schools to everyone, confuse the idea that all should have equal chance with the notion that all have equal endowments.   -*ADLAI STEVENSON*

If one cannot state a matter clearly enough so that even an intelligent twelve-year-old can understand it, one should remain within the cloistered walls of the university and laboratory until one gets a better grasp of one's subject matter.

*-MARGARET MEAD, American anthropologist (1901 - 1978)*

Speaking simply and in the broadest sense, the teacher shows the student how to discern, evaluate, judge, and recognize the truth. He does not impose a fixed content of ideas and doctrines that the student must learn by rote. He teaches the student how to learn and think for himself. He encourages rather than suppresses a critical and intelligent response.

The student's response and growth is the only reward suitable for such a labor of love. Teaching, the highest of the ministerial or cooperative arts, is devoted to the good of others. It is an act of supreme generosity. St. Augustine calls it the greatest act of charity.

*-MORTIMER ADLER, American philosopher, educator*

The university is the only institution in Western society whose business it is to search for and transmit truth regardless of all competing or conflicting pressures and demands; pressures for immediate usefulness, for social approval, pressures to serve the special interests of government, a class, a professional group, a race, a faith, even a nation.

*-HENRY STEELE COMMAGER, American historian*

We cannot have a society half slave and half free; nor can we have thought half slave and half free. If we create an atmosphere in which men fear to think independently, inquire fearlessly, express themselves freely, we will in the end create the kind of society in which men no longer care to think independently or to inquire fearlessly. If we put a premium on

conformity we will, in the end, get conformity.
*-HENRY STEELE COMMAGER*

Our schools must encourage brains, for our world needs brains. We can no longer be content with mediocrity, with the second rate. There is nothing undemocratic about this. To develop an intellectual elite is no more undemocratic than to develop an athletic elite or journalistic elite. We must learn to take brains in our stride, as we do expertness on the football field, the basketball floor, the state, or the newsroom.   *-HENRY STEELE COMMAGER*

We have rudiments of reverence for the human body, but we consider as nothing the rape of the human mind.
*-ERIC HOFFER, American author (1902 - 1983)*

The education explosion is producing a vast number of people who want to live significant, important lives but lack the ability to satisfy this craving for importance by individual achievement. The country is being swamped with nobodies who want to be somebodies.   *-ERIC HOFFER*

Everyone who remembers his own educational experience remembers teachers, not methods and techniques. The teacher is the kingpin of the educational situation. He makes or breaks programs.
*-SIDNEY HOOK, American philosopher, educator (1902 - 1989)*

The school is a place or institution for teaching and learning.
Underneath this definition in every standard dictionary is another definition: School is a large

number of fish of the same kind swimming together in the same direction.
-*HARRY GOLDEN, American editor, writer (1903 - 1981)*

No school can offset the evil influence not merely of a bad home, but of a home with low moral, disciplinary and intellectual standards. If fathers and mothers offer their children no more intellectual fare than comic books, a television set, and picture magazines; if they make of the home merely a place to sleep, drink and eat - and not the center of life - they have no right to complain of the schools.
-*GRAYSON KIRK, American educator*

Secrecy strikes at the very root of what science is, and what it is for. It is not possible to be a scientist unless you believe that it is good to learn. It is not good to be a scientist, and it is not possible, unless you think that it is of the highest value to share your knowledge, to share it with anyone who is interested. It is not possible to be a scientist unless you believe that the knowledge of the world, and the power which this gives, is a thing of intrinsic value to humanity, and that you are using it to help in the spread of knowledge, and are willing to take the consequences.
-*J. ROBERT OPENHEIMER, American physicist, author (1904 - 1967)*

When you read a classic, you do not see more in the book than you did before; you see more in you than there was before.
-*CLIFTON FADIMAN, American author, editor*

A college education is not a quantitative body of memorized knowledge   salted  away  in a card file.  It is a taste for knowledge, a taste for philosophy, if you will; a capacity to explore, to question, to perceive relationships, between fields of knowledge and experience.

*-A. WHITNEY GRISWOLD, American historian, educator (1906 - 1963)*

There is no lack of opportunity for learning among us. What is lacking is a respect for it, an honest respect such as we now have for technical competence or business success. ... We honor learning, but do not believe in it. We reward it with lengthy obituaries and a wretched living wage. Rather than submit to it ourselves, we hire substitutes; rather than cultivate our own brains, we pick theirs. We spend as much time and energy on short-cuts to learning and imitations of learning as we do on learning itself.  *-A. WHITNEY GRISWOLD*

In the long run of history, the censor and the inquisitor have always lost. The only sure weapon against bad ideas is better ideas. The source of better ideas is wisdom. The surest path to wisdom is a liberal education.  *-A. WHITNEY GRISWOLD*

Give me another drink and I'll tell you all you want to know.

*-FATS WALLER, American jazz musician (1904 - 1943)*

Unless an individual is free to obtain the fullest education with which his society can provide him, he is being injured by society.

*- W. H. AUDEN, American poet (1907 - 1973)*

Curiosity is free-wheeling intelligence. ... It endows the people who have it with a generosity in argument

and a serenity in their own mode of life which springs from the cheerful willingness to let life take the forms it will.
-*ALISTAIR COOKE, American essayist, journalist*

The test and the use of man's education is that he finds pleasure in the exercise of his mind.
-*JACQUES BARZUN, American writer, teacher*

Teaching is not a lost art, but the regard for it is a lost tradition. -*JACQUES BARZUN*

Youngsters and adults cannot learn if information is pressed into their brains. You can teach only by creating interest, by creating an urge to know. Knowledge has to be sucked into the brain, not pushed into it. First, one must create a state of mind that craves knowledge, interest and wonder.
-*VICTOR WEISSKOPF, American physicist, author*

I know this is heresy. People who teach reading are dead against what they call "verbalizing." If you verbalize, you lose time. What time are they talking about. Time is one of the great hobgoblins of our day. There is really no time except the single, fleeting moment that slips by us like water, and to talk about losing time, or saving time, is often a very dubious argument. When you are reading you cannot save time, but you can diminish your pleasure by trying to do so. What are you going to do with this time when you have saved it. Have you anything to do more important than reading? You are reading for pleasure, you see, and pleasure is very important. Incidently, your reading may bring you information, or enlightenment, but unless it brings pleasure first you should think carefully about why you are doing it.

*-ROBERTSON DAVIES, Canadian editor, novelist (1913 - 1995)*

The primary purpose of a liberal education is to make one's mind a pleasant place in which to spend one's leisure.

*-SYDNEY J. HARRIS, American newspaper columnist (1917 - 1986)*

The smaller the mind, the more interested it is in the rare, the extraordinary, the sensational; the larger the mind, the more interested it is in studying the obvious, examining the ordinary, and investigating the commonplace. *-SYDNEY J. HARRIS*

Why do most Americans look up to education and look down upon educated people? (Our national schizophrenia.) *-SYDNEY J. HARRIS*

Students need to learn far more than the basic skills. Children who have just started school may still be in the labor force in the year 2030. For them, nothing could be more wildly impractical than an education designed to prepare them for specific vocations or professions or to facilitate their adjustment to the world as it is. To be practical, an education should prepare a man for work that doesn't yet exist and whose nature cannot even be imagined. This can be done only by teaching people how to learn, by giving them the kind of intellectual discipline that will enable them to apply man's accumulated wisdom to new problems as they arise, the kind of wisdom that will enable them to *recognize* new problems as they

arise.
-*CHARLES E. SILBERMAN, American editor, author*

The condition of the true artisan, perhaps, is most nearly akin to the gifted schoolteacher's: an all but anonymous calling that allows for mastery, even for a sort of genius, but rarely for fame, applause, or wealth, whose chief reward must be the mere superlative doing of the thing.
-*JOHN BARTH, American novelist*

Modern cynics and skeptics see no harm in paying those to whom they entrust the minds of their children a smaller wage than is paid to those to whom they entrust the care of their plumbing.
-*JOHN F. KENNEDY, 35th President of the United States (1917 - 1963)*

At the desk where I sit, I have learned one great truth. The answer for all our national problems - the answer for all the problems of the world - comes to a single word. That word is "education."
-*LYNDON B. JOHNSON, 36th President of the United States (1908 - 1973)*

We must open the doors of opportunity. But we must also equip our people to walk through those doors.
-*LYNDON B. JOHNSON*

Education is not the means of showing people how to get what they want. Education is an exercise by means of which enough men, it is hoped, will learn to want what is worth having.
-*RONALD REAGAN, 40th President of the United States*

When I need some information, my first thought is still of a book - and the library. When I have an inquiry, I still turn first to the telephone. The latter has served with improvement but no basic change for rather more than a century; books have survived for far longer. They will endure the information revolution; they will not be lost on that superhighway. The problem will still be finding the relevant and sorting out the true from the false. Our problem, to repeat, is not a shortage of information or in its transfer. It is in deciding what is useful and what is right.

*-JOHN KENNETH GALBRAITH, American economist*

Educators insist computers are valuable in school but admit they can't say yet whether technology actually improves achievement or merely lays the foundation to learn by sparking imagination, motivation, and enthusiasm.

... "The use of technology will never replace the traditional skills that students need to have - whether we're talking about reading, mathematics or science," says Linda Roberts of the U.S. Department of Education. "But I would argue that this is a new basic, a new literacy that complements the traditional curriculum."

Don Tapscott, author of *Growing Up Digital: The Rise of the Net Generation*, agrees, noting that the Net Generation is beginning to think, learn, work, play, communicate, shop and create in fundamentally different ways from their parents. Tapscott says computers and the Net are simply preconditions for moving to a new way to learn.

*-TAMARA HENRY, American writer. In USA TODAY*

A coach's discipline is different in kind from

a regular teacher's, because the coach wants the same thing the class wants - to win. There is no such clear goal for a regular teacher. Whether a student pays attention in class is pretty much up to him. It's a one-on-one affair between student and authority figure, with the student, if anything, holding the edge, surrounded by allies, most of whom have no special desire to go where the teacher is going and are only too happy to keep the pace slow.

But the coach starts out with his class already at white heat: these kids will work for him to degree unimaginable in a classroom, and with an eagerness and excitement that only creative kids in school ever experience. An English teacher looking at a football drill or pep rally must overflow with envy: if he could capture just one ounce of such energy for his poetry class, his students would be the wonder of the nation. But in the classroom, the teacher is the only one who works as hard as that - like a coach doing solitary pushups and kneebends, while the students look on idly, waiting for something to interest them.

*-WILFRED SHEED, American essayist, novelist*

If you believe that no one was ever corrrupted by a book, you have also to believe that no one was ever improved by a book, (or a play or a movie). You have to believe, in other words, that all art is morally trivial and that, consequently, all education is morally irrelevant.

*-IRVING KRISTOL, American editor, educator*

I have never met anyone who was funny and stupid.

*-BARBARA WALTERS, American journalist, television personality*

As it now stands, our classrooms tend to reflect conditions prevailing in the larger society, e.g., the disintegration of the nuclear family, the high degree of mobility - and sometimes rootlessness - that characterizes our society, and the erosion of community life. It is not easy for teachers to motivate students to learn if learning is not respected in the home. If at home or in the community the work of the school is regarded with indifference, then whatever the level of dedication, commitment and ability possessed by the teachers, the salvage rate will be low.

In contrast, if students come principally from homes where there are books, a respect for education and learning, and reasonable expectations about how students spend their time, the salvage rate will be much higher. Although students from these different home enviroments may have equal opportunity on paper, or under the law, there is no equality in reality. Schools cannot solve these problems alone, nor should they be expected to. The failures and shortcomings of our society cannot be placed at the doorstep of the nation's schools. They have a role to play, but they cannot play it on a field where only the schools have fielded a team.

*-DAVID GARDNER, American educator*

If the massive numbers of college students reflected a national boom in love of learning and a prevalent yen for self-improvement, America's investment in the classroom might make sense. These are introspective qualities that can enrich any society in ways beyond the material. But one need look no further than the curricular wars to understand that most students are not looking to broaden their spiritual or intellectual horizons. ... Students are demanding courses that reflect and affirm their own identities in the most literal way. Rather than read a Greek dramatist of 2,000 years ago and thrill to the discovery that some ideas and emotions are universal, many insist on reading writers of their own gender or ethnicity or sexual preference, ideally writers of the present or the recent past.

*-WILLIAM A. HENRY III, American writer, critic (1950 - 1994)*

I've seen kids, whose behavior and lack of academic progress tormented their parents and teachers, finally catch fire and go on to be successes. And I've seen perfect high school students, whose parents would constantly boast about them, collapse later and never really hook on in the real world.

America is a country of endless chances when it comes to education. Even the worst case scenario is never that bad. The child who totally messes up in grammer school can expunge his record with a good high school performance. The kid who is a disaster in high school can have his transcript erased by hard work at a junior college and then can transfer to a four year school.

We as parents, have to remember our own paths: the false starts, the blunders, the second and third chances that were all a part of getting where we are, and to trust that our children - guided but not overwhelmed by us - will have the same resilience.

*-PATRICK WELSH, American teacher, writer*

Even the most enlightened reforms will not make

much of a difference until American education deals with the basic philosophical bind in which it is trapped - namely, how do we insist that everyone is entitled to a publc education and still uphold the moral and academic standards that are essential if schools are going to work. The reformers talk a great deal about standards, but most high schools and colleges back off when it comes to the crunch. We are obsessed about the drop-out rate in our high schools but refuse to admit, in spite of mounting evidence everywhere, that the kick-out rate must go up if our schools are going to be serious institutions rather than "the place I go to be with my friends," as so many kids now see them.  *-PATRICK WELSH*

Many Americans believe their schools are doing a satisfactory job, mostly because their children are able to go on to college. What Americans don't realize is that their kids get into college because many colleges don't have high standards. There is a college for just about every achievement level, from barely passable to first rate. Ability to pay, not achievement, is the main admissions criterion in all too many of our higher education institutions. And if one looks at the low achievement levels in high school and the high school attendance rates, it's clear that the overwhelming majority of our students are getting their high-school education in college.
*-ALBERT SHANKER, President, American Federation of Teachers (1928 - 1997)*

We desperately need to recover a sense of the fundamental purpose of education, which is to provide for the intellectual and moral education of the young. From the ancient Greeks to the founding fathers, moral instruction was *the* central task of education. "If you ask what is the good of education," Plato said, "the answer is easy - that education makes good men, and that good men act nobly." Jefferson believed that education should aim at improving one's "morals" and "faculties." And of education, John Locke said this, "Tis virtue that we aim at, hard virtue, and the subtle arts of shifting." Until a quarter-century or so ago, this consensus was so deep as to go virtually unchallenged. Having departed from this time-honored belief, we are now reaping the whirlwind. And so we talk not about education as the architecture of souls, but about "skills facilitation" and "self-esteem" and about being "comfortable with ourselves."

*- WILLIAM BENNETT, American educator, philosopher*

It is the aim of education to teach the citizen that he must first of all rule himself.

*- WINTHROP ALDRICH, American writer*

It isn't what people think that is important, but the reason they think what they think.

*- EUGENE IONESCO, French playwright*

The world is divided into people who think they are right.

*- UNKNOWN*

Good judgement comes from experience, and experience comes from bad judgement.

*- UNKNOWN*

It is one thing to recognize the right - and responsibility - of parents to educate their children as members of a family, and quite another to claim this right of familial education extends to a right of parents to insulate their children from exposure to ways of life or thinking that conflict with their own. Children are not simply the property or the responsibility of their parents, they are also our future citizens.

-*AMY GUTMANN, American educator*

Schools have a much greater capacity than most parents and voluntary associations for teaching children to reason out loud about disagreements that arise in democratic politics and to understand the political morality appropriate to a democracy. Since many of the virtues defended by conservatives - honesty, respect for law, fairness, self-discipline - are necessary for students to appreciate the advantages of democratic politics, schools should do their best to inculcate these virtues. But if character is, as Noah Webster defines it, "strength of mind, individuality, independence, moral quality," then teaching students how to defend democracy, to think about the demands of fairness, and to reason about our political disagreements is no less essential to developing moral character than instilling the less intellectual virtues of fidelity, kindness, respect for law, diligence and self-discipline. Schools have more of a comparative advantage in teaching the former set of virtues than they do in teaching the latter.   -*AMY GUTMANN*

The more you read, the smarter you grow. The smarter you grow, the longer you stay in school. The longer you stay in school, the more money you earn.

The more you earn, the better your children will do in school. So if you hook a child with reading, you influence not only his future but also that of the next generation.
-*JIM TRELEASE,* American author

Today, education is perhaps the most important function of state and local governments. Compulsory school attendance laws and the great expenditures for education both demonstrate our recognition of the importance of education to our democratic society. It is required in the performance of our most basic public responsibilities, even service in the armed forces. It is the very foundation of good citizenship. Today, it is a principal instrument in awakening the child to cultural values, in preparing him for later professional training, and in helping him to adjust normally to his environment. In these days, it is doubtful that any child may reasonably be expected to succeed in life if he is denied the opportunity of an education. Such an opportunity, where the state has undertaken to provide it, is a right which must be made available to all on equal terms.
-*U.S. SUPREME COURT,* in Brown v. Board of Education. 1954

Since democratic schools are impossible without an aware and supportive public, defending them requires us to tell the public the truth. Schools never did the needed job for many people. Most Americans didn't get the education they deserved. The nation tolerated it as long as the economy offered the poorly educated a measure of dignity and hope through unskilled or semi-skilled industrial work. But the fact remains that schools sold short those Americans who were not members of the elite. Schools did the job they were asked to do - but they've never before done what is needed today. If America can commit itself to this next task - educating all children well - the historic promise of free public schooling will finally, for the first time, be fulfilled.

-*DEBORAH MEIER*, American writer

# CHAPTER - 6

## *WORK*

### ***

Bowmen bend their bows when they wish to shoot; unbrace them when the shooting is over. Were they kept strung they would break, and fail the archer in time of need. So it is with men. If they give themselves constantly to serious work, and never indulge awhile in pastime or sport, they lose their senses, and become mad or moody.

-*HERODOTUS, Greek historian (c.484 - c.425 B.C.)*

Nothing is so certain as that the evils of idleness can be shaken off by hard work.

-*SENECA, Roman statesman, philosopher (c.4 B.C. - 65 A.D.)*

One must not always think so much about what one should do, but rather what one should be. Our works do not ennoble us; but we must ennoble our works.

-*MEISTER ECKEHART, German theologian (c.1260 - 1328)*

This noble precept is often cited by Plato: "Do thine own work, and know thyself." Each of these two parts generally cover the whole duty of man, and each includes the other. He who will do his own work well, discovers that his first lesson is to know himself, and what is his duty.

-*MICHEL DE MONTAIGNE, French moralist, essayist (1533 - 1592)*

Being is something we hold dear, and being consists in movement and action. Wherefore each man in some sort exists in his work.  -*MICHEL DE MONTAIGNE*

One man is no more than another if he does no more than another.
-*MIGUEL DE CERVANTES, Spanish novelist (1547 - 1616)*

If all the year were playing holidays,
To sport would be as tedious as to work.
-*WILLIAM SHAKESPEARE, English playwright, poet (1564 - 1616)*

Wheras many men, by accident inevitable, become unable to maintain themselves by their labor, they ought not to be left to the charity of private person, but to be provided for, as far forth as the necessities of nature require, by the laws of the Commonwealth. For as it is uncharitableness in any man to neglect the impotent; so it is in the sovereign of a Commonwealth, to expose them to the hazard of such uncertain charity.
But for such as have strong bodies the case is otherwise; they are to be forced to work; and to avoid the excuse of not finding employment, there ought to be such laws as may encourage all manner of arts; as navigation, agriculture, fishing, and all manners of manufacture that require labor.
-*THOMAS HOBBES, English philosopher (1588 - 1679)*

The labor of the body relieves us from the fatigues of the mind; and this it is which forms the happiness of the poor.
-*FRANÇOIS DE LA ROCHEFOUCAULD, French moralist (1613 - 168)*

It is not so strange as, perhaps, before

consideration it may appear, that the property of labour should be able to overbalance the community of land, for it is labour indeed that puts the difference of value on everything; and let anyone consider what the difference is between an acre of land planted with tobacco or sugar, sown with wheat or barley, and an acre of the same land lying in common without any husbandry upon it, and he will find that the improvement of labour makes the far greater part of the value.

I think it will be but a very modest computation to say, that of the products of the earth useful to the life of man, nine-tenths are the effects of labour. Nay, if we will rightly estimate things as they come to our use, and cast up the several expenses about them - what in them is purely owing to Nature and what to labour - we shall find that in most of them ninety-nine hundredths are wholly to be put on the account of labour.

*-JOHN LOCKE, English philosopher (1632 - 1704)*

There are only two ways by which to rise in this world, either by one's own industry or by the stupidity of others.

*-JEAN DE LA BRUYÈRE, French writer, moralist (1645 - 1696)*

Work keeps us from three great evils, boredom, vice, and need.

*-VOLTAIRE, French author, philosopher (1694 - 1778)*

When men are employed, they are best contented; for on the days they worked they were good-natured and cheerful, and, with the consciousness of having done a good day's work, they spent the evening jollily; but

on our idle days they were mutinous and quarrelsom.
-*BEN FRANKLIN, American statesman, writer, scientist (1706 - 1790)*

I never knew a man who was good at making excuses who was good at anything else. -*BEN FRANKLIN*

Excellence in any department can be attained only by labor of a lifetime; it is not to be purchased at a lesser price.
-*SAMUEL JOHNSON, English lexicographer, writer (1709 - 1784)*

Great labour, either of mind or body, continued for several days together, is in most men naturally followed by a great desire of relaxation, which, if not restrained by force or by some strong necessity, is almost irresistable. It is the call of nature, which requires to be relieved by some indulgence, sometimes of ease only, but sometimes, too, of dissipation and diversion.
-*ADAM SMITH, Scottish economist (1723 - 1790)*

People of the same trade seldom meet together but the conversation ends in a conspiracy against the public, or in some diversion to raise prices.
-*ADAM SMITH*

Excellence is never granted to man, but as a reward of labor. It argues, indeed, no small strength of mind to persevere in the habits of industry without the pleasure of perceiving those advantages, which, like the hand of a clock, while they make hourly approaches to their point, yet proceed so slowly as to escape observation.
-*JOSHUA REYNOLDS, English painter (1723 - 1792)*

I'm a great believer in luck, and I find the harder I work the more I have of it.
-*THOMAS JEFFERSON, 3rd President of the United States (1743 - 1826)*

Everyone loves his own country, customs, language, wife, children, not because they are the best in the world, but because they are his established property, and he loves in them himself, and the labor he has bestowed on them.
-*JOHANN GOTTFRIED VON HERDER, German cleric, writer (1744 - 1803)*

One must *be* something to be able to *do* something.
-*JOHANN WOLFGANG VON GOETHE, German poet, playwright (1749 - 1832)*

Men give me some credit for genius. All the genius I have lies just in this: when I have a subject in hand, I study it profoundly. Day and night it is before me. I explore it in all its bearings. My mind becomes pervaded with it. Then the effort which I make the People are pleased to call the fruit of genius. It is the fruit of labor and thought.
-*ALEXANDER HAMILTON, American statesman (1755 - 1804)*

Labour, like all other things which are purchased and sold, has its natural and its market price. ... The market price of labour is the price which is really paid for it, from the natural operation of the proportion of the supply to the demand.
-*DAVID RICARDO, English economist (1772 - 1823)*

There is no way of keeping profits up but by keeping wages down.   -*DAVID RICARDO*

Employment gives health, sobriety, and morals. Constant employment and well-paid labor produce, in

a country like ours, general prosperity, content, and cheerfulness.
*-DANIEL WEBSTER, American lawyer, statesman, orator (1782 - 1852)*

"A fair day's wages for a fair day's work"; it is as just a demand as governed men ever made of governing. It is the everlasting right of man.
*- THOMAS CARLYLE, Scottish essayist, historian (1795 - 1881)*

Blessed is he who has found his work; let him ask no other blessedness. He has a work, a life-purpose; he has found it and will follow it. *-THOMAS CARLYLE*

Every man's task is his life-preserver.
*- GEORGE BARRELL EMERSON, American educator (1797 - 1881)*

Every really able man, in whatever direction he work, if you talk sincerely with him, considers his work, however much admired, as far short of what it should be.
*-RALPH WALDO EMERSON, American essayist, poet (1803 - 1882)*

The crowning fortune of a man is to be born with a bias to some pursuit which finds him in employment and happiness. *-RALPH WALDO EMERSON*

The crime which bankrupts men and states is jobwork - declining from your main design, to serve a turn here or there. *-RALPH WALDO EMERSON*

When a workman is unceasingly and exclusively engaged in the fabrication of one thing, he ultimately does his work with singular dexterity; but at the same time he loses the general faculty of applying his mind to the direction of the work. He every day becomes more adroit and less industrious; so that it may be said of him that in proportion as the workman improves, the man is degraded. What can be expected of a man who has spent twenty years of his life in making heads for pins? And to what can that mighty human intelligence which has so often stirred the world be applied in him except it be to investigate the best method of making pins' heads? When a workman has spent a considerable portion of his existence in this manner, his thoughts are forever set upon the object of his daily toil; his body has contracted certain fixed habits, which it can never shake off; in a word, he no longer belongs to himself, but to the calling that he has chosen.

*-ALEXIS DE TOCQUEVILLE, French politician, historian, writer (1805 - 1859)*

Inasmuch as most good things are produced by labor, it follows that all such things of right belong to those whose labor has produced them. But it has so happened in all the ages of the world, that some have labored, and others have, without labor, enjoyed a large proportion of the fruits. This is wrong, and should not continue. To secure to each laborer the whole product of his labor, or as nearly as possible, is a most worthy object of any good government.

*-ABRAHAM LINCOLN, 16th President of the United States (1809 - 1865)*

It is assumed that labor is available only in conection with capital; that nobody labors unless somebody else, owning capital, somehow by the use of it, induces him to labor. This assumed, it is next considered whether it is best that capital shall hire laborers, and thus induce them to work by their consent. Having proceeded so far, it is naturally concluded that all laborers are either hired laborers or what we call slaves.

Now, there is no such relation between capital and labor as here assumed. ... Labor is prior to and independent of capital. Capital is only the fruit of labor and could never have existed if labor had not first existed. Labor is the superior of capital, and deserves much the higher consideration.
*-ABRAHAM LINCOLN*

My father taught me to work, but not to love it. I never did like to work, and I don't deny it. I'd rather read, tell stories, crack jokes, talk, laugh - anything but work.  *-ABRAHAM LINCOLN*

Manual labour, though an unavoidable duty, though designed as a blessing, and naturally both a pleasure and a dignity, is often abused, till, by its terrible excess, it becomes really a punishment and a curse. It is only a proper amount of work that is a blessing. Too much of it wears out the body before its time; cripples the mind, debases the soul, blunts the senses and chills the affections. It makes a man a spinning-jenny, or a ploughing-machine, and not "a being of a large discourse, that looks before and after." He ceases to be a man, and becomes a thing.
*- THEODORE PARKER, American clergyman (1810 - 1860)*

I cannot forget that the laboring class, so-called, must, like any other, stand up for its rights, or be content to see them trampled underfoot; and that the strength given it by organization, superintended upon numbers, is its only effectual defense against the else unchecked tyranny of capital, greedy for profit and reckless of others' rights. The power developed by combination may be abused, like any other power; but labor is helpless and a prey without it.

-*HORACE GREELEY, American journalist, political leader (1811 - 1872)*

Most men, even in this comparatively free country, through mere ignorance and mistake, are so occupied with the factitious cares and superfluously coarse labors of life that its finer fruits cannot be plucked by them. Their fingers, from excessive toils, are too clumsy and tremble too much for that.

-*HENRY DAVID THOREAU, American essayist, naturalist (1817 - 1862)*

Business! I think there is nothing - not even crime - more opposed to poetry, to philosophy, to life itself, than this incessant business.   -*HENRY DAVID THOREAU*

It is not enough to be industrious - so are the ants. What are you industrious about?

-*HENRY DAVID THOREAU*

In proportion as the bourgeoisie, i.e. capital, is developed, in the same proportion is the proletariat, the modern working class, developed - a class of laborers, who live only so long as they find work, and who find work only so long as their labour increases capital. These labourers, who must sell themselves piecemeal, are a commodity like every other article of commerce, and are consequently exposed to all the vicissitudes of competition, to all the fluctuations of the market.

-*KARL MARX, German philosopher, economist, socialist (1818 - 1883)*

In order that people may be happy in their work, these three things are needed: They must be fit for it.

---

They must not do too much of it. And they must have a sense of success in it.
*-JOHN RUSKIN, English author (1819 - 1900)*

God gives every bird its food, but he does not throw it into the nest.
*-J.G. HOLLAND, American editor, author (1819 - 1881)*

As a remedy against all ills - poverty, sickness, and melancholy - only one thing is absolutely necessary: a liking for work.
*-CHARLES BAUDELAIRE, French poet (1821 - 1867)*

Business is really more agreeable than pleasure; it interests the whole mind, the aggregate nature of man, more continuously, and more deeply. But it does not *look* as if it did.
*-WALTER BAGEHOT, English economist, journalist (1826 - 1877)*

All men's instincts, all their impulses in life, are efforts to increase their freedom. Wealth and poverty, health and disease, culture and ignorance, labor and leisure, repletion and hunger, virtue and vice, are all only terms for greater or less degree of freedom.
*-LEO TOLSTOY, Russian writer (1828 - 1910)*

The more is given the less the people will work for themselves, and the less they work the more their poverty will increase.   *-LEO TOLSTOY*

The Bible legend tells us that the absence of labor - idleness - was a condition of the first man's blessedness before the Fall. Fallen man has retained a love of idleness, but the curse weighs on the race

not only because we have to seek our bread in the sweat of our brows, but because our moral nature is such that we cannot be both idle and at ease. An inner voice tells us we are in the wrong if we are idle. If man could find a state in which he felt that though idle he was fulfilling his duty, he would have found one of the conditions of man's primitive blessedness.
*-LEO TOLSTOY*

Money is the symbol of duty, it is the sacrament of having done for mankind that which mankind wanted.
*-SAMUEL BUTLER, English writer (1835 - 1902)*

I can hire one-half the working class to kill the other half.
*-JAY GOULD, American businessman (1836 - 1892)*

So long as all the increased wealth which modern progress brings goes but to build up great fortunes, to increase luxury and make sharper the contrast between the House of Have and the House of Want, progress is not real and cannot be permanent.
*-HENRY GEORGE, American economist, writer (1839 - 1897)*

It is not labor in itself that is repugnant to man; it is not the natural necessity for exertion which is a curse. It is only labor which produces nothing - exertion of which he cannot see the result.

The fact is that the work which improves the condition of mankind, the work which extends knowledge and increases power and enriches literature, and elevates thought, is not done to secure a living. It is not the work of slaves, driven to their task either by the lash of a master or by animal necessities. It is the work of men who perform it for their own sake, and not that they may get more to eat or drink, or wear, or display. In a state of society where want is abolished, work of this sort could be enormously increased. -*HENRY GEORGE*

Man must be doing something, or fancy that he is doing something, for in him throbs the creative impulse; the mere basker in the sunshine is not a natural, but an abnormal man. -*HENRY GEORGE*

Few persons realize how much of their happiness is dependent upon their work, upon the fact that they are kept busy and not left to feed upon themselves. Happiness comes most to persons who seek her least, and think least about it. It is not an object to be sought, it is a state to be induced. It must follow and not lead. It must overtake you, and not you overtake it. How important is health to happiness, yet the best promoter of health is *something to do.* Blessed is the man who has some congenial work, some occupation in which he can put his heart, and which affords a complete outlet to all the forces there are in him.
-*JOHN BURROUGHS, American naturalist (1837 - 1921)*

We need some imaginative stimulus, some not impossible ideal such as may shape vague hope, and transform it into effective desire, to carry us year after year, without disgust, through the routine work which is so large a part of life.
-*WALTER PATER, English essayist, critic (1839 - 1894)*

One of the eternal conflicts of which life is made up is that between the effort of every man to get the

most he can for his services, and that of society, disguised under the name of capital, to get his services for the least possible return.
-*OLIVER WENDELL HOLMES, JR., U.S. Supreme Court Justice (1841 - 1935)*

Men seldom die of hard work; activity is God's medicine. The highest genius is willingness and ability to do hard work. Any other conception of genius makes it a doubtful, if not a dangerous possession.
-*ROBERT MACARTHUR, American clergyman (1841 - 1923)*

There is no passion like that of a functionary for his function.
-*GEORGES CLEMENCEAU, French politician (1841 - 1929)*

The right and interests of laboring men will be protected and cared for - not by the labor agitators but by the Christian men to whom God in his infinite wisdom has given control of the property interests of this country.
-*GEORGE F. BAER, American industrialist (1842 - 1914)*

I never did anything worth doing by accident; nor did any of my inventions come by accident; they came by work.
-*THOMAS EDISON, American inventor (1847 - 1931)*

When a little capital or a new idea was enough to start a man in business for himself, workingmen were constantly becoming employers and there was no hard and fast line between the two classes. Labor unions were needless then, and general strikes were out of the question. But when the era of small concerns with small capital was succeeded by that of

the great aggregations of capital, all this was changed. The individual laborer, who had been relatively important to the small employer, was reduced to insignificance and powerlessness over against the great corporation, while at the same time the way upward to the grade of empoyer was closed to him. Self-defense drove him to union with his fellows.
-*EDWARD BELLAMY, American author (1850 - 1898)*

To protect the workers in their inalienable rights to a higher and better life; to protect them, not only as equals before the law, but also in their health, their homes, their firesides, their liberties as men, as workers, and as citizens; to overcome and conquer prejudices and antagonism; to secure to them the right to life, and the opportunity to maintain that life; the right to be full sharers in the abundance which is the result of their brain and brawn, and the civilization of which they are the founders and the mainstay. The attainment of these is the glorious mission of the trade unions.
-*SAMUEL GOMPERS, American labor leader (1850 - 1924)*

Show me the country in which there are no strikes and I'll show you that country in which there is no liberty. -*SAMUEL GOMPERS*

The worst crime against working people is a company which fails to operate at a profit.
-*SAMUEL GOMPERS*

As if a man's soul were not too small to begin with, they have dwarfed and narrowed theirs by a life of all

work and no play; until here they are at forty, with a listless attention, a mind vacant of all material of amusement, and not one thought to rub against another, while they wait for the train.
-*ROBERT LEWIS STEVENSON, Scottish novelist, essayist (1850 - 1894)*

The fact is, that civilization requires slaves. The Greeks were quite right there. Unless there are slaves to do the ugly, horrible, uninteresting work, culture and contemplation become almost impossible. Human slavery is wrong, insecure, and demoralizing. On mechanical slavery, on the slavery of the machine, the future of the world depends.
-*OSCAR WILDE, Irish poet, playwright, wit (1854 - 1900)*

Work is the refuge of people who have nothing better to do.    -*OSCAR WILDE*

No other technique for the conduct of life attaches the individual so firmly to reality as laying emphasis on work; for his work at least gives him a secure place in a portion of reality, in the human community.
-*SIGMUND FREUD, Austrian neurologist, psychoanalyst (1856 - 1939)*

Any man who has a job has a chance.
-*ELBERT HUBBARD, American writer, publisher (1856 - 1915)*

One machine can do the work of fifty ordinary men. No machine can do the work of one extraordinary man.    -*ELBERT HUBBARD*

The world cares very little about what a man or woman knows; it is what the man or woman is able to

do that counts.
-*BOOKER T. WASHINGTON, American educator, writer (1856 - 1915)*

The employer puts his money into business and the workman his life. The one has as much right as the other to regulate that business.
-*CLARENCE DARROW, American lawyer (1857 - 1938)*

If I were a factory employee, a working man on the railroad, or a wage earner of any sort, I would undoubtedly join the union of my trade. If I disapproved of its policy, I would join in order to fight that policy; if the union leaders were dishonest, I would join in order to put them out. I believe in the union and I believe that all men who are benefited by the union are morally bound to help to the extent of their powers in the common interests advanced by the union.
-*THEODORE ROOSEVELT, 26th President of the United States (1858 - 1919)*

I don't pity any man who does hard work worth doing. I admire him. I pity the creature who does not work, at whichever end of the social scale he may regard himself as being.   -*THEODORE ROOSEVELT*

I don't pay good wages because I have a lot of money; I have a lot of money because I pay good wages.
-*ROBERT BOSCH, German inventor, industrialist (1861 - 1942)*

It is not work that men object to, but the element of drudgery. We must drive out drudgery wherever we find it. We shall never be wholly civilized until we remove the treadmill from the daily job.
-*HENRY FORD, American industrialist (1863 - 1947)*

There is nothing in saving money. The thing to do with it is to put it back into yourself, into your work, into the thing that is important, into whatever you are so much interested in that it is more important than money.   *-HENRY FORD*

The dictionary is the only place where success comes before work.
*-ARTHUR BRISBANE, American journalist (1864 - 1936)*

Failure is not the only punishment for laziness; there is also the success of others.
*-JULES RENARD, French writer (1864 - 1910)*

The test of a vocation is the love of the drudgery it involves.
*-LOGAN PEARSALL SMITH, American essayist (1865 - 1946)*

A man with a career can have no time to waste upon his wife and friends; he has to devote it wholly to his enemies.
*-JOHN OLIVER HOBBES, English novelist, dramatist (1867 - 1906)*

The return from your work must be the satisfaction which that work brings you and the world's need of that work. With this, life is heaven, or as near heaven as you can get. Without this - with work which you despise, which bores you, and which the world does not need - this life is hell.
*- W.E.B. DU BOIS, American educator, writer (1868 - 1963)*

All this life is senseless and tragic in which the endless slaving labor of one man constantly goes to supply another with more bread than he can use.
*-MAXIM GORKY, Russian novelist, playwright (1868 - 1936)*

The manager's brains are under the workman's cap.
- *WILLIAM D. HAYWOOD, American labor leader (1869 - 1928)*

As to the great mass of working girls and women, how much independence is gained if the narrowness and lack of freedom of the home are exchanged for the narrowness and lack of freedom of the factory, sweatshop, department store, or office?
- *EMMA GOLDMAN, American editor, activist, anarchist (1869 - 1940)*

It is easy to believe that life is long and one's gifts are vast - easy at the beginning, that is. But the limits of life grow more evident; it becomes clear that great work can be done rarely, if at all.
- *ALFRED ADLER, Austrian psychologist (1870 - 1937)*

Society can progress only if men's labors show a profit - if they yield more than is put in.
- *BERNARD M. BARUCH, American businessman, diplomat (1870 - 1965)*

Work is of two kinds: first, altering the position of matter at or near the earth's surface relatively to other such matter; second, telling other people to do so. The first kind is unpleasant and ill paid; the second is pleasant and highly paid.
- *BERTRAND RUSSELL, English philosopher (1872 - 1970)*

Skilled work, of no matter what kind, is only done well by those who take a certain pleasure in it, quite apart from its utility, either to themselves in earning a living, or to the world through its outcome.
- *BERTRAND RUSSELL*

The primary aim of all government regulation of the economic life of the community should be, not to

supplant the system of private economic enterprise, but to make it work.
-*CARL BECKER,  American historian (1873 - 1945)*

Some regard private enterprise as if it were a predatory tiger to be shot. Others look upon it as a cow that they can milk. Only a handful see it for what it really is - the strong horse that pulls the whole cart.
-*WINSTON CHURCHILL,  Prime Minister of Great Britain, author (1874 - 1965)*

Too many Americans are dependent for everything on a 'job'. Americans don't own their high standard of living, they only rent it, which means that they are likely to lose it suddenly as so many did in the Depression.
-*GERTRUDE STEIN,  American author (1874 - 1946)*

It is difficult to get a man to understand something when his salary depends upon his not understanding it.
-*UPTON SINCLAIR,  American writer, reformer (1878 - 1968)*

When a man tells you he got rich through hard work, ask him *whose*?
-*DON MARQUIS,  American journalist (1878 - 1937)*

The work of the working people, and nothing else, produces the wealth, which, by some hocus-pocus arrangement, is transferred to me, leaving them bare. While they support me in splendid style, what do I do for them? Let the candid upholder of the present order answer, for I am not aware of doing anything for them.
-*JOSEPH PATTERSON,  American publisher (1879 - 1946)*

How do I work? I grope.
-*ALBERT EINSTEIN, American physicist (1879 - 1955)*

Any man with a superior air, the intelligence of a stockbroker, and the resolution of a hat-check girl can cadge enough money, in this glorious republic of morons, to make life soft for him.
-*H.L. MENCKEN, American editor, satirist (1880 - 1956)*

Wealth in modern societies is distributed according to opportunity.
-*RICHARD TAWNEY, English economic historian (1880 - 1962)*

The program of the CIO has a two-fold purpose. The first is to bring security and liberty to those who work for their living. In achieving this it is our conviction that we implement the second purpose, the creation of economic and social stability. It is only upon such economic stability that a lasting democratic form of government can exist.
-*JOHN L. LEWIS, American labor leader (1880 - 1969)*

Labor Day symbolizes our determination to achieve an economic freedom for the average man which will give his political freedom reality.
-*FRANKLIN D. ROOSEVELT, 32nd President of the United States (1882 - 1945)*

I see an America where the workers are really free and through their great unions, undominated by any outside force or any dictator within, can take their proper place at the council tables with the owners and managers of business; where the dignity and security of the working man and woman are guaranteed by their strength and fortified by the safeguards of law.   -*FRANKLIN D. ROOSEVELT*

No business which depends for its existence on paying less than living wages to its workers has any right to continue in this country. By living wages I mean more than a bare subsistence level - I mean the wages of decent living.   *-FRANKLIN D. ROOSEVELT*

Happiness lies not in the mere possession of money; it lies in the joy of achievement, in the thrill of creative effort. The joy and moral stimulation of work no longer must be forgotten in the mad chase of evanescent profits.   *-FRANKLIN D. ROOSEVELT*

Your plan for work and happiness should be big, imaginative and daring. Strike out boldly for the things you honestly want more than anything else in the world. The mistake is to put your sights too low, not to raise them too high. The definite, faraway goal will supercharge your whole body and spirit; it will awaken your mind and spirit; it will awaken your mind and creative imagination, and put meaning into otherwise lowly step-by-step tasks you must go through in order to attain your final success.
*-HENRY J. KAISER, American industrialist (1882 - 1967)*

A life spent in constant labor is a life wasted, save a man be such a fool as to regard a fulsome obituary as an ample reward.
*-GEORGE NATHAN, American writer, critic (1882 - 1958)*

An *unemployed* existence is a worse negation of life than death itself. Because to live means to have something definite to do - a mission to fulfill - and in the measure in which we avoid setting our life to something, we make it empty. Human life, by its

very nature, has to be dedicated to something.
-*JOSE ORTEGA Y GASSET, Spanish philosopher (1883 - 1955)*

Work and Love - these are the basics. Without them there is neurosis.
-*THEODOR REIK, American psychologist (1888 - 1969)*

When the accumulation of wealth is no longer of high social importance, there will be great changes in the code of morals. We shall be able to rid ourselves of many of the psuedo-moral principles which have hag-ridden us for two-hundred years, by which we have exalted some of the most distasteful of human qualities into the position of highest virtues.
-*JOHN MAYNARD KEYNES, English economist (1883 - 1946)*

Most people like hard work. Particularly when they are paying for it.
-*FRANKLIN P. JONES, American lawyer (1887 - 1929)*

Each honest calling, each walk of life, has its own elite, its own aristocracy based upon excellence of performance.
-*JAMES BRYANT CONANT, American educator (1893 - 1978)*

A society that gives to one class all the opportunities for leisure, and to another all the burdens of work, dooms both classes to spiritual sterility.
-*LEWIS MUMFORD, American author, cultural historian (1895 - 1990)*

The cleverly expressed opposite of any generally accepted idea is worth a fortune to somebody.
-*F. SCOTT FITZGERALD, American novelist (1896 - 1940)*

Whatever women do they must do twice as well as

men to be thought half as good.  Luckily, this is not difficult.
-*CHARLOTTE WHITTEN, Canadian journalist, author, social worker (1896 - 1975)*

What most people don't seem to realize is that there is just as much money to be made out of the wreckage of a civilization as from the upbuilding of one.
-*MARGARET MITCHELL, American novelist (1900 - 1949)*

If you mean by capitalism the God-given right of a few big corporations to make all the decisions that will affect millions of workers and consumers and to exclude everyone else from discussing and examining those decisions, then the unions are threatening capitalism.
-*MAX LERNER, American newspaper columnist (1902 - 1992)*

If you don't want to work you have to work to earn enough money so that you won't have to work.
-*OGDEN NASH, American humorist, poet (1902 - 1971)*

People who work sitting down get paid more than people who work standing up.    *-OGDEN NASH*

A man who works with his hands is a laborer; a man who works with his hands and his brain is a craftsman; but a man who works with his hands and his brain and his heart is an artist.
-*LOUIS NIZER, English lawyer, author (1902 - 1994)*

Our greatest weariness comes from work not done.
-*ERIC HOFFER, American author, philosopher (1902 - 1983)*

Work expands so as to fill the time available for its

completion. The thing to be done swells in importance and complexity in a direct ratio with the time to be spent.

-*CYRIL PARKINSON, English historian, author (1909 - 1993)*

So much of what we call management consists in making it difficult for people to work.

-*PETER DRUCKER, American writer, consultant*

If you aren't fired with enthusiasm, you'll be fired with enthusiasm.

-*VINCE LOMBARDI, American football coach (1913 - 1970)*

It's easy to have faith in yourself and have discipline when you're a winner, when you're number one. What you got to have is faith and discipline when you're not a winner.   -*VINCE LOMBARDI*

Work is accomplished by those employees who have not yet reached their level of incompetence. ... In a hierarchy, every employee tends to rise to his level of incompetence; the cream rises until it sours.

-*LAURENCE J. PETER, Canadian-born American writer*

It is easy to fool yourself. It is possible to fool the people you work for. It is more difficult to fool the people you work with. But it is almost impossible to fool the people who work under you.

-*HARRY B. THAYER, American businessman*

When did I make my greatest hiring mistakes? When I put intelligence and energy ahead of morality. In choosing people for top positions, you have to try to make sure that they have a clear sense of what is right and wrong, a willingness to be truthful, the courage to say what they think and to do what they think is right, even if the politics mitigate against that. This is the quality that really should be at the top.

*- W. MICHAEL BLUMENTHAL, American businessman*

Executives in their 30s and 40s are valuable because they're eager and keen and aware of what can, should, needs to be done. Executives in their 50s and 60s are valuable because they're more relaxed and experienced and often aware of what can't, shouldn't, needn't be done.

*- MALCOM FORBES, American publisher (1919 - 1990)*

Almost all surveys indicate that the vast majority of Americans - over 80 percent - are satisfied with their jobs. There has been no significant change in these figures over time. Many people, of course, do object to specific aspects of their jobs, complaining about boredom, pay, opportunity for advancement, the way that work is organized, and so forth.

Daniel Yankelovich reports that almost 90 percent of all American workers say that it is important to work hard; 78 percent indicate an inner need to do their very best. His research also suggests that the motives driving people to work have changed; the proportion saying that they work primarily or solely for money has declined, while the younger and better educated emphasize the expressive side of work. To summarize Yankelovich, such workers increasingly believe that work, rather than leisure, can give them what they are looking for: an outlet for self-expression as well as material rewards.

*- SEYMOUR MARTIN LIPSET, American sociologist*

We can say without exaggeration that the present national ambition of the United States is unemployment. People live for quitting time, for weekends, for vacations, and for retirement.

-WENDELL BERRY, American poet, writer

If there is one secret to survival - note that I'm saying survival, not success - in business, it is tenacity. If you have some minimal talent, bathe with regularity and aren't certifiably insane, you can survive in any field if you simply are determined to hold on. I was astonished to discover in the theater that although some talent was necessary, the fellow who lived, slept and ate the theater, wanting to be part of it above all else, might not become a star but was certain to endure.

-CHARLES PETERS, American editor

The price one pays for pursuing any profession, or calling, is an intimate knowledge of its ugly side.

-JAMES BALDWIN, American novelist (1924 - 1987)

A worker is a part-time slave. The boss says when to show up, when to leave, and what to do in the meantime. He tells you how much work to do and how fast. He is free to carry his control to humiliating extremes, regulating, if he so desires, the clothes you wear or how often you go to the bathroom. With a few exceptions he can fire you for any reason, or no reason. He spies on you by means of snitches and supervisors; he amasses a dossier on you. If you talk back you are accused of insubordination, just as if you were a naughty child.

This demeaning system rules at least half those waking hours of a majority of men and women for most of their lives. Anybody who says these people are "free" is lying or stupid. You are what you do. If you do boring, stupid, montonous work, chances are you'll end up boring, stupid and montonous. Work is a much better explanation for the creeping cretinization around us than even such significant moronizing mechanisms as television and education. People who are regimented all their lives are psychologically enslaved. Their aptitude for autonomy is so atrophied that they develop an acute fear of freedom. The obedience training at their jobs carries over into the families *they* start, thus reproducing the system. Once you drain the vitality from people at work, they'll likely submit to hierarchy in politics, culture, and everything else. They're used to it.

-*BOB BLACK, American writer*

What we discovered was that beneath the surface, widespread pain pervades thousands of families. In general, the pain springs from the illusion that their personal life should make up for everything else that is unfulfilling; that it should be a "haven in a heartless world" unaffected by the daily frustrations of the working world. Most importantly, people believe that the "right" relationship will provide that haven. Yet most people in this society fail to find the magical relationship that they believe will compensate for the alienation of the larger world.

People typically return home from work feeling tense, often upset, sometimes depressed, almost always with a deep sense of frustration, for which they blame themselves. Typically, these feelings are buried beneath a surface level of relief at getting home, and most workers attempt to present themselves as "not letting it get to them." They try to pretend that they are unaffected by stupid bosses, arrogant supervisors, new processes that they aren't sure they can master and feel they must, sales that didn't go through, people they aren't sure they have impressed enough, co-workers with whom they must compete for praise or promotion, or changes in the economy that may make their product less desirable and their jobs less secure. Most frequently I found that people don't want to know about the psychic costs of work, or even begin to think about them. They tell themselves that all this can be quickly forgotten in some form of "relaxation" at home.

-*MICHAEL LERNER, American writer, editor*

The restive middle-class majority of Americans is seeking a more stable economy in which a new balance is found among the competing values of opportunity, security, and responsibility. The emphasis during the 1980s on entrepreneurship, though in many ways healthy, also distorted our view of how wealth is created. Economics in the 1980s so romanticized the brave risk-taking souls who provide investment capital that it overlooked the much larger group that ultimately makes a company successful: the people who work for it. For the last decade we have given honor of place not to those who labored daily for wages and salaries but to those who attained instant wealth, instant fame, and instant luxury. In our economic life, no less than in our political life, we have forgotten the old values of loyalty, hard work, and craftsmanship.

*-E.J. DIONNE, American journalist, author*

Unlike workers of the past, the new generation may not see managers as the enemy or members of a different social class, but possibly as team leaders with an important job to do. They do, however, like the idea of the union pushing managers to behave better, stop favoritism, increase training, and widen participation in decision making. They want to be motivated by fair rewards, challenging jobs, and respectful relationships. They want to be listened to and treated as individuals. They do no want to be part of a culture where one marches in lockstep to the commands of a tough-talking boss, be it management or union. They want a participatory union leadership to cooperate, to make the company more competitive, and at the same time, to defend their rights vigorously.

The values of these employees fit well with the needs of companies that consider their frontline employees as resources to be developed rather than as commodities to be exploited.

*-MICHAEL MACCOBY, American educator, writer*

The American women's movement has long been asking for equal rights, but its conception of equality has never had anything to do with "sameness". Pregnancy, after all, is like nothing else.

What we have always maintained is that women bring extra responsibilities to the work place and if women are ever going to have equality, they need equal access to opportunity. If that means instituting special, compensatory policies so that women can compete on an equal footing with men, and still be able to take time out to bear children, so be it.

Take another example: The person who is confined to a wheelchair will never get the job if ramps aren't cut into the curb so that they can gain access to the office building. If they can do the job, we, as a society, need to do whatever it takes to assure that they have the opportunity to succeed.

...People think that we can put the family in the freezer; that children can wait until we have time to be with them. They cannot wait. And though government action is not the prescription for all of America's family ills, to underestimate the role it can play in helping the famly accommodate to changed social and economic realities is a dangerous mistake.

*-PATRICIA SCHROEDER, American politician*

Businesses want plans and controls. The new workers want options and individual treatment. Indeed, this may be the ultimate challenge that women initiate in the workplace.

*-ELLEN GOODMAN, American journalist, author*

I have yet to hear a man ask for advice on how to combine a marriage and a career.

*-GLORIA STEINEM, American writer, feminist*

We don't want to see a female Einstein become an assistant professor. We want a woman schlemiel to get promoted as quickly as a male schlemiel.

*-BELLA ABZUG, American politician, feminist (1920 - 1998)*

In a competitive economy, companies that can't control their costs won't survive; but neither will those that are so callous that they demoralize their workers and can't draw new workers. The tension is ongoing and reflects a deeper dilemma. An economy that's flexible - that produces higher efficiencies, new technologies and rising living standards - can't provide absolute security. It never has and, quite probably, never will.

*-ROBERT J. SAMUELSON, American journalist, author*

It's amazing that the basic cause of downsizing is so rarely acknowledged: these companies have more workers than they really need - or can afford to pay.

CEO's aren't callous Scrooges shouting "Bah humbug" as they shove loyal workers out the door; they are responding to a competitive situation that demands they become more productive.

If we must blame somebody for the layoffs, it ought to be you and me. All of us are looking for the best deals in clothing, computers, and telephone service - and rewarding the high-quality low-cost providers with our business. I haven't met one person who would agree to pay AT&T twice the going rate for phone service if AT&T would promise to stop laying people off.

These companies are responding to the constant pressure from consumers and shareholders.

*-PETER LYNCH, American portfolio manager, author*

It is undeniable, I think, that some kinds of contemporary religious extremism also represent a generalized nebulous consciousness of dissent, an inarticulate, perhaps inexpressible critique of the political and moral economy of today's world. But the question remains, even if this is true why are these movements so easily pushed over the edge, why are they so violent, so destructive, and why is their thinking so filled with intolerance and hate?

Today, for the first time in history, a single ideal commands something close to absolute hegemony in the world: the notion that human existence must be permanently and irredeemably subordinated to the functioning of the impersonal mechanisms of a global marketplace. Realized in varying degrees in various parts of the world, this ideal enjoys the vigorous support of universities, banks, vast international corporations, and an increasingly interconnected global communications network. However, the market ideal as a cultural absolute, untempered by any other ethical, political, or spiritual ideals, is often so inhuman and predatory in its effects that it cannot but generate dissent. It is simply not conceivable that the majority of human beings will ever willingly give their assent to the idea that the search for profit should be the sole or central organizing principle of society.

*-ANITAV GHOSH, Indian novelist, journalist*

Before we are swept away by enthusiasm for well intentioned businesses as a new phenomenon that can save the world, it's worth recalling the 100 year-old lesson of George Pullman, the 18th-century railway car magnate. When Pullman built his model factory town near Chicago in 1880, he was hailed as a farsighted humanitarian. But in 1894 his workers went on strike because Pullman had repeatedly cut wages while keeping rents unchanged. It led to a nationwide rail shutdown, stopped only with federal troops and the jailing of union leaders.

Even the most morally motivated businessperson will continually feel the pressure of banks, stockholders, competitors and greed to compromise on responsibility in favor of profits.

*-DAVID MOBERG, American editor, writer*

If companies have a moral responsibility not to fill the movie theater and airwaves with violence and moral degradation, do they not also have a responsibility to keep workers employed when profits are rising? A moral responsibility to upgrade worker skills, an obligation to fully fund pension plans, to provide health care?

The CEO's are remarkably quiet. We are acting as if the economy had nothing to do with values. We need a serious national discussion about corporate responsibility.

*-ROBERT REICH, American educator, writer, government official*

As the median male wage began to decline in the late Seventies, American workers developed a number of coping mechanisms. The first one was for women to go into the workforce in great numbers. Women did not go into the workforce because of the wonderous opportunities suddenly open to them but to prop up family incomes. The second coping mechanism, which emerged in the Eighties, was for people to have smaller families. Not because they loved children less, but because they couldn't afford larger families. And then that coping mechanism was exhausted. In the late Eighties, the third coping mechanism was to work longer. We saw the workweek become longer, and we saw a lot of people take on second, even third jobs. ...

People tell me they're worried. They're worried about their jobs. They're worried about keeping their jobs. These are kitchen-table conversations that Americans all across the land are having.

*-ROBERT REICH*

As technologies and markets rapidly evolve, the best preparation for careers of the future will be through cumulative learning on the job rather than formal training completed years before.

This means that academic degrees and professional credentials will count for less; on-the-job training, for more. American college students have it backwards. The courses to which they now gravitate - finance, law, accounting, management, and other practical arts - may be helpful to understand how a particular job is *now* done (or, more accurately, how your instructors did it years ago when they held such jobs or studied the people who held them), but irrelevant to how such a job *will* be done. The intellectual equipment needed for the job of the future is an ability to define problems, quickly assimilate relevant data, conceptualize and reorganize the information, make deductive and inductive leaps with it, ask hard questions about it, discuss findings with colleagues, work collaboratively to find solutions, and then convince others. And *these* sorts of skills can't be learned in career-training courses. To the extent they can be found in universities at all, they're more likely to be found in subjects such as history, literature, philosophy, and anthropology - in which students can witness how others have grappled for centuries with the challenge of living good and productive lives. Tolstoy and Thucydides are far more relevant to the management jobs of the future, for example, than are Hersey and Blanchard.   *-ROBERT REICH*

Armies it has been said, are always trying to fight the last war, not the present one. Non-military organizations, too, are essentially conservative. And the more successful they have been in the past, the more difficult it is for them to pick up the clues that signal a sea change in how work is going to be done in the future. It was so in the Nineteenth Century, when industrialism transformed work into jobs. It is so today when jobs are being transformed into something else.

You may not notice the change in the rules until you leave your present situation, for until then your assumptions and expectations may be protected by the refusal of everyone around you to deal with the new realities.   This brings to mind the story of Balmung, the magic sword of the Germanic hero Siegfried. Balmung was so sharp that it could slice an armoured warrior in two, from the top of his helmet to the soles of his iron boots. But the cut was so fine that the wounded man could not even feel it. Until he moved. And then he fell into two pieces. Today's jobholders may likewise feel that nothing has happened. But just wait until they leave their jobs.

*- WILLIAM BRIDGES, American educator, author*

America has lept headlong into the information age, and our careers will never be the same. "We are in the midst of a historical transition in the way work is organized and carried out," says Thomas Malone, a professor in the Sloan School of Management at MIT. As technology allows companies to accomplish more with fewer people - and as it transforms the way work happens in virtually every discilpline - millions of people will find themselves working for "one-person companies," he says. Many who are cut loose, will literally strike out on their own. But even those with full-time jobs will increasingly be lone rangers within their companies, traveling from one project to the next, working alone and in virtual teams, rarely settling into one long-term position. At no time in modern history have so many workers been so totally reliant on their own wits and resources to thrive.

Although the digital revolution has clearly unsettled many, workers with vision are already capitalizing on the same advances that helped precipitate massive corporate restructuring. The new technologies have given one-person companies the power to accomplish tasks once handled by flocks of folks in big organizations, and they have granted employees new flexibility - to telecommute, for example. The upshot: You Inc. may be the fastest growing employment segment in the economy. According to a new poll conducted for *U.S. News* and Bozell Worldwide by KRC Research & Consulting, 55 percent of Americans want to be their own boss.

-AMY SALTZMAN, American writer. In U.S. News & World Report

I do not believe we can repair the basic fabric of

society until people who are willing to work have work. Work organizes life.
-*BILL CLINTON,* 42nd President of the United States

A man's work is his dilemma: his job is his bondage, but it also gives him a fair share of his identity and keeps him from being a bystander in somebody else's world.
-*MELVIN MADDOCKS,* American writer

Most people work just hard enough not to get fired and get paid just enough money not to quit.
-*GEORGE CARLIN,* American comedian

We all have a basic need to be active, engaged in meaningful pursuits, and valued by other people. In an important sense, these things constitute the true value of work more than money or power.
-*BRAD EDMUNSON,* American writer, editor

It's incredibly easy to get caught up in an activity trap, in the busyness of life, to work harder and harder at climbing the ladder of success only to discover it's leaning against the wrong wall.
-*STEPHEN COVEY,* American educator, author

If you find something you like to do, and somehow make it your job, you'll never have to work a day in your life.
-*UNKNOWN*

# CHAPTER - 7

# *HAPPINESS*

### ***

Little by little does the trick.
*-AESOP, legendary Greek fabulist (c.620 - 560 B.C.)*

When a child is born [to the Trausi] all its kindred sit around it in a circle and weep for the woes it will have to undergo now that it is come into the world, making mention of every ill that falls to the lot of humankind; when, on the other hand, a man has died, they bury him with laughter or rejoicings, and say that now he is free from a host of sufferings, and enjoys the completest happiness.
*-HERODOTUS, Greek historian (c.484 - c.425 B.C.)*

Scarcely, indeed, can any man unite all advantages; as there is no country which contains within it all that it needs, but each, while it possesses some things, lacks others, and the best country is that which contains the most; so no single human being is complete in every respect - something is always lacking. He who unites the greatest number of advantages, and retaining them to the day of his death, then dies peaceably, that man alone, sire, is, in my judgement, entitled to bear the name of 'happy'. But in every matter it behooves us to mark well the

end: for oftentimes God gives men a gleam of happiness, and then plunges them into ruin.
-*HERODOTUS*

Call no man happy till you know the end of his life. Till then, at most, he can only be called fortunate.
-*HERODOTUS*

The way to gain a good reputation is to endeavor to be what you desire to appear.
-*SOCRATES, Greek philosopher (c.469 - c.399 B.C.)*

What then is the result of what has been said? Is not this the result - that other things are indifferent, and that wisdom is the only good, and ignorance the only evil?

Let us consider a further point: Seeing that all men desire happiness, and happiness, as has been shown, is gained by a use, and a right use, of the good things of life, and the right use of them, and good fortune in the use of them, is given by knowledge, - the inference is that everybody ought by all means to try and make himself as wise as he can.   *-SOCRATES*

How many things there are which I don't want.
-*SOCRATES*

He who is of a calm and happy nature will hardly feel the pressure of age, but to him who is of an opposite disposition youth and age are equally a burden.
-*PLATO, Greek philosopher (c.428 - c.347 B.C.)*

With those who identify happiness with virtue or some one virtue our account is in harmony; for to virtue belongs virtuous activity. But it makes, perhaps, no small difference whether we place the chief good in possession or in use, in state of mind or in activity. For the state of mind may exist without producing any good result, as in a man who is asleep or in some other way quite inactive, but the activity cannot; for one who has the activity will of necessity be acting, and acting well, and as in the Olympic Games, it is not the most beautiful and the strongest that are crowned but those who compete. ... So those who act win, and rightly win, the noble and good things in life.

*-ARISTOTLE, Greek philosopher (384 - 322 B.C.)*

Happiness must be some form of contemplation. But, being a man, one will also need external prosperity; for our nature is not self-sufficient for the purpose of contemplation, but our body also must be healthy and must have food and other attention. Still, we must not think that the man who is to be happy will need many things or great things, for self-sufficiency and action do not involve excess, and we can do noble acts without ruling earth and sea.    *-ARISTOTLE*

The ultimate value of life depends upon awareness, and the power of contemplation rather than upon mere survival.    *-ARISTOTLE*

What we said before will apply now; that which is proper to each thing is by nature best and most pleasant for each thing; for man, therfore, the life according to reason is best and pleasantest, since reason more than anything else *is* man. This life therfore is also the happiest.    *-ARISTOTLE*

"Know Thyself" is a good saying, but not in all situations. In many it is better to say "Know Others."
-*MENANDER, Greek dramatist (c.342 - c.291 B.C.)*

Living is not the good, but living well. The wise man therfore lives as long as he should, not as long as he can. He will think of life in terms of quality, not quantity.
-*SENECA, Roman statesman, philosopher (c.4 B.C. - 65 A.D.)*

And seeing the multitudes, he went up into a mountain: and when he was set, his disciples came unto him:

And he opened his mouth, and taught them, saying,

Blessed are the poor in spirit: for theirs is the kingdom of heaven.

Blessed are they that mourn: for they shall be comforted.

Blessed are the meek: for they shall inherit the earth.

Blessed are they which do hunger and thirst after righteousness: for they shall be filled.

Blessed are the merciful: for they shall obtain mercy.

Blessed are the pure in heart: for they shall see God.

Blessed are the peacemakers: for they shall be called the Children of God.

Blessed are they which are persecuted for righteousness' sake: for their's is the kingdom of heaven.

Blessed are ye, when men shall revile you, and persecute you, and shall say all manner of evil against you falsely, for my sake.

Rejoice, and be exceeding glad: for great is your reward in heaven: for so persecuted they the prophets which were before you.
*-MATTHEW, 5:1-12*

What is a man profited, if he shall gain the whole world, and lose his own soul?
*-MATTHEW, 6:26*

A man grows most tired while standing still.
*-CHINESE PROVERB*

The art of living is more like wrestling than dancing.
*-MARCUS AURELIUS, Roman emperor, philosopher (121 - 180)*

We cannot ask to be happy when our actions have not earned us happiness; the good, only, are happy; divine beings are happy only because they are good.
*-PLOTINUS, Roman philosopher (205 - 270)*

I have reigned above fifty years in victory and peace, beloved by my subjects, dreaded by my enemies, and respected by my allies. Riches and honors, power and pleasure, have waited on my call, nor does any earthly blessing appear to be wanting for my felicity. In this situation, I have diligently numbered the days of pure and genuine happiness which have fallen to my lot: they amount to fourteen. O man, place not thy confidence in this present world.
*-ABD-AR-RAHMAN III, Caliph of Cordoba (912 - 961)*

It is impossible for any created good to constitute man's happiness. For happiness is the perfect good, which quiets the appetite altogether since it would not be the last end if something yet remained to be desired. Now the object of the will, that is, of man's appetite, is the universal good, just as the object of the intellect is the universal true. Hence it is evident that nothing can quiet man's will except the universal good. This is to be found not in any creature, but in God alone, because every creature has goodness by participation. Therfore God alone can satisfy the will of man.

-SAINT THOMAS AQUINAS, Italian scholastic philospher (1225 - 1274)

There is no greater sorrow than to recall, in misery, the time when we were happy.

-DANTE, Italian poet (1265 - 1321)

Habit is overcome by habit.

-THOMAS À KEMPIS, Dutch ecclesiastic, writer (1380 - 1471)

It is the chiefest point of happiness that a man is willing to be what he is.

-ERASMUS, Dutch scholar (1466 - 1536)

We are great fools. "He has spent his life in idleness," we say; "I have done nothing today." What, have you not lived. That is not only the fundamental but the most illustrious of your occupations. "If I had been placed in a position to manage great affairs, I would have shown what I could do." Have you been able to think out and manage your own life? You have done the greatest task of all. To show and exploit her resources Nature has no need of fortune; she shows herself equally on all levels and behind a curtain as well as without one.To compose our character is our duty, not to compose books, and to win, not battles and provinces, but order and tranquility in our conduct. Our great and glorious masterpiece is to live appropriately. All other things, ruling, hoarding, building, are only little appendages and props, at most.

-*MICHEL DE MONTAIGNE, French moralist, essayist (1533 - 1592)*

He who loses wealth loses much; he who loses a friend loses more; but he who loses courage loses all.

-*MIGUEL DE CERVANTES, Spanish novelist (1547 - 1616)*

We know what we are, but know not what we may be.

- *WILLIAM SHAKESPEARE, English playwright (1564 - 1616)*

If you are too fortunate, you will not know yourself. If you are too unfortunae, nobody will know you.

- *THOMAS FULLER, English clergyman (1608 - 1661)*

A man who finds no satisfaction in himself, seeks for it in vain elsewhere.

-*FRANÇOIS DE LA ROCHEFOUCALD, French moralist (1613 - 1680)*

Before we passionately desire anything which another possesses, we should examine as to the happiness of the possessor.   -*LA ROCHEFOUCALD*

Happiness lies in the taste, and not in the things; and it is from having what we desire that we are happy - not from having what others think desirable.

-*LA ROCHEFOUCALD*

Few things are needful to make the wise man happy, but nothing satisfies the fool; - and this is the reason why so many of mankind are miserable.

-*LA ROCHEFOUCALD*

Sometimes in life situations develop that only the half-crazy can get out of.   *-LA ROCHEFOUCALD*

All solitary enjoyments quickly pall, or become painful.
*-JAMES SHARP, Scottish clergyman (1618 - 1679)*

Solomon and Job have best known and best spoken of the misery of man; the former the most fortunate, and the latter the most unfortunate of men; the former knowing the vanity of pleasures from experience, the latter the reality of evils.
*-BLAISE PASCAL, French scientist and philosopher (1623 - 1662)*

All men seek happiness. This is without exception. Whatever different means they employ, they all tend to this end. The cause of some going to war, and of others avoiding it, is the same desire in both, attended with different views. The will never takes the least step but to this object. This is the motive of every action of every man, even those who hang themselves.   *-BLAISE PASCAL*

A trifle consoles us because a trifle upsets us.
*-BLAISE PASCAL*

The last thing one knows is what to put first.
*-BLAISE PASCAL*

Happy the Man, and happy he alone,
He who can call today his own;
He who, secure within, can say,
Tomorrow, do thy worst, for I have liv'd today.
*-JOHN DRYDEN, English poet, critic (1631 - 1700)*

A sound mind in a sound body, is a short but full description of a happy state in this world.
-*JOHN LOCKE, English philosopher (1632 - 1704)*

If we live according to the guidance of reason, we shall desire for others the good which we seek for ourselves.
-*BARUCH SPINOZA, Dutch philosopher (1632 - 1677)*

He that leaveth nothing to chance will do few things ill, but he will do very few things.
-*SIR GEORGE SAVILE, English politician, essayist (1633 - 1695)*

Happy the man who, unknown to the world, lives content with himself in some retired nook, whom the love of this nothing called Fame has never intoxicated with its vain smoke; who makes all his pleasure dependent on his liberty of action, and gives an account of his leisure to no one but himself.
-*NICOLAS BOILEAU-DESPRÉAUX, French poet, critic (1636 - 1711)*

The true happiness is of a retired nature, and an enemy to pomp and noise; it arises, in the first place, from the enjoyment of one's self; and in the next, from the friendship and conversation of a few select companions; it loves shade and solitude, and naturally haunts groves and fountains, fields and meadows; in short, it feels everything it wants within itself, and receives no addition from the multitudes of witnesses and spectators. On the contrary, false happiness loves to be in a crowd, and to draw the eyes of the world upon her. She does not receive satisfaction from the applauses which she gives herself, but from the admiration which she raises in

others. She flourishes in courts and palaces, theatres and assemblies, and has no existence but when she is looked upon.
-*JOSEPH ADDISON, English essayist (1672 - 1719)*

A good conscience is to the soul what health is to the body; it preserves a constant ease and serenity within us, and more than countervails all the calamities and afflictions that can possibly befall us.
-*JOSEPH ADDISON*

I conceive that the great part of the miseries of mankind are brought upon them by false estimates they have made of the value of things.
-*BEN FRANKLIN, American statesman, writer, scientist (1706 - 1790)*

I believe long habits of virtue have a sensible effect on the countenance.   -*BEN FRANKLIN*

Human felicity is produced not so much by great pieces of good fortune that seldom happen, as by little advantages that occur every day.
-*BEN FRANKLIN*

"If you want nothing," said Imlac, "how are you unhappy?"

"That I want nothing," said the prince, "or that I know not what I want, is the cause of my complaint; if I had any known want, I should have a certain wish; that wish could excite endeavor, and I should not then repine to see the sun move so slowly towards the western mountain, or lament when the day breaks, and sleep will no longer hide me from myself. When I see the kids and the lambs chasing one another, I fancy that I should be happy if I had something to pursue. But, possessing all that I can want, I find one day and one hour exactly like another, except that the latter is still more tedious than the former. Let your experience inform me how the day may now seem as short as in my childhood, while nature was yet fresh and every moment showed me what I never had observed before. I have already enjoyed too much; give me something to desire."

The old man was suprised at this new species of affliction and knew not what to reply, yet was unwilling to be silent. "Sir," said he, "if you had seen the miseries of the world you would know how to value your present state." "Now," said the prince, "you have given me something to desire. I shall long to see the miseries of the world, since the sight of them is necessary to happiness."

*-SAMUEL JOHNSON, English writer, lexicographer (1709 - 1784). From* Rasselas

The love of life is necessary to the vigorous prosecution of any undertaking. *-SAMUEL JOHNSON*

Hope is itself a species of happiness, and perhaps the chief happiness which this world affords; but, like all other pleasures immoderately enjoyed, the excesses of hope must be expiated by pain, and expectations improperly indulged must end in disappointment. If it be asked, what is the improper expectation which it is dangerous to indulge, experience will quickly answer that it is such expectation as is dictated not by reason, but by desire; expectations raised, not by the common occurrences of life, but by the wants of the expectant; an expectation that requires the common course of things to be changed, and the general rules of action to be broken. *-SAMUEL JOHNSON*

Few enterprises of great labor or hazard would be undertaken if we had not the power of magnifying the advantages we expect from them.  *-SAMUEL JOHNSON*

Resolve not to be poor: whatever you have, spend less. Poverty is a great enemy to human happiness; it certainly destroys liberty, and it makes some virtues impracticable, and others extremely difficult.
*-SAMUEL JOHNSON*

Human happiness seems to consist in three ingredients; action, pleasure and indolence. And though these ingredients ought to be mixed in different proportions, according to the disposition of the person, yet no one ingredient can be entirely wanting without destroying in some measure the relish of the whole composition.
*-DAVID HUME, Scottish philosopher (1711 - 1776)*

Good and ill are common to all, but in varying proportions. The happiest is he who suffers least; the most miserable is he who enjoys least. Ever more sorrow than joy - this is the lot of all of us. Man's happiness in this world is but a negative state; it must be reckoned by the fewness of his ills.
*-JEAN-JACQUES ROUSSEAU, French philosopher (1712 - 1778)*

Supreme happiness consists in self-content; that we may gain this self-content we are placed upon this earth and endowed with freedom, we are tempted by our passions and restrained by conscience. What more could divine power itself have done in our behalf?  *-JEAN-JACQUES ROUSSEAU*

Inasmuch as  virtue and happiness together constitute

the possession of the *summum bonum* in a person, and the distribution of happiness in exact proportion to morality (which is the worth of the person, and his worthiness to be happy) constitutes the *summum bonum* of a possible world; hence this *summum bonum* expresses the whole, the perfect good, in which, however, virtue as the condition is always the supreme good, since it has no condition above it; wheras happiness, while it is pleasant to the possessor of it, is not of itself absolutely and in all respects good, but always presupposes morally right behavior as its condition.

*-IMMANUEL KANT, German philosopher (1724 - 1804)*

When the thinking man has conquered the temptations to vice, and is conscious of having done his (often hard) duty, he finds himself in a state of peace and satisfaction which may well be called *happiness,* in which virtue is her own reward.

*-IMMANUEL KANT*

Yes, you moralists morose and imprudent, there is happiness on earth, there is a lot of it, and each has his own. It's not permanent, no. It passes, it comes back, and passes you again, by that law which is inherent in the nature of all created things, the movement, the eternal rotation of man and thing. And it may be that the sum total of ill, consequence of our imperfection, our physical and intellectual imperfection, surpases the sum total of each individual's happiness. All that is possible, but it does not follow that there is no happiness, and a great deal of happiness. If there were not happiness on earth, the creation would be a monstrosity and

Voltaire would have been right when he called our planet the latrines of the universe. An evil pleasantry, which is no more than an absurdity, or rather meaningless, if not a jet of poetic bile.

Yes, there is happiness, and much of it. I repeat that today I know it only by remembrance. Those who admit candidly what they feel are worthy of having it. Those who are not worthy of it are those who have it and yet deny it, and those who are able to get it, yet neglect it. I have no reproach to make to myself on either score.

*-CASANOVA, Italian adventurer (1725 - 1798)*

It has been a thousand times observed, and I must observe it once more, that the hours we pass with happy prospects in view are more pleasing than those crowned with fruition.

*-OLIVER GOLDSMITH, British poet, novelist (1728 - 1774)*

It is necessary to the happiness of a man that he be mentally faithful to himself.

*-THOMAS PAINE, American political philosopher, writer (1737 - 1809)*

It is neither wealth nor splendor but tranquility and occupation, which give happiness.

*-THOMAS JEFFERSON, 3rd President of the United States (1743 - 1826)*

I am retired to Monticello, where, in the bosom of my family, and surrounded by my books, I enjoy a repose to which I have been long a stranger. My mornings are devoted to correspondence. From breakfast to dinner, I am in my shops, my garden, or on horseback among my farms; from dinner to dark, I give to society and recreation with my neighbors and

friends; and from candle light to early bedtime, I read. My health is perfect; and my strength considerably reinforced by the activity of the course I pursue. ... I talk of ploughs and harrows, of seeding and harvesting, with my neighbors, and of politics too, if they choose with as little reserve as the rest of my fellow citizens, and feel, at length, the blessing of being free to say and do what I please.
*- THOMAS JEFFERSON*

A man can stand almost anything except a succession of ordinary days.
*-JOHANN WOLFGANG VON GOETHE, German poet, playwright (1749 - 1832)*

It is an aspect of all happiness to suppose that we deserve it.
*-JOSEPH JOUBERT, French moralist (1754 - 1824)*

All that is good in man lies in youthful feeling and mature thought.　*-JOSEPH JOUBERT*

No man chooses evil because it is evil; he only mistakes it for happiness, the good he seeks.
*-MARY WOLLSTONECRAFT, English writer, feminist (1759 - 1797)*

I am more convinced that our happiness or unhappiness depends far more on the way we meet events of life, than on the nature of those events themselves.
*-ALEXANDER VON HUMBOLDT, German naturalist, statesman (1769 - 1859)*

No enjoyment, however inconsiderable, is confined to the present moment. A man is the happier for life from having made once an agreeable tour, or lived for any length of time with pleasant people, or enjoyed any considerable interval of innocent pleasure.

-SYDNEY SMITH, English clergyman, writer (1771 - 1845)

A great deal of talent is lost to the world for want of a little courage. Every day sends to their graves obscure men whom timidity prevented from making a first effort.    -SYDNEY SMITH

For what do we live, but to make sport for our neighbors, and laugh at them in our turn?

-JANE AUSTEN, English novelist (1775 - 1817)

Even in the common affairs of life, in love, friendship, and marriage, how little security have we when we trust our happiness in the hands of others!

- WILLIAM HAZLITT, English essayist, critic (1778 - 1830)

Almost all our misfortunes in life come from the wrong notions we have about the things that happen to us. To know men thoroughly, to judge events sanely is, therfore, a great step towards happiness.

-STENDHAL, French novelist (1783 - 1842)

In a world where all is unstable, and nought can endure, but is swept onwards at once in the hurrying whirlpool of change; where a man, if he is to keep erect at all, must always be advancing and moving, like an acrobat on a rope - in such a world, happiness is inconceivable. How can it dwell where, as Plato says, *continual Becoming and never Being* is the sole form of existence. In the first place, a man never is happy, but spends his whole life in striving after something which he thinks will make him so; he seldom attains his goal, and when he does, it is only to be disappointed; he is mostly shipwrecked in the end, and comes into harbour with masts and rigging gone. And then, it is all one whether he has been happy or miserable; for his life was never anything more than a present moment always vanishing; and now it is over.

-*ARTHUR SCHOPENHAUER,  German philosopher (1788 - 1860)*

Necessity is the constant scourge of the lower classes, ennui of the higher ones.   -*ARTHUR SCHOPENHAUR*

The tragedy of life is not so much what men suffer, but rather what they miss.

-*THOMAS CARLYLE,  Scottish essayist, historian (1795 - 1881)*

Young men for some time have an idea that such a thing as happiness is to be had and therfore are extremely impatient under any unpleasant restraining - in time, however, of such stuff is the world about them, they know better and instead of striving from Uneasiness greet it as an habitual sensation.

-*JOHN KEATS, English poet (1795 - 1821)*

In vain do they talk of happiness who never subdued an impulse in obedience to a principle. He who never sacrificed a present to a future good, or a personal to a general one, can speak of happiness only as the blind do of colors.

-*HORACE MANN, American educator (1796 - 1859)*

All happiness depends on courage and work. I have had many periods of wretchedness, but with energy, and above all with illusions, I pulled through them all.

-*HONORÉ DE BALZAC, French novelist (1799 - 1850)*

People do not lack strength; they lack will.
*- VICTOR HUGO, French author (1802 - 1885)*

The supreme happiness of life is the conviction that we are loved.   *-VICTOR HUGO*

The purpose of life is not to be happy. It is to be useful, to be honorable, to be compassionate, to have it make some difference that you have lived and lived well.
*-RALPH WALDO EMERSON, American poet, essayist (1803 - 1882)*

A man must consider what a rich realm he abdicates when he becomes a conformist.   *-RALPH WALDO EMERSON*

Character is that which can do without success.
*-RALPH WALDO EMERSON*

The bitterest tragic element in life from an intellectual source is the belief in a brute Fate or Destiny.   *-RALPH WALDO EMERSON*

No man, for any considerable period, can wear one face to himself and another to the multitude without finally getting bewildered as to which may be true.
*-NATHANIEL HAWTHORNE, American writer (1804 - 1864)*

When it is positively asserted to be impossible that human life should be happy, the assertion, if not something like a verbal quibble, is at least an exaggeration. If by happiness be meant a continuity of highly pleasurable excitement, it is evident enough that this is impossible. A state of exalted pleasure lasts only moments, or in some cases, and with some intermissions, hours or days, and is the occasional brillant flash of enjoyment, not its permanent and steady flame. Of this the philosophers who have taught that happiness is the end of life were as fully aware as those who taunt them. The happiness which they meant was not a life of rapture; but moments of such, in an existence made up of few and transitory pains, many and various pleasures, with a decided predominance of the active over the passive, and having as the foundation of the whole, not to expect more from life than it is capable of bestowing.

A life thus composed, to those who have been fortunate enough to obtain it, has always appeared worthy of the name of happiness. And such an existence is even now the lot of many, during some considerable portion of their lives. The present wretched education, and wretched social arrangements, are the only real hindrance to its being attainable by almost all.

*-JOHN STUART MILL, English philosopher (1806 - 1873)*

Believe me, every heart has its secret sorrows, which the world knows not; and oftentimes we call a man cold when he is only sad.

*-HENRY WADSWORTH LONGFELLOW, American poet (1807 - 1882)*

If we could read the secret history of our enemies, we should find in each sorrow and suffering enough to disarm all hostility.   *-HENRY WADSWORTH LONGFELLOW*

With most men life is like backgammon - half skill and half luck.

*-OLIVER WENDELL HOLMES, SR., American physician, writer (1809 - 1894)*

The great thing is this world is not so much where we

stand as in what direction we are moving.
-*OLIVER WENDELL HOLMES, SR.*

Happiness is not the end of life; character is.
-*HENRY WARD BEECHER, American clergyman (1813 - 1887)*

I know of no more encouraging fact than the unquestionable ability of man to elevate his life by a conscious endeavor.
-*HENRY DAVID THOREAU, American essayist, naturalist (1817 - 1862)*

I would rather sit on a pumpkin and have it all to myself than be crowded on a velvet cushion.
-*HENRY DAVID THOREAU*

One half the troubles of this life can be traced to saying yes too quickly and not saying no soon enough.
-*JOSH BILLINGS, American humorist (1818 - 1885)*

My advice to those who are about to begin, in earnest, the journey of life, is to take their heart in one hand and a club in the other.    -*JOSH BILLINGS*

There ain't much fun in medicine, but there's a good deal of medicine in fun.    -*JOSH BILLINGS*

We act as though comfort and luxury were the chief requirements of life, when all that we need to make us really happy is something to be enthusiastic about.
-*CHARLES KINGSLEY, English clergyman, novelist (1819 - 1875)*

There is the greatest practical benefit in making a few failures early in life.
-*THOMAS H. HUXLEY, English biologist, writer (1825 - 1895)*

And if ye say there is no law, ye shall also say there is no sin. And if ye say there is no sin, ye shall also say there is no righteousness. And if there be no righteousness there be no happiness.
-*THE BOOK OF MORMON, Written 1827 - 1830*

If you want to be happy, be.
-*LEO TOLSTOY, Russian novelist (1828 - 1910)*

Necessity is the mother of taking chances.
-*MARK TWAIN, American writer, humorist (1835 - 1910)*

Grief can take care of itself, but to get the full value of a joy you must have somebody to divide it with.
-*MARK TWAIN*

Good friends, good books, and a sleepy conscience: this is the ideal life.   -*MARK TWAIN*

There are two great rules of life, the one general and the other particular. The first is that everyone can, in the end, get what he wants, if he only tries. This is the general rule. The particular rule is that every individual is, more or less, an exception to the rule.
-*SAMUEL BUTLER, English writer (1835 - 1902)*

The men who start out with the notion that the world owes them a living generally find that the world pays its debt in the penitentiary or the poor house.
-*WILLIAM GRAHAM SUMNER, American economist, sociologist (1840 - 1910)*

People talk fundamentals and superlatives and then make some changes of detail.
-*OLIVER WENDELL HOLMES, JR., U.S. Supreme Court Justice (1841 - 1935)*

Who can decide offhand which is absolutely better,

to live or to understand life. We must do both alternately, and a man can no more limit himself to either than a pair of scissors can cut with a single one of its blades.

*-WILLIAM JAMES, American philosopher, psychologist (1842 - 1910)*

How to gain, how to keep, how to recover happiness is in fact for most men at all times the secret motive of all they do, and of all they are willing to endure.

*-WILLIAM JAMES*

The greatest discovery of my generation is that a human being can alter his life by altering his attitude.

*-WILLIAM JAMES*

Happiness, like every other emotional state, has blindness and insensibility to opposing facts given it as its instinctive weapon for self-protection against disturbance.   *-WILLIAM JAMES*

If merely 'feeling good' could decide, drunkenness would be the supremely valid human experience.

*-WILLIAM JAMES*

Happiness, n. An agreeable sensation arising from contemplating the misery of another.

*-AMBROSE BIERCE, American journalist, writer (1842 - c.1914)*

Calamity, n. A more than commonly plain and unmistakable reminder that the affairs of this life are not of our own ordering. Calamities are of two kinds: misfortune to ourselves, and good fortune to others.   *-AMBROSE BIERCE*

Live all you can; it's a mistake not to. It doesn't so

much matter what you do in particular, so long as you have your life. If you haven't had that, what have you had?

-*HENRY JAMES, American writer (1843 - 1916)*

What is happiness? The feeling that power *increases* - that resistance is being overcome.

-*FRIEDRICH WILHELM NIETZSCHE, German philosopher, poet (1844 - 1900)*

If we have our own "why" of life, we can bear almost any "how". -*FRIEDRICH WILHELM NIETZSCHE*

Love for life is still possible, only one loves differently; it is like love for a woman whom one does not trust. -*FRIEDRICH WILHELM NIETZSCHE*

The thought of suicide is a great consolation; with the help of it, one has got through many a bad night.

-*FRIEDRICH WILHELM NIETZSCHE*

It is the mark of a good action that it appears inevitable in retrospect.

-*ROBERT LOUIS STEVENSON, Scottish novelist, poet (1850 - 1894)*

Most people are other people. Their thoughts are someone else's opinion, their lives a mimicry, their passions a quotation.

-*OSCAR WILDE, Irish poet, playwright, wit (1854 - 1900)*

Selfishness is not living as one wishes to live. It is asking others to live as one wishes to live.

-*OSCAR WILDE*

This is the true joy of life - the being used for a purpose recognized by yourself as a mighty one, the being thoroughly worn out before you are thrown to

the scrap-heap; the being a force of nature, instead of a feverish, selfish clod of ailments and grievances!
    -*GEORGE BERNARD SHAW, British playwright, critic (1856 - 1950)*

Take care to get what you like or you will be forced to like what you get.    -*GEORGE BERNARD SHAW*

What we do during our working hours determines what we have; what we do in our leisure hours determines what we are.
    -*GEORGE EASTMAN, American inventor, industrialist (1854 - 1932)*

In every individual the two trends, one towards personal happiness and the other towards unity with the rest of humanity, must contend with each other.
    -*SIGMUND FREUD, Austrian neurologist, psychoanalyst (1856 - 1939)*

When making a decision of minor importance, I have always found it advantageous to consider all the pros and cons. In vital matters, however, such as the choice of a mate or profession, decisions should come from the unconscious, from somewhere within ourselves. In the important decisions of our personal lives we should be governed by the deep inner needs of our nature.    -*SIGMUND FREUD*

To find out what one is fitted to do and to secure an opportunity to do it is the key to happiness.
    -*JOHN DEWEY, American philosopher, educator (1859 - 1952)*

Whether you think you can or think you can't, you're right.
    -*HENRY FORD, American industrialist (1863 - 1947)*

My best friend is the one who brings out the best in

me.  *-HENRY FORD*

In spite of illness, in spite even of the archenemy sorrow, one *can* remain alive long past the usual date of disintegration if one is unafraid of change, insatiable in intellectual curiosity, interested in big things, and happy in small ways.

*-EDITH WHARTON, American novelist (1862 - 1937)*

Love is but a prelude to life, an overture in which the theme of the impending work is exquisitely hinted at, but which remains nevertheless only a symbol and a promise.  What is to follow, if all goes well, begins presently to appear.  Passion settles down into possession, courtship into partnership, pleasure into habit.  A child, half mystery and half plaything, comes to show us what we have done and to make its consequences perpetual.  We see that by indulging our inclinations we have woven about us a net from which we cannot escape: our choices, bearing fruit, begin to manifest our destiny.  That life which once seemed to spread out infinetly before us is narrowed to one mortal career.  We learn that in morals the infinite is a chimera, and that in accomplishing anything definite a man renounces everything else.  He sails henceforth for one point of the compass.

*-GEORGE SANTAYANA, American philosopher, poet (1863 - 1952)*

Character is the basis of happiness and happiness the sanction of character.  *-GEORGE SANTAYANA*

Wealth must justify itself in happiness.

*-GEORGE SANTAYANA*

Society is like the air, necessary to breathe, but

insufficient to live on. *-GEORGE SANTAYANA*

One's friends are that part of the human race with which one can be human. *-GEORGE SANYAYANA*

America is the greatest of opportunities and the worst of influences. *-GEORGE SANTAYANA*

Don't be afraid to take a big step if one is indicated. You can't cross a chasm in two small jumps.
*-DAVID LLOYD GEORGE, British statesman (1863 - 1945)*

Real happiness is not dependent on external things. The pond is fed from within. The kind of happiness that springs from inward thoughts and emotions. You must cultivate your mind if you wish to achieve enduring happiness. You must furnish your mind with interesting thoughts and ideas. For an empty mind seeks pleasure as a substitute for happiness.
*-WILLIAM LYON PHELPS, American educator, critic (1865 - 1943)*

Those who decide to use leisure as a means of mental development, who love good music, good books, good pictures, good plays, good company, good conversation - what are they? They are the happiest people in the world. *-WILLIAM LYON PHELPS*

People have many different kinds of pleasure. The real one is that for which they will forsake the others.
*-MARCEL PROUST, French novelist (1871 - 1922)*

To be without some of the things you want is an indispensable part of happiness.
*-BERTRAND RUSSELL, English philosopher (1872 - 1970)*

The good life, as I conceive it, is a happy life. I do

not mean that if you are good you will be happy - I mean that if you are happy you will be good.
 *-BERTRAND RUSSELL*

One should respect public opinion in so far as it is necessary to avoid starvation and to keep out of prison, but anything that goes beyond this is voluntary submission to an unnecessary tyranny.
 *-BERTRAND RUSSELL*

Real life is, to most men, a long second best, a perpetual compromise between the ideal and the posssible.   *-BERTRAND RUSSELL*

Pain and suffering do not enoble the human spirit. Pain and suffering breed meanness, bitterness, cruelty. It is only happiness that ennobles.
 *- W. SOMERSET MAUGHAM, English novelist, playwright (1874 - 1965)*

The common idea that success spoils people by making them vain, egotistic, and self-complacent is erroneous; on the contrary, it makes them, for the most part, humble, tolerant, and kind. Failure makes people cruel and bitter.   *-W. SOMERSET MAUGHAM*

The value of money is that with it we can tell any man to go to the devil. It is the sixth sense which enables you to enjoy the other five.
 *- W. SOMERSET MAUGHAM*

The unfortunate thing about this world is that good habits are so much easier to give up than bad ones.
 *- W. SOMERSET MAUGHAM*

In three words I can sum up everything I've learned

about life. It goes on.
-*ROBERT FROST, American poet (1874 - 1963)*

Happiness makes up in height what it lacks in length.
-*ROBERT FROST*

One thing I know: the only ones among you who will be really happy are those who will have sought and found how to serve.
-*ALBERT SCHWEITZER, French clergyman, physician, philosopher (1875 - 1965)*

There are as many nights as days, and the one is just as long as the other in the year's course. Even a happy life cannot be without a measure of darkness, and the word "happy" would lose its meaning if it were not balanced by sadness. It is far better to take things as they come along with patience and equanimity.
-*CARL JUNG, Swiss psychiatrist (1875 - 1961)*

I would rather be ashes than dust. I would rather that my spark should burn out in a brilliant blaze than it should be stifled by dry-rot. I would rather be a superb meteor, every atom of me in magnificent glow, than a sleepy and permanent planet. The proper function of man is to live, not to exist. I shall not waste my days in trying to prolong them. I shall use my time.
-*JACK LONDON, American novelist (1876 - 1916)*

Happiness is a how, not a what; a talent, not an object.
-*HERMANN HESSE, German author, (1877 - 1962)*

Time is the coin of your life. It is the only coin you

have, and only you can determine how it will be spent. Be careful lest you let other people spend it for you.
-*CARL SANDBURG, American writer (1878 - 1967)*

One of the greatest necessities in America is to discover creative solitude.   -*CARL SANDBURG*

The optimist proclaims that we live in the best of all possible worlds; and the pessimist fears this is true.
-*JAMES BRANCH CABELL, American novelist, essayist (1879 - 1958)*

Avoiding danger is no safer in the long run than outright exposure.   The fearful are caught as often as the bold.
-*HELEN KELLER, American author, lecturer (1880 - 1968)*

Security is mostly a superstition. It does not exist in nature, nor do the children of men as a whole experience it. Avoiding danger is no safer in the long run than outright exposure. Life is either a daring adventure, or nothing. To keep our faces toward change and behave like free spirits in the presence of fate is strength undefeatable.
-*HELEN KELLER*

When one door of happiness closes, another opens; but often we look so long at the closed door that we do not see the one which has been opened for us.
-*HELEN KELLER*

The one permanent emotion of the inferior man is fear - fear of the unknown, the complex, the inexplicable. What he wants beyond everything else is safety.   -*H.L. MENCKEN, American editor, satirist (1880 - 1956)*

If at first you don't succeed, try again. Then quit. No use being a damn fool about it.
- *W.C. FIELDS, American comedian, actor (1880 - 1946)*

The most radical division that is possible to make of humanity is that which splits it into two classes of creatures: those who make great demands on themselves, piling up difficulties and duties; and those who demand nothing special of themselves, but for whom to live is to be every moment what they already are, without imposing on themsleves any effort toward perfection, mere buoys that float on waves.
- *JOSÉ ORTEGA Y GASSET, Spanish philosopher, writer (1883 - 1955)*

We cannot put off living until we are ready. The most salient characteristic of life is its coerciveness: it is always urgent, "here and now" without any possible postponement. Life is fired at us point blank.     - *JOSÉ ORTEGA Y GASSET*

If you want the present and the future to be different from the past, Spinoza tells us, study the past, find out the causes that made it what it was and bring different causes to bear.
- *WILL DURANT, American historian (1885 - 1981)*

Some men *must* be too spiritual, some *must* be too sensual. Some *must* be too sympathetic, and some *must* be too proud. We have no desire to say what men *ought* to be. We only wish to say there are all kinds of ways of being, and there is no such thing as human perfection.
- *D.H. LAWRENCE, English novelist (1885 - 1930)*

Nothing splendid has ever been achieved except by those who dared believe that something inside them was superior to circumstances.
*-BRUCE BARTON, American businessman, writer (1886 - 1967)*

Many men would take the death-sentence without a whimper to escape the life-sentence which fate carries in her other hand.
*-T.E. LAWRENCE, British archaeologist, soldier, writer (1888 - 1935)*

None of us can help the things life has done to us. They're done before you realize it, and once they're done they make you do other things until at last everything comes between you and what you'd like to be, and you have lost your true self forever.
*-EUGENE O'NEILL, American playwright (1888 - 1953)*

The ideas I stand for are not mine. I borrowed them from Socrates. I swiped them from Chesterfield. I stole them from Jesus. And I put them in a book. If you don't like their rules, whose would you use?
*-DALE CARNEGIE, American writer, speaker (1888 - 1955)*

Happiness, after all, is an inner state of mind. It is little dependent on outside environment. Happiness has very little to do, for instance, with whether you are rich or not rich. Some of the most miserable persons I have come across in my life are the rich people. It is true that poverty makes one miserable in a very acute way. But my point is that it is not wealth but co-ordination of one's thought and action which removes inner conflicts. It is in that way that integration of personality is achieved.
*-JAWAHARLAL NEHRU, Prime Minister of India (1889 - 1964)*

Adventure is something you seek for pleasure, or even for profit, like a gold rush or invading a country; for the illusion of being more alive than ordinarily, the thing you *will* to occur; but experience is what really happens to you in the long run; the truth that finally overtakes you.
  -*KATHERINE ANNE PORTER, American novelist (1890 - 1980)*

There are three ingredients in the good life; learning, earning, and yearning.
  -*CHRISTOPHER MORLEY, American novelist, journalist (1890 - 1957)*

Too much of a good thing can be wonderful.
  -*MAE WEST, American actress (1893 - 1980)*

to be nobody but yourself - in a world which is doing its best, night and day, to make you everybody else - means to fight the hardest battle which any human being can fight, and never stop fighting.
  -*e.e. cummings, American poet, painter (1894 - 1962)*

Humor is one of God's most marvelous gifts. Humor gives us smiles, laughter, and gaiety. Humor reveals the roses and hides the thorns. Humor makes our heavy burdens light and smooths the rough spots in our pathways. Humor endows us with the capacity to clarify the obscure, to simplify the complex, to deflate the pompous, to chastise the arrogant, to point a moral, and to adorn a tale.
  -*SAM ERVIN, U.S. Senator, writer (1896 - 1985)*

Anybody can do just about anything with himself that he really wants to and makes up his mind to do. We are capable of greater things than we realize. How much one actually achieves depends largely on:

1) Desire. 2) Faith. 3) Persistent Effort. 4) Ability. But if you are lacking the first three factors, your ability will not balance out the lack. So concentrate on the first three and the results will amaze you.
*-NORMAN VINCENT PEALE, American clergyman, author (1898 - 1993)*

There is no meaning to life except the meaning man gives his life by the unfolding of his powers.
*-ERICH FROMM, American psychoanalyst, philosopher (1900 - 1980)*

We have developed a phobia of being alone. We prefer the most trivial and even obnoxious company, the most meaningless activities, to being alone with ourselves; we seem to be frightened at the prospect of facing ourselves.  *-ERICH FROMM*

To every man his chance, to every man, regardless of his birth, his shining golden opportunity - to every man the right to live, to work, to be himself, and to become whatever thing his manhood and his vision can combine to make him - this is the promise of America.
*-THOMAS WOLFE, American novelist (1900 - 1938)*

The secret of happiness is to find a congenial monotony.
*-V.S. PRITCHETT, English novelist*

When people are free to do as they please, they usually imitate each other.
*-ERIC HOFFER, American author, philosopher (1902 - 1983)*

There is little difference in people, but that little difference makes a big difference. The little difference is attitude. The big difference is whether

it is positive or negative.
-*W. CLEMENT STONE, American businessman, philanthropist, publisher*

Those who say life is worth living at any cost have already written for themselves an epitaph of infamy, for there is no cause and no person they will not betray to stay alive. Man's vocation should be the use of the arts of intelligence in behalf of human freedom.
-*SIDNEY HOOK, American philosopher, author (1902 - 1989)*

The pursuit of happiness, which American citizens are obliged to undertake, tends to involve them in trying to perpetuate the moods, tastes and aptitudes of youth.
-*MALCOLM MUGGERIDGE, English writer, editor (1903 - 1990)*

No human being can really understand another, and no one can arrange another's happiness.
-*GRAHAM GREENE, English author (1904 - 1991)*

In philosophical terminology, every object has an essence and an existence. An essence is an intelligible and unchanging unity of properties; an existence is a certain actual presence in the world. Many people think that the essence comes first and then the existence: that peas, for example, grow and become round in conformity with the idea of peas, and that gherkins are gherkins because they participate in the essence of gherkins. This idea originated in religious thought: It is a fact that the man who wants to build a house has to know exactly what kind of object he's going to create - essence precedes existence - and for all those who believe that God created men, he must have done so by referring to his idea of them. But even those who have no religious faith have maintained this traditional view that the object never exists except in conformity with its essence; and everyone in the 18th century thought that all men had a common essence called human nature. Existentialism, on the contrary, maintains that in man - and in man alone - existence precedes essence.

This simply means that man first *is*, and only subsequently is this or that. In a word, man must create his own essence: It is throwing himself into the world, suffering there, struggling there, that he gradually defines himself. And the definition always remains open ended: We cannot say what *this* man is before he dies, or what mankind is before it has disappeared. It is absurd in this light to ask whether existentialism is fascist, conservative, communist, or democratic. ... All I can say - without wanting to insist too much on the similarities - is that it isn't too far from the conception of man found in Marx. For is it not a fact that Marx would accept this motto of ours for man: *make, and in making make yourself, and be nothing but what you have made of yourself.*

-JEAN-PAUL SARTRE, *French philosopher, writer (1905 - 1980)*

If one sets aside time for a business appointment or shopping expedition, that time is accepted as inviolable. But if one says, "I cannot come because that is my hour to be alone," one is considered rude, egotistical, or strange. What commentary on our civilization.

-ANNE MORROW LINDBERGH, *American writer*

I never said, "I want to be alone." I only said, "I want to be left alone." There is all the difference.
-GRETA GARBO, American actress (1905 - 1990)

One face to the world, another at home makes for misery.
-AMY VANDERBILT, American columnist, radio-TV hostess (1908 - 1974)

To be happy, we must not be too concerned with others. -ALBERT CAMUS, French philosopher, novelist (1913 - 1960)

There is no fate that cannot be surmounted by scorn.
-ALBERT CAMUS

It's a kind of spiritual snobbery that makes people think they can be happy without money.
-ALBERT CAMUS

Wealth is not without its advantages and the case to the contrary, although it has often been made, has never proved widely persuasive.
-JOHN KENNETH GALBRAITH, American economist

The only people who claim that money is not important are people who have enough money so that they are relieved of the ugly burden of thinking about it.
-JOYCE CAROL OATES, American novelist

Nothing confers freedom like a buck in the bank.
-MALCOM FORBES, American publisher (1919 - 1990)

The pessimist sees only the tunnel; the optimist sees the light at the end of the tunnel; the realist sees the tunnel and light - and the next tunnel.
-SYDNEY J. HARRIS, American newspaper columnist (1917 - 1986)

If I didn't have spiritual faith, I would be a pessimist. But I'm an optimist. I've read the last page in the Bible. It's all going to turn out all right.
  -*BILLY GRAHAM, American evangelist*

At the age of five I had become a skeptic and began to sense that any happiness that came my way might be the prelude to some grim cosmic joke.
  -*RUSSELL BAKER, American columnist, author*

For some good advice on how to live ask someone who knows he's dying.
  -*ABAGAIL VAN BUREN, American advice columnist*

What's terrible is to pretend that the second-rate is first-rate. To pretend that you don't need love when you do; or you like your work when you know quite well you're capable of better.
  -*DORIS LESSING, English novelist*

It is not the mountain we conquer but ourselves.
  -*EDMUND HILLARY, New Zealand mountaineer, writer*

If you want to win anything - a race, your self, your life - you have to go a little beserk.
  -*GEORGE SHEEHAN, American physician, public speaker*

John Locke's general philosophy has obvious implications for a theory of morals. The traditional view was that some sort of moral knowledge was innate. Locke thought otherwise. What God had given men was a faculty of reason and a sentiment of self-love. Reason combined with self-love produced morality. Reason could discern the principles of ethics, or natural law, and self-love should lean men to obey them.

Locke wrote in one of his notebooks that "it is a man's proper business to seek happiness and avoid misery. Happiness consists in what delights and contents the mind, misery in what disturbs, discomposes or torments it." He would "make it my business to seek satisfaction and delight and avoid uneasiness and disquiet." But he knew that "if I prefer a short pleasure to a lasting one, it is plain I cross my own happiness."

For Locke, in other words, Christian ethics was natural ethics. The teaching of the New Testament was a means to an end - happiness in this life and the next. The reason for doing what the Gospel demanded about loving one's neighbor, etc. was not just that Jesus said it. By doing these things one promoted one's happiness; men were impelled by their natural self-love to desire it.

Wrongdoing was thus for Locke a sign of ignorance or folly. People did not always realize that long-term happiness could usually only be bought at the cost of short-term pleasure. If people were prudent and reflective, not moved by the winds of impulse and emotion, they would have what they most desired.

*-MAURICE CRANSTON, English political scientist, philosopher, author (1920 -1993)*

I firmly believe that if you follow a path that interests you, not to the exclusion of love, sensitivity, and cooperation with others, but with the strength of conviction that you can move others by your own efforts, and do not make success or failure the criteria by which you live, the chances are you'll be a person worthy of your own respect.

-*NEIL SIMON, American playwright*

The trick in living against the grain of your closest associates is in hanging on firmly but good-humoredly to your own identity.

-*WILLIAM SAFIRE, American journalist, author*

Things equal out pretty well. Our dreams seldom come true, but then neither do our nightmares.

-*CHARLES KENNEDY, American publisher (1935 - 1984)*

Hope is not the conviction that something will turn out well but the certainty that something makes sense, regardless of how it turns out.

-*VACLAV HAVEL, Czech writer, President of Czech Republic*

Václav Havel writes that modern society is held together by fear - fear of loss, mostly; so we accumulate more and more things with which to assure ourselves that it isn't necessary to be afraid and that our compromises haven't been for nothing. It is fear, Havel believes, that drives us to accept corruption and dishonesty, to pretend we are what we aren't.

Ultimately, having given away almost everything that matters, we end up defining ourselves by our possessions. Gradually we become incapable of imagining goals higher or more meaningful than a fine house or a fine car. We abandon hope without even realizing we've done so.

-*G.J. MEYER. American writer. In Harper's*

Ability is what you're capable of doing. Motivation determines what you do. Attitude determines how

well you do it.
-*LOU HOLTZ, American football coach*

You've got to think it and believe it in order to achieve it.
-*UNKNOWN*

I don't know the key to success, but the key to failure is trying to please everybody.
-*BILL COSBY, American actor, comedian, author*

You don't get to choose how you are going to die or when. You can only decide how you're going to live.
-*JOAN BAEZ, American folksinger, activist*

What many people deny, especially macho men, is the element of luck in life. Few successful people like to mention it, but let's be honest. Luck plays a big part in everything. Right place, right time, left turn rather than right turn, avoidance of illness, the right genes, all luck. We ought to think about it more before we pound our chests.
-*PAUL NEWMAN, American actor*

Modern Americans travel light, with little philosophical baggage other than a fervent belief in their right to the pursuit of happiness.
-*GEORGE F. WILL, American columnist, commentator*

To think of American life today without television taxes the imagination. One extraordinary social fact about television is that it is both ubiquitous and, on the scale of social goods, disappointing. Television has the virtues of being cheap and accesible, and does not require much engagement - it is therfore most popular among children, the old, the poor, and the less educated. Society's most powerless receive television as a consolation prize. Even many of these, and most other people most of the time, think watching it an activity not so much valuable in itself as preferable, perhaps, to other choices near at hand. Yet, in several social experiments, many people have refused large sums of money for volunteering to do without television for one month. But even these diehards, like most people, rank television low among their pleasures. It is an enjoyment that turns out to be not so enjoyable after all. *What are you doing? Nothing, just watching television. How was the program? OK.* Watching television is something to do, but it is also and always *just* watching television.

*- TODD GITLIN, Ameican sociologist, author*

That happiness is to be attained through limitless material acquisition is denied by every religion and philosophy known to humankind, but it is preached incessantly by every American television set.

*-ROBERT BELLAH, American sociologist*

Personal responsibility is the brick and mortar of power. The responsible person knows that the quality of his life is something that he will have to make inside the limits of his fate. Some of these limits he can push back, some he cannot, but in any case the quality of his life will pretty much reflect the quality of his efforts. When this link between well-being and action is truely accepted, the result is power. With this understanding and the knowledge that he is responsible, a person can see his margin of choice. He can choose and act, choose and act again, without illusion. He can create himself and make himself felt in the world. Such a person has power.

*- SHELBY STEELE, American educator, author*

Most of us in America believe a few simple propositions that seem so clear and self-evident they scarcely need be said. Choice is a good thing in life, and the more of it we have, the happier we are. Authority is inherently suspect, nobody should have the right to tell others what to think or how to behave. Sin isn't personal, it's social; individual human beings are creatures of the society they live in.

Those ideas are the manifesto of an entire generation in America, the generation born in the baby boom years and now in its thirties and forties. They are powerful ideas. They all have a ring of truth. But in the past quarter-century, taken to excess they have landed us in a great deal of trouble.

The worship of choice has brought us a world in which nothing we choose seems good enough to be permanent, and we are unable to resist the endless pursuit of new selections - in work, in marriage, in front of the television set. The suspicion of authority has meant the erosion of standards of conduct and civility, visible most clearly in schools where teachers who dare to discilpline pupils risk a profane response. The repudiation of sin has given us a collection of wrongdoers who insist that they are not responsible for their actions because they have been dealt bad cards in life. When we declare that there are no sinners, we are a step away from deciding that there is no such thing as right and wrong.

We have grown fond of the saying that there is no free lunch, but we forget that it applies to moral as well as economic matters. Stable relationships, civil classrooms, safe streets - the ingredients of what we call community - all come at a price. The price is rules, and people who can enforce them; limits on the choices we can make as individuals; and a willingness to accept the fact that there are bad people in the world, and sin even in the best of us. The price is not low, but the life it makes possible is no small achievement.
*-ALAN EHRENHALT, American writer, editor*

At sixteen I was stupid, confused, insecure and indecisive. At twenty-five I was wise, self-confident, prepossessing and assertive. At forty-five I am stupid, confused, insecure and indecisive. Who would have supposed that maturity is only a short break in adolescence.
*-JULES FEIFFER, American playwright, cartoonist.* Caption to a cartoon.

The man who views the world at 50 the same as he did at 20 has wasted 30 years of his life.
*-MUHAMMAD ALI, American boxer*

We believe that a worthwhile life is defined by a kind of spiritual journey and a sense of obligation that is, for us, not burdensome. It's liberating, it's wonderful, it's fun. *-HILLARY CLINTON, American First Lady*

If you can't be yourself, why get up in the morning.
*-DENNIS RODMAN, American basketball player*

Happiness in the older years of life, like happiness in every year of life, is a matter of choice - *your* choice for yourself.
*-HAROLD AZINE, American writer*

Whatever you do, don't give up. Because all you can do once you've given up is bitch. I've known some great bitchers in my time. With some it's a passion, with others an art.
*-MOLLY IVINS, American newspaper columnist, author*

Courage is the power to let go of the familiar.
*-UNKNOWN*

The greatest contribution which any of us can make to the world is just to be ourselves at our best.
*-UNKNOWN*

Everybody needs beauty as well as bread, places to play in and pray in, where Nature may heal and cheer and give strength to body and soul alike.
*-JOHN MUIR, American naturalist*

The life of sensation is the life of greed, it requires more and more. The life of the spirit requires less and less; time is ample and its passage sweet.
*-ANNIE DILLARD, American writer*

Out of our beliefs are born deeds. Out of our deeds we form habits; out of our habits grow our character; and on our character we build our destination.
*-HENRY HANCOCK, American educator*

# AUTHOR INDEX